SUCCESS IN MATHS

CW00524346

pupil's book

Rob Kearsley Bullen
Andrew Edmondson
Tony Ward

Longman

F2

CONTENTS

Brush Up Your Number 1

Place Value and Ordering with Whole Numbers

Learn About It

The table shows the names of some numbers up to one billion.

1	one	100	one hundred
2	two	120	one hundred and twenty
3	three	125	one hundred and twenty-five
9	nine	200	two hundred
10	ten	999	nine hundred and ninety-nine
11	eleven	1000	one thousand
12	twelve	10 000	ten thousand
19	nineteen	100 000	one hundred thousand
20	twenty	1 000 000	one million
25	twenty-five	10 000 000	ten million
30	thirty	100 000 000	one hundred million
99	ninety-nine	1 000 000 000	one billion (thousand million)

These numbers are called **digits**:
0, 1, 2, 3, 4, 5, 6, 7, 8, 9.

This diagram shows what each digit in the number **one million, two hundred and thirty-five thousand, six hundred and twenty-four** stands for.

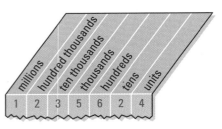

Group the digits in threes to show thousands, millions and billions.

This number is **five billion, thirteen million, forty thousand, three hundred and five**.

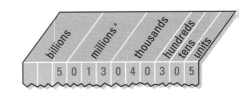

Try It Out

(A) Write these numbers in words.

1 74	**2** 493	**3** 502
4 6000	**5** 3504	**6** 16 425
7 249 050	**8** 6 023 504	**9** 178 362 591

B Write these numbers in numerals (using digits).

 1 nine hundred and twenty-four
 2 eight thousand, nine hundred and fifteen
 3 seventy-nine thousand and twenty-one
 4 one hundred and thirty-three thousand
 5 one million and one
 6 seventeen million, two hundred and three thousand and fifty-eight
 7 nine billion, sixteen million, three thousand and twenty-nine

Learn More About It

You can use columns to write these numbers in order.

8450   8435   549   21 034   9251

	8	4	5	0
	8	4	3	5
		5	4	9
2	1	0	3	4
	9	2	5	1

From largest to smallest:

21 034   9251   8450   8435   549

From smallest to largest:

549   8435   8450   9251   21 034

Try It Out

C **1** Write these numbers in order, from largest to smallest.

  (a) 5821, 98, 643 145, 785, 3 230 432, 98 040
  (b) 11 298, 9949, 13 100, 8625, 9329, 8695

 2 Write these numbers in order, from smallest to largest.

  (a) 6477, 7476, 6774, 7746, 6747, 7647, 7467
  (b) 1 394 826, 982 000, 1 385 999, 899 999, 1 396 492

Practice

D **1** Write these numbers in order, from smallest to largest.

  (a) 129 000, 4 132 505 050, 7982, 49 000 000, 380, 160 500 293, 92 400, 7 920 059
  (b) 8277, 2872, 8272, 2287, 7282, 2278, 8227, 7822, 2782, 7228
  (c) 314 269 578, 314 629 758, 324 156 798, 312 469 578, 324 165 978, 312 469 758, 314 627 985

 2 Write the numbers in question 1(a) in words.

Finished Early?
⇨ Go to page 321

1 Negative Numbers

In this chapter you will learn about …
1. working with negative numbers
2. adding and subtracting negative numbers

1 Working with Negative Numbers

Remember?

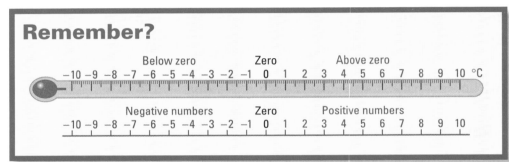

Try It Out

A Copy this temperature scale.

1. Find the new temperature when …
   (a) 5 °C falls by 9 °C (Start at 5 °C and count down 9.)
   (b) −7 °C increases by 5 °C (Start at −7 °C and count up 5.)
   (c) −3 °C falls by 4 °C
   (d) −8 °C increases by 10 °C.

2. Find the difference between the temperatures in each pair.
   (a) 9 °C and 6 °C (Start at 9 °C and count how far to 6 °C.)
   (b) −4 °C and 5 °C
   (c) −3 °C and −7 °C
   (d) 8 °C and −8 °C

3 **(a)** Write down the numbers shown by the arrows on the number line below.

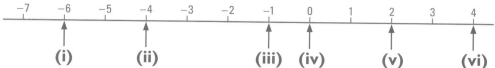

(b) Write down the numbers on the number line which are ...

(i) more than zero **(ii)** less than 2

(iii) less than −3 **(iv)** more than −5.

4 In each pair, how much bigger is the first number than the second?

(a) 2 and −3 (Start at −3 and count how far to 2.)

(b) −4 and −7 **(c)** 4 and −5 **(d)** −1 and −6

Learn About It

Sharna calculates 3 − 5 using a number line.

She starts at 3 and moves 5 spaces left.

The answer is −2 so she writes 3 − 5 = −2.

Paul calculates 3 − 5 a different way.

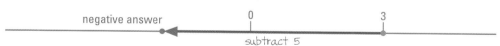

Paul knows that the answer will be negative, because 5 is bigger than 3.

First he calculates the **difference** between 5 and 3: 5 − 3 = 2.

Then he makes the answer negative: −2.

Paul's method works for large numbers too. He has to calculate −21 + 63.

> **Word Check**
> **difference** bigger number minus smaller number

The answer will be positive because 63 is bigger than 21.

He calculates the difference: 63 − 21 = 42.

Try It Out

B 1 Use a number line like Sharna's to calculate the following.

    (a) 4 – 7   **(b)** –3 + 6   **(c)** –5 + 3   **(d)** –5 + 5

    (e) 0 – 3   **(f)** 2 – 4   **(g)** 7 – 10   **(h)** –5 – 5

2 Use Paul's method to calculate the following.

    (a) 10 – 40   **(b)** –20 + 30   **(c)** –30 + 10

    (d) –30 + 30   **(e)** –15 + 25   **(f)** –25 + 12

    (g) 18 – 35   **(h)** –14 + 37   **(i)** 200 – 800

Learn More About It

Emma has to calculate –10 – 30.

She says 'I start at –10 and go down by 30. I'm at –40.'

She writes –10 – 30 = –40.

Emma checks her answer using a number line.

Try It Out

C 1 Calculate the following using Emma's method. Draw a number line.

    (a) –3 – 6   **(b)** –5 – 9   **(c)** –20 – 50

    (d) –40 – 40   **(e)** –15 – 25   **(f)** –200 – 100

    (g) –21 – 7   **(h)** –15 – 12   **(i)** –37 – 54

    (j) –32 – 29   **(k)** –120 – 250   **(l)** –2000 – 3000

2 Calculate the following using Emma's or Paul's method.
Draw a number line.

    (a) –30 + 10   **(b)** –10 – 9   **(c)** –15 + 25

    (d) 57 – 100   **(e)** –24 – 25   **(f)** –130 + 460

Practice

D Jason opens a bank account with £5.

The amount in his bank account is called his **balance**.

He writes a cheque for £8. Now he has £5 − £8 = −£3 in his bank account.

A negative balance means he owes the bank money.

Jason **deposits** (puts in) £9 in his account. His balance is now −£3 + £9 = £6.

Copy the table.

Write down each calculation.

Write the answer in the table.

		Calculation	Balance
Deposit			£5
Cheque	£8	5 − 8	−£3
Deposit	£9	−3 + 9	£6
Cheque	£7		
Cheque	£4		
Deposit	£2		
Deposit	£13		
Cheque	£40		
Cheque	£20		
Deposit	£35		
Cheque	£32		
Cheque	£28		
Deposit	£63		
Cheque	£100		
Deposit	£160		

E Work out the following long calculations from left to right.

Example 4 − 7 − 2 + 8

Working 4 − 7 − 2 + 8 (Work out the first two numbers.)
= −3 − 2 + 8 (Write down the answer. Repeat.)
= −5 + 8 (Repeat.)
= 3 (Check using a number line.)

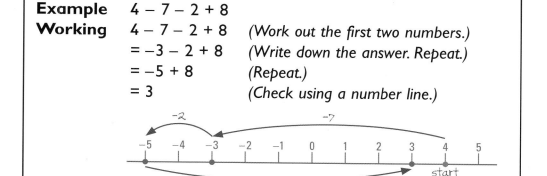

Answer 3

1 4 − 8 + 3   **2** −2 + 7 − 3   **3** −2 + 5 − 1 + 3
4 4 − 5 − 6 + 3   **5** −15 + 12 + 5   **6** −10 − 20 − 30
7 15 − 20 − 10 + 25   **8** 40 − 60 + 30 − 70 + 80

Finished Early?
 Go to page 321

Further Practice

F The Ocean Hotel has floors above and below sea level. The table below shows some journeys of the Ocean Hotel lift.

Write a calculation for each journey.

Work out which floor the lift ends up at.

Example	Starting floor 6. Journey: ↑2 ↓12
Working	The lift starts at floor 6. It goes up 2 floors then down 12 floors.
	6 + 2 − 12
	= 8 − 12 (*Remember: work from left to right.*)
	= −4
	A negative number shows the floor is below sea level.
Answer	Finishing floor −4

	Starting floor	Journey	Finishing floor
	6	↑2 ↓12	−4
1	−5	↑9	
2	7	↓10	
3	−4	↓11	
4	19	↓26	
5	−3	↓16	
6	−15	↑32	
7	2	↓6 ↓8	
8	−3	↑9 ↓14	
9	20	↓28 ↓10	
10	−17	↑32 ↓26	
11	−6	↑10 ↓15 ↑21	
12	14	↓27 ↑19 ↓13	

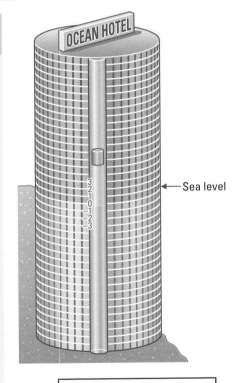

← Sea level

Finished Early?
➡ Go to page 321

❷ Adding and Subtracting Negative Numbers

Learn About It

Josh has to add 3 and −5. He writes the negative number in brackets to make it clearer.

He replaces + − by − because adding a negative number makes the answer smaller.

He uses these rules when adding:

Different signs give −	Same signs give +
+ − gives − − + gives −	+ + gives + − − gives +

Josh can also check his answer using a calculator.
Negative numbers are written inside brackets.
For example, −5 is written (−5).

Example (−2) − (+3)
Working (−2) − (+3)
= (−2) − 3   (Replace − + by −.)
= −5
Answer   −5

Try It Out

G Calculate the following.

1 4 − (−3)	2 (−1) − (+3)	3 6 − (+3)
4 (−2) − (−5)	5 0 + (−5)	6 8 − (−7)
7 (−20) − (+30)	8 1 − (−5) + 7	9 12 + (−12)
10 (−2) + 4	11 3 − (−5)	12 (−4) + (−3)
13 0 − (−3)	14 (−5) + 5	15 2 − (−3)
16 0 − (−2)	17 (−3) + (−3)	18 (−6) − (−6)

Practice

H Calculate the following.

1	$(-25) + (-17)$	**2**	$(-13) + 28$
3	$50 - 60$	**4**	$37 - (-25)$
5	$(-57) - (-57)$	**6**	$(-100) - (-45)$
7	$150 - (-200)$	**8**	$(-126) - (+48)$
9	$(-120) + (-420)$	**10**	$3 - 5 + (-2)$
11	$3 - (-8) + 2$	**12**	$(-3) + (-3) - (-1)$
13	$(-2) - (-2) - (-2)$	**14**	$(-4) - (-2) - (-3)$
15	$(-5) - (-5) - 5$	**16**	$20 + (-30) - (-50)$
17	$25 - 65 + (-90)$	**18**	$(-2) + (-2) - (-2) + 2$

Further Practice

> **Finished Early?**
> ➡ Go to page 322

I In each question below, two parts have the same answer and one is different. Find the odd one out.

Example	**(a)** $6 - (-4)$ **(b)** $(-4) + (-6)$ **(c)** $(-6) + (-4)$
Working	**(a)** $6 - (-4) = 6 + 4 = 10$
	(b) $(-4) + (-6) = (-4) - 6 = -10$
	(c) $(-6) + (-4) = (-6) - 4 = -10$
Answer	**(a)** is the odd one out.

1	**(a)** $5 + (-2)$	**(b)** $(-2) - (-5)$	**(c)** $(-5) - (-2)$
2	**(a)** $(-4) - (+7)$	**(b)** $(-7) + (-4)$	**(c)** $(-4) - (-7)$
3	**(a)** $7 + (-3)$	**(b)** $3 - (-7)$	**(c)** $(-3) - (-7)$
4	**(a)** $20 + (-30)$	**(b)** $(-30) - 20$	**(c)** $10 + (-20)$
5	**(a)** $(-100) + (-200)$	**(b)** $(-100) - 200$	**(c)** $(-200) - (-100)$
6	**(a)** $(-25) - (-25)$	**(b)** $75 - (-50)$	**(c)** $25 - (-100)$
7	**(a)** $(-56) + (-25)$	**(b)** $(-42) + (-36)$	**(c)** $15 + (-93)$
8	**(a)** $(-194) + (-63)$	**(b)** $252 - (+145)$	**(c)** $(-273) - (-16)$
9	**(a)** $500 + (-250) - (-150)$	**(b)** $(-200) - (-100) + 100$	
	(c) $50 + 500 - 150$		
10	**(a)** $(-52) - 34 + (-24)$	**(b)** $14 + (-26) - 56$	
	(c) $(-74) + (-32) + 38$		

> **Finished Early?**
> ➡ Go to page 322

Unit 1 *Negative Numbers*
Summary of Chapter 1

- A number line can help you to add and subtract numbers.

$(-2) + 5 = 3$

$21 - 63 = -42$
(because $63 - 21 = 42$)

$(-20) - 10 = -30$
(because $20 + 10 = 30$)

$(-7) + 9 - 3 = -1$

- Use these rules to replace two signs by one sign:

Examples:
$2 - (-3) = 2 + 3 = 5$
$2 - (+3) = 2 - 3 = -1$

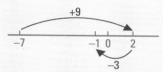

Different signs give −	Same signs give +
+ − gives −	+ + gives +
− + gives −	− − gives +

- Negative numbers are written inside brackets, e.g. -2 is written (-2).

$3 + (-5)$
$= 3 - 5$ (+ − gives −.)
$= -2$

Brush Up Your Number 2

Addition and Subtraction of Whole Numbers

Learn About It

There are lots of different ways of adding whole numbers. Here are three ways to work out 346 + 183.

Split 183 into 3, 80 and 100.

Add 3
346 + 3 = 349
Add 80
349 + 80 = 429
Add 100
429 + 100 = 529

Add the hundreds, tens and units separately.

300 + 100 = 400
40 + 80 = 120
6 + 3 = 9
529

Then add the answer.

Set it out in columns.

```
   346
+  183
   529
     1
```

1 carried from the 10s column.

Try It Out

Ⓐ Work out the following.

1 247 + 145	**2** 261 + 172	**3** 358 + 722
4 149 + 4576	**5** 2583 + 176	**6** 2345 + 3671

Learn More About It

You can also subtract in different ways. Here are three ways to work out 347 − 275.

Split 275 into 5, 70 and 200.

Subtract 5
347 − 5 = 342
Subtract 70
342 − 70 = 272
Subtract 200
272 − 200 = 72

Count on in steps.

275 [+5] 280
280 [+20] 300
300 [+40] 340
340 [+7] 347
72

Add up the steps.

Set it out in columns.

```
  2 1
  ̸3̸47      1 borrowed
- 275
   72
```

Try It Out

Ⓑ Work out the following.

1 456 − 234	**2** 362 − 143	**3** 671 − 490
4 234 − 153	**5** 2456 − 1937	**6** 1226 − 875

Practice

C A shop puts money in the bank from sales and takes out money for costs. Copy and complete this table. You add on sales and subtract costs.

Money in the bank			New bank balance
£10 000	Sales	£2 500	£12 500
£13 500	Costs	£3 500	
£7 245	Sales	£2 754	
£12 624	Costs	£5 436	
£34 576	Costs	£16 285	
£125 360	Sales	£58 243	
£234 576	Costs	£108 628	

D In each question below there are three calculations. Two have the same answers and one is different. Write down the answer to the odd one out in each set.

1 (a) 275 + 377 **(b)** 1002 − 350 **(c)** 204 + 385

2 (a) 398 + 477 **(b)** 1597 − 703 **(c)** 2380 − 1486

3 (a) 365 + 498 + 221 **(b)** 23 682 − 22 348 **(c)** 16 374 + 8923 − 24 213

4 (a) 56 784 − 23 265
(b) 127 264 − 94 112
(c) 623 242 + 12 456 − 602 546

E This map shows six towns and their populations.

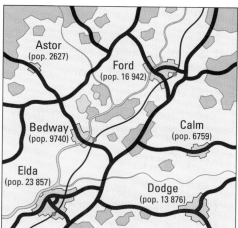

1 What is the total population of Calm and Dodge?

2 What is the total population of Elda and Ford?

3 How much bigger is the population of Bedway than of Astor?

4 How much smaller is the population of Astor than of Ford?

5 How much bigger is the population of Elda than the total population of Calm and Dodge?

6 What is the difference between the total population of the three smallest towns and the total population of the three largest towns?

7 What is the total population of all six towns?

Finished Early?
 Go to page 323

2 Coordinates and Graphs

In this chapter you will learn about ...
1. coordinates
2. reading graphs
3. drawing graphs

T 1 Coordinates

Remember?

The x-axis goes across the page.
It is horizontal (→).

The y-axis goes up the page.
It is vertical (↑).

Two numbers called **coordinates** give the position of a point.

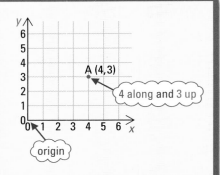

A (4,3)

4 along and 3 up

origin

The coordinates of point **A** are (4, 3).
It is 4 along and 3 up.
The first number is always along the x-axis and the second number is up the y-axis.

Axes meet at the **origin** (0, 0).

Try It Out

A 1 Write down ...
- **(a)** the x-coordinate of A
- **(b)** the y-coordinate of B
- **(c)** the x-coordinate of C
- **(d)** the x-coordinate of D
- **(e)** the y-coordinate of E
- **(f)** the y-coordinate of F
- **(g)** the y-coordinate of G
- **(h)** the x-coordinate of H.

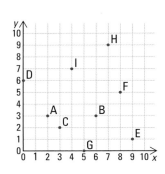

2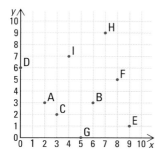

Write down the letter at each of the following coordinates:
(3, 2), (9, 1), (2, 3), (6, 3), (8, 5), (0, 6), (7, 9), (5, 0).

Learn About It

Squared paper

The numbers on the axes can be **negative** as well as positive.

The point **P** has coordinates $(1, -5)$.
From the origin, **P** is right 1 and down 5.

The point **Q** has coordinates $(-2, 3)$.
From the origin, **Q** is left 2 and up 3.

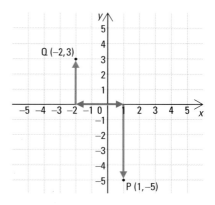

Example	Mark the point **R** $(-4, -5)$.
Working	From the origin, **R** is left 4 and down 5.
Answer	

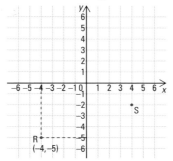

Example	What are the coordinates of **S**?
Working	From the origin, **S** is right 4 and down 2.
Answer	$(4, -2)$

Try It Out

Squared paper

B 1 Draw axes on squared paper. The x- and y-axes should be from −5 to 5.

2 Plot these points:
$(-4, -3) \rightarrow (-2, 3) \rightarrow (0, 1) \rightarrow (2, 3) \rightarrow (4, -3)$

3 Join up the points in the order shown. Use straight lines.

4 What letter have you made?

Practice

C 1 Each triangle below has three corners, A, B and C.
Write down the coordinates of the corners of each triangle.

(a)

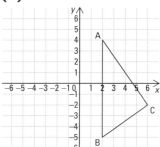

(b)

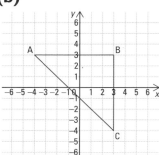

(c)

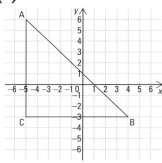

(d)

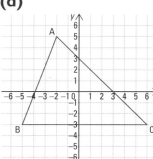

(e)

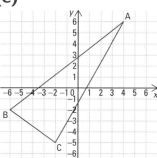

(f)

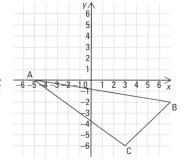

2 Write down the coordinates of:

(a) ○
(b) ✛
(c) ■
(d) □
(e) ●
(f) ▲
(g) △
(h) ✚

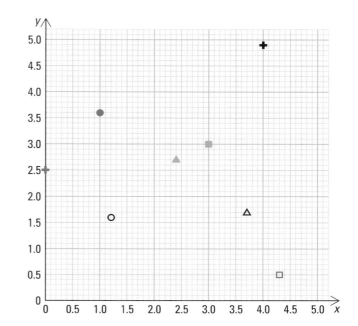

D

A4 graph paper

1 Draw a grid with x- and y- axes from 0 to 100.
(*Scale:* 1 cm to 10 units.)
This grid represents a map.

2 The **church** is at (38, 58). Mark it and label it **C**.

3 The **school** is at (51, 73). Mark it and label it **S**.

4 The **railway station** is at (68, 52). Mark it and label it **R**.

5 The **railway line** goes from the station to the edges of the grid in a straight line. It goes off the edges at (40, 0) and (100, 92). Mark these points and draw the railway line.

6 The main **road** goes from (6, 100) to (100, 53) in a straight line. Mark these points and draw the road.

7 There is a **level crossing** where the road crosses the railway. Mark this point and label it **L**.
Write down the coordinates of **L**.

8 The **playing field** has four corners. They are at (40, 44), (48, 42), (45, 30) and (37, 32).
Mark the corners and join them up. Label the field **F**.

Finished Early?
➡ Go to page 324

Further Practice

E Write down the coordinates of the corners of these shapes.

1
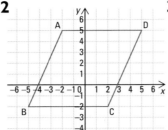

2

3
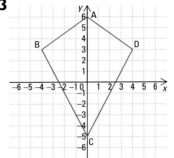

4
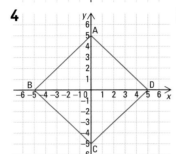

5
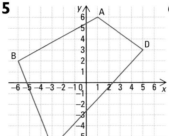

6
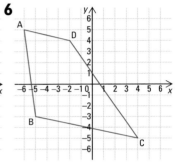

F

Squared paper

For each question below:

(a) draw a grid with x- and y- axes from −8 to 8
  (*Scale:* 1 cm to 1 unit.)

(b) plot the points in the question

(c) join the points linked by arrows with straight lines

(d) name the letter you have drawn.

1 $(-5, -4) \rightarrow (-3, 3) \rightarrow (0, 0) \rightarrow (3, 3) \rightarrow (5, -4)$

2 $(-6, 1) \rightarrow (-2, -6) \rightarrow (2, 1)$

3 $(-4, 6) \rightarrow (3, 6) \rightarrow (-4, -2) \rightarrow (3, -2)$

4 $(-4, -4) \rightarrow (-4, 3) \rightarrow (1, -4) \rightarrow (1, 3)$

5 $(-2, 4) \rightarrow (-6, 4) \rightarrow (-6, -6) \rightarrow (-2, -6)$
  then $(-6, -1) \rightarrow (-3, -1)$

> **Finished Early?**
> ➡ Go to page 324

❷ Reading Graphs

Learn About It

On a line graph, straight lines join points.

The scales on the axes do not have to start from 0. You show this with a **broken axis**.

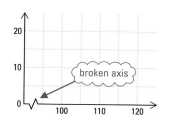

A graph shows a **connection** between two things. One thing is shown on each **axis** of a graph.

Jason weighed himself on his birthday every year and drew this graph. The graph shows the connection between his age and his weight.

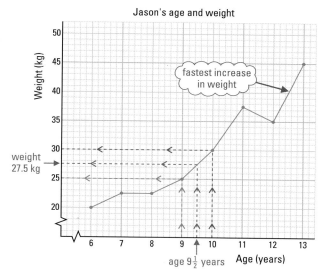

Jason's age and weight

When Jason was 9 he weighed 25 kg.
When he was 10 he weighed 30 kg.
When he was $9\frac{1}{2}$ the graph shows $27\frac{1}{2}$ kg. He might not have been exactly this weight. This is an **estimate**.

Jason's weight goes up most quickly when the graph is steepest. His fastest increase is between the ages of 12 and 13.

Word Check

estimate a guess at a value, based on what you know

Key Fact

The steeper the line on the graph, the faster the increase or decrease.

Try It Out

G While Kate was in hospital, her temperature was recorded every hour on this graph.

1 What was Kate's temperature at 11am?
2 What was Kate's temperature at 2pm?
3 What was Kate's highest temperature?
4 What was Kate's lowest temperature?
5 When was Kate's temperature 38 °C?
6 When was Kate's temperature 36.5 °C?
7 How much did Kate's temperature fall between 11am and 12 noon?
8 How much did Kate's temperature rise between 1pm and 3pm?

Learn More About It

This is a graph of Pat's earnings and the time she works.

It is a **conversion graph**. The line is straight because time and wages are connected by a rule. The rule is that, for every hour Pat works, she earns £6.

Suppose you know the hours Pat worked. You can read off her wages from the graph.

If Pat works $7\frac{1}{2}$ hours, she earns £45. Follow the red lines on the graph.

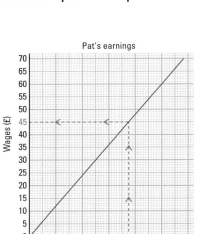

Word Check
_____
conversion change from one thing to another

Try It Out

H This graph shows the cost of Petrolco Petrol.

1 How much money is shown by each small division on the **cost** axis?

2 How much do 10 litres cost?

3 How much do 15 litres cost?

4 How much do 7 litres cost?

5 How much petrol do you get for £7?

6 How much petrol do you get for £4.50?

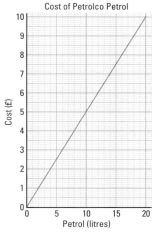

Cost of Petrolco Petrol

Practice

I 1 This graph shows the temperature of a cup of coffee. As it cools, a measurement is made every 2 minutes.

(a) What is the temperature of the coffee at the start?

(b) What is the temperature of the coffee after 4 minutes?

(c) What is the temperature of the coffee after 10 minutes?

(d) When is the temperature 53 °C?

(e) Estimate the temperature after 3 minutes.

(f) Estimate the temperature after 11 minutes.

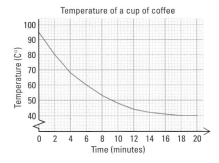

Temperature of a cup of coffee

2 This graph shows the sales of two cars, the Aurora and the Branco, for six months.

(a) What were the sales of the Aurora in January?

(b) What were the sales of the Branco in January?

(c) What was the smallest sale of the Aurora?

(d) When were the sales of the two cars equal?

(e) For what months were the sales of the Branco more than those of the Aurora?

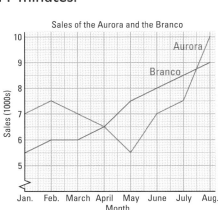

Sales of the Aurora and the Branco

J **1** Fairphone is a mobile phone company. Fairphone's charges are shown in red.

(a) What is the cost of 5 hours of calls?

(b) What is the cost of 3 hours of calls?

(c) How much time would £15 of calls take?

(d) How much time would £24 of calls take?

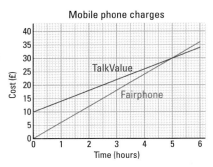

Mobile phone charges

2 TalkValue is another mobile phone company. TalkValue charges are shown in blue on the graph in question 1.

(a) What is the cost of 5 hours of calls?

(b) What is the cost of 3 hours of calls?

(c) How much time would £15 of calls take?

(d) How much time would £24 of calls take?

(e) For one number of hours, Talkvalue and Fairphone cost the same. How many hours is this?

3 Which of the phone companies in questions 1 and 2 would be cheaper if you made . . .

(a) 2 hours of calls

(b) 6 hours of calls

(c) just a few phone calls

(d) a lot of phone calls?

Finished Early?
➡ Go to page 324

Further Practice

K Every two minutes a TV company recorded the number of people watching Megamovies and produced this graph.

1 What was the largest number of viewers?

2 Estimate how many viewers there were after 11 minutes.

3 Estimate how many viewers there were after 25 minutes.

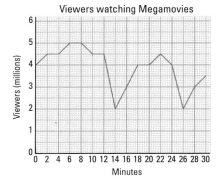

Viewers watching Megamovies

4 Estimate when 3.5 million viewers were watching.

5 When do you think the advertisements were being shown?

L This graph shows the connection between deutschmarks (DM) and pounds (£).

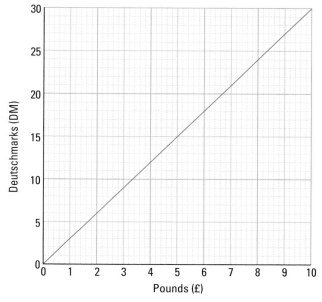

1 How much money is shown by each small division on the **pounds** axis?

2 How many DM would you get for ...
   (a) £3
   (b) £8
   (c) £5.40?

3 How many pounds would you get for ...
   (a) DM 6
   (b) DM 21
   (c) DM 7?

4 There is a rule to convert pounds to deutschmarks. What is it? Use the graph to help you.

Finished Early?
➡ Go to page 324

P ③ Drawing Graphs

Graph paper

Learn About It

Jason recorded the sales in his school shop over an eight-week half term.

Week	1	2	3	4	5	6	7	8
Sales (£)	27	30	33	31	30	33	34	35

1 Copy these axes on graph paper.

2 Plot the data from the table. Start with (1, 27), then (2, 30), etc.
Mark each point with a small cross (x).

3 Join the points, in order, with straight lines.

4 The plotted points are all at the top. They go across the full width of the **Week** axis, but a lot of the **Sales** axis is wasted.

Draw a new graph with a *broken* Sales axis.
Keep everything else the same as in stage 1, but change the Sales axis as follows:

Scale: 1cm to £1.
Range: 25→35.

> *Remember: put a **break** in an axis if it doesn't start at 0.*

5 Plot the points on your new graph.

Both ways of drawing the graph are correct but the second looks better.

Key Fact

Always **label** the axes.
Always write the **units**, if any (e.g. metres, hours).
Give the graph a **title**.

Try It Out

 The table shows the number of ice-creams sold by a shop each month for a year.

Month	Jan.	Feb.	Mar.	Apr.	May	Jun.	Jul.	Aug.	Sep.	Oct.	Nov.	Dec.
Ice-creams sold	12	11	15	37	26	47	50	75	55	31	35	20

1 Draw and label axes for a graph of the sales.

→ Horizontal axis:
Label: 'Month'.
Scale: 1 cm to 1 month.

↑ Vertical axis:
Label: 'Ice-creams sold'.
Scale: 2 cm to 10 sales.
Range: 0→80.

2 Plot the data.

3 Use your graph to find the month in which …
   (a) sales were highest   **(b)** sales increased the most
   (c) sales decreased the most.

Learn More About It

1 You can draw a conversion graph for metres and feet. One metre is about 3 feet. Suppose you want to convert lengths up to 12 m. The **metres** axis must go up to 12 m. The **feet** axis must go up to 12 × 3 = 36 feet. Round this number off: 40 feet.

2 Draw and label axes for the graph.

→ Horizontal axis:
Label: 'metres'.
Scale: 1 cm to 1 m.
Range: 0→12 m.

↑ Vertical axis:
Label: 'feet'.
Scale: 1 cm to 5 feet.
Range: 0→40 feet.

3 Now you can work out the number of feet and copy this table.

2 × 3 = 6
5 × 3 = 15
10 × 3 = 30

Metres	2	5	10
Feet	6	15	30

4 Now mark three points: (2, 6), (5, 15) and (10, 30). You should find they are in a straight line. Draw the line with a ruler.

5 Use the line to convert any two lengths from metres to feet and two from feet to metres.

Key Fact

When you draw a conversion graph:
- work out the range of numbers you need
- draw the axes
- choose three numbers for the table
- work out the conversions
- plot three points
- join the points with a straight line.

Try It Out

Ⓝ A **pint** is an imperial unit of capacity. One litre is about 2 pints.

1 You are going to draw a conversion graph that will change up to 20 litres into pints.
Work out what range of numbers you need on your axes.
Draw the axes.

Litres	5	10	15
Pints			

2 Copy and complete this table.

3 Plot the points on the graph. Join them with a straight line.

4 Use your graph to answer these questions.
  (a) What is 7 litres in pints?
  (b) What is 33 pints in litres?

Practice

1 Jagdesh heated a liquid then allowed it to cool. He recorded the temperature of the liquid every five minutes.

Time (minutes)	0	5	10	15	20	25	30	35	40	45	50	55	60
Temperature (°C)	40	50	55	75	80	100	65	60	60	60	55	35	40

(a) Draw a line graph to show how the temperature changed over time.

→ Horizontal axis: ↑ Vertical axis:
Label: 'Time (minutes)'.   *Label*: 'Temp. (°C)'.
Scale: 1 cm to 5 minutes.   *Scale*: 1 cm to 5 °C.
Range: 0→60 minutes.   *Range*: 0→100 °C.

(b) What was the highest temperature?
(c) What was the lowest temperature?
(d) Estimate the temperature after 12 minutes.
(e) When was the temperature 65 °C?

2 To find the number of minutes needed to cook a joint of meat, calculate:

weight in kilograms $\boxed{\times 40}$ → $\boxed{+ 30}$ time in minutes.

(a) Find the time needed to cook a joint weighing . . .
   (i) 2 kg   (ii) 4 kg   (iii) 6 kg.
(b) Draw a conversion graph to give the cooking times of joints weighing up to 6 kg.
(c) What is the cooking time of a joint weighing 5 kg?
(d) What is the cooking time of a joint weighing 2.5 kg?

Finished Early?
➡ Go to page 325

Further Practice

P **1** When Andy was in hospital, his temperature was taken every hour.

   (a) Draw a line graph to show this information.

Time	9am	10am	11am	12noon	1pm	2pm	3pm	4pm
Temperature (°C)	36	35	37	38	38	39	38	37.5

   (b) When was Andy's temperature lowest?
   (c) What was Andy's highest temperature?
   (d) When was Andy's temperature 37 °C?

2 A distance of 5 miles is approximately equal to 8 km.

   (a) Draw a graph to convert distances of up to 20 miles
       to kilometres.
   (b) What is 12 miles in km?
   (c) What is 40 km in miles?
   (d) What is 23 km in miles?

Finished Early?
➡ Go to page 325

Unit 2 *Coordinates and Graphs*
Summary of Chapter 2

- Two numbers called **coordinates** give the position of a point.

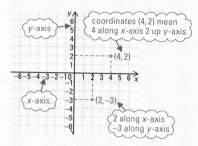

- There are many real-life situations in which **line graphs** are used. Points are plotted and joined, in order with a straight line. The temperature of a patient in a hospital is recorded in this way.

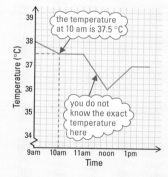

- A **conversion graph** is a straight-line graph that shows the relationship between two sets of data.

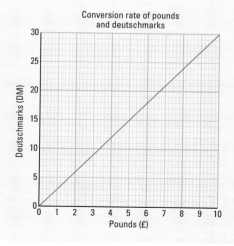

Brush Up Your Number 3

T ● Multiplication Tables

Learn About It

It is important to know your multiplication tables by heart. Practise them every day. Ask someone to test you.

Try It Out

A Answer these questions.

1 3×2	**2** 4×5	**3** 2×2	**4** 3×4
5 7×3	**6** 4×6	**7** 9×2	**8** 5×8
9 6×9	**10** 8×7	**11** 9×8	**12** 7×6

Practice

B Answer these questions.

1 There are six cars in a car park. Each has four wheels. How many wheels are there altogether?
2 Stamps cost 7p each. How much do nine stamps cost?
3 There are 10 mm in 1 cm. How many millimetres are there in 8 cm?
4 Building bricks are 2 cm high. How high is a column of seven bricks?
5 Bradley has six hours of lessons a day. How many hours of lessons does he have in six days?
6 There are five school days in a week. How many are there in three weeks?
7 A chocolate bar has eight squares. How many do five bars have?
8 Hattie has saved nine 5p pieces. How much has she saved altogether?
9 Each box contains six eggs. How many eggs are there in nine boxes?
10 Eight pupils wear gym shoes. How many gym shoes are there in all?
11 Tim and Pak each buy a bus ticket each week. How many tickets do they buy in six weeks?
12 What is the total length of nine rolls of fence if each roll is 9 m long?
13 Pies are cut into four pieces. How many pieces are there in two pies?
14 How many days are there in eight weeks?
15 Five people drink four cups of tea each. How many cups are drunk altogether?
16 Jamie cycles 2 km each day. How far does he cycle in five days?

17 It takes four apples to make a pie. How many are needed to make nine pies?

18 May Ling gets £3 a week for pocket money. How much does she get in eight weeks?

19 A can holds 5 litres of oil. How much do six cans hold?

20 Nine playing cards are dealt to each of five children. How many cards are dealt altogether?

21 A bush grows 6 cm every year. How much does it grow in two years?

22 A lift can hold six people. How many people can it carry in three journeys?

23 Umbrellas cost £9 each. How much do three cost?

24 A snail crawls 7 cm a minute. How far can it get in seven minutes?

25 There are nine sausages in a pack. How many are in two packs?

26 A swimming pool is 8 m wide. Pete swims seven widths. How far does he swim?

27 Batteries are sold in packs of four. How many are in ten packs?

28 It takes nine hours to make a kite. How long would it take to make four?

29 A bracelet is made of eight links. How many links are in two bracelets?

30 Jo works eight hours a day. How long does she work in ten days?

31 Seven apples weigh 1 kg. How many apples weigh 6 kg?

32 Mahood takes three minutes to make a sandwich. How long will he take to make four?

33 A minibus can take nine passengers. How many passengers can seven minibuses take?

34 There are seven servings in a box of cereal. How many servings are there in four boxes?

35 It rained six hours a day for four days. How long did it rain in total?

C

A 1–10 dice

1 Throw the dice in turn. Multiply the numbers and write the answer.

2 When you have ten multiplication facts each, check each other's answers.

> **Finished Early?**
> ➡ Go to page 325

3 Angles

In this chapter you will learn about ...
1. estimating, measuring and drawing angles
2. angle facts
3. triangles
4. quadrilaterals

T 1 Estimating, Measuring and Drawing Angles

Remember?

- An angle measures the turn between lines that meet at a point.
- An angle of 90° is called a right angle.
- You can **estimate** the size of angles by comparing them to right angles.
- This angle is between 0° and 90°.

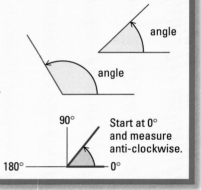

angle

angle

90°   Start at 0° and measure anti-clockwise.

180° ——— 0°

Try It Out

A Write whether each angle is:

(a) between 0 and 90°   **(b)** between 90° and 180°

(c) between 180° and 270°   **(d)** between 270° and 360°.

1   2   3

        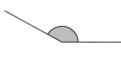

4   5

   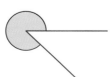

Learn About It

Tracing paper

For a more accurate estimate use this:

All these angles are 45°.

 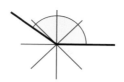

You can trace this to
help you estimate angles.

> ## Word Check
>
> **estimate** a guess at a value,
> based on what you know

This angle is a little more than 45° + 45° + 45° = 135°.
So a sensible estimate might be 150°.

Try It Out

B Estimate the size of these angles.

1

2

3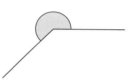

4

5

6

Protractor

Learn More About It

You measure and draw angles
accurately using
a **protractor**.

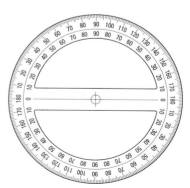

Estimate the size of this angle.
It is more than 135°.

Use a protractor to measure the angle. Line up zero on one of the arms of the angle. Here you use the outside scale. The angle is 150°, which is about the same as the estimate.

arm of the protractor
on one arm
of the angle

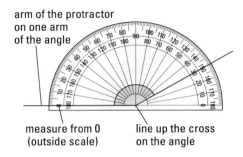

measure from 0   line up the cross
(outside scale)   on the angle

To **draw** an angle of 70°, first estimate its size –
it will look roughly like this.

Draw a base line and mark a point on it.

Line up the base of the protractor over the line and place the centre on the point you marked.
Read off 70° and mark the angle.

use the inside scale

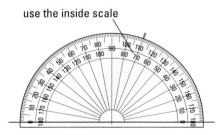

Remove the protractor and use a ruler to join up the points. Label the angle.
Check your angle is about the same as the estimate.

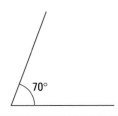

70°

Try It Out

Measure these angles.

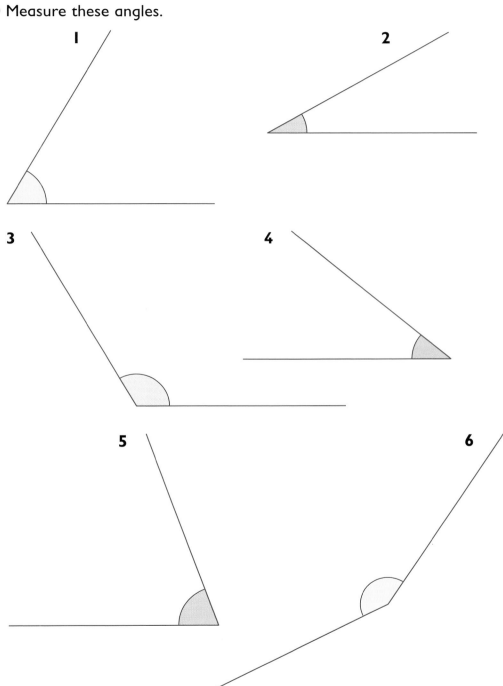

D Draw these angles.

1 60°   **2** 30°   **3** 120°   **4** 150°   **5** 40°

Practice

E Draw these angles by estimating, without using a protractor. Then measure your angles using a protractor.

1 45°   **2** 65°   **3** 80°   **4** 100°   **5** 130°   **6** 150°

F Measure the angles marked by numbers in this abstract painting.

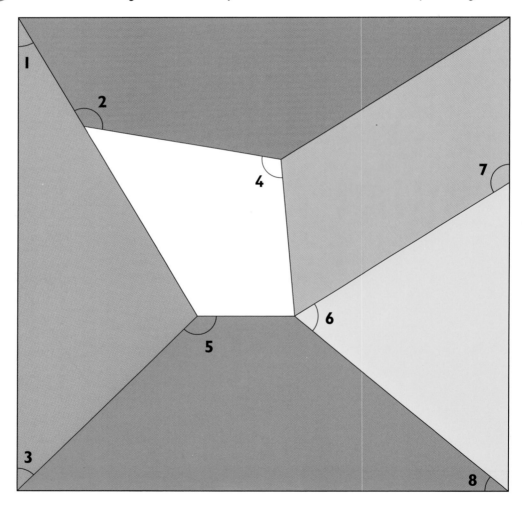

G Draw each triangle accurately and measure the missing angle. Draw the 10 cm line first, then use a protractor to draw the two angles.

1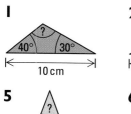

2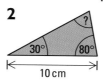

3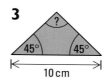

4

5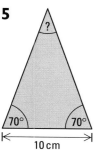

6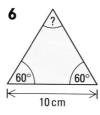

Finished Early?
➡ Go to page 325

Further Practice

H 'The Plough' is a group of stars. Measure the numbered angles.

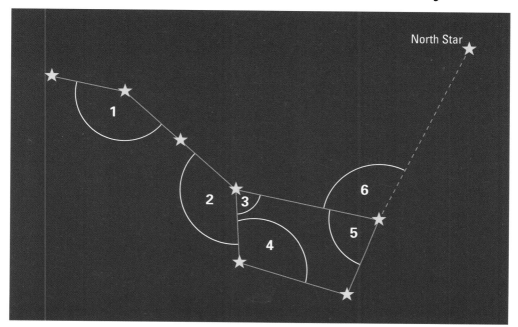

I Draw these angles.

1 25°	**2** 55°	**3** 70°
4 110°	**5** 140°	**6** 160°

Finished Early?
➡ Go to page 325

❷ Angle Facts

Learn About It

Angles on a straight line add up to 180°.
The red and the blue angles add up to 180°.
Angles that meet at a point add up to 360°.

180°

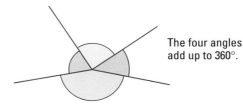
The four angles add up to 360°.

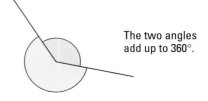
The two angles add up to 360°.

You can use these facts to find unknown angles.

Example   Find the missing angle.

(a)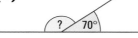
? 70°

(b)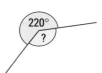
220°
?

Working   (a) The angles add up to 180°.

? = 180° − 70° = 110°

(b) The angles add up to 360°.

? = 360° − 220° = 140°

Answer   (a) 110°   (b) 140°

Try It Out

Ⓙ Find the missing angles.

1
? 50°

2
? 100°

3
60° ?

4
140° ?

5
240°
?

6
140°
?

7
200° ?

8
? 150°

Key Fact

Angles on a straight line add up to 180°.
Angles at a point add up to 360°.

Practice

K Work out the missing angles.

Example

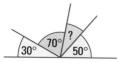

Working   Angles on a straight line add up to 180°.
30° + 70° + 50° = 150°
? = 180° − 150° = 30°
Answer   30°

1   **2**   **3**   **4**

5   **6**   **7**   **8**

L Work out the missing angles.

1   **2**   **3**   **4**

5   **6**   **7**   **8**

Finished Early?
➡ Go to page 326

Further Practice

 M Copy this diagram. Your drawing does not need to be accurate. Calculate and label the missing angles.

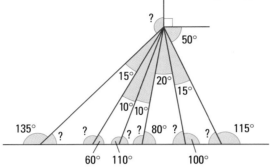

Finished Early?
➡ Go to page 326

P ③ Triangles

Learn About It

Scrap paper or card, scissors

1 Draw a large triangle.

2 Cut out your triangle and mark the angles with letters.

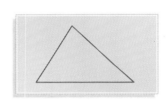

3 Tear off the corners of the triangle.

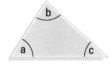

4 Fit the corners together so they meet at a point and note the angle they make.

5 Draw and cut out three different triangles. Again, tear off the corners and put them together. What do you notice about the angle the corners of a triangle make? Write down your result.

Try It Out

 N In each question below, write *yes* if the three angles **could** make a triangle. Write *no* if the three angles **could not** make a triangle.

1 30°, 40°, 110°   **2** 70°, 20°, 90°   **3** 60°, 60°, 60°
4 40°, 40°, 90°   **5** 70°, 30°, 70°   **6** 85°, 65°, 30°

Key Fact

Angles in a triangle add up to 180°.

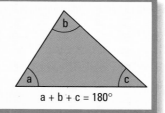

$$a + b + c = 180°$$

Learn More About It

Scrap paper or card, scissors

1 Draw these triangles. Triangles that have two equal sides are called **isosceles** triangles.

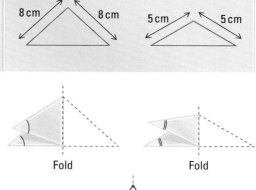

8 cm   8 cm   5 cm   5 cm

2 Cut out the triangles and fold them as shown. What do you notice about the marked angles?

Fold   Fold

3 An **equilateral** triangle has all its sides equal. If you fold it different ways, what can you say about the angles?

All sides equal

Key Fact

In an isosceles triangle, two angles are equal.

In an equilateral triangle, each angle is 60°.

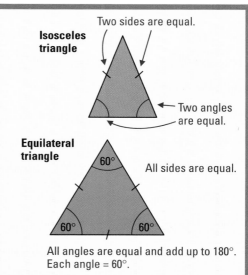

Two sides are equal.

Isosceles triangle

Two angles are equal.

Equilateral triangle

60°

All sides are equal.

60°   60°

All angles are equal and add up to 180°.
Each angle = 60°.

Try It Out

◉ In each question below . . .
if the angles can make an isosceles triangle, write *isosceles*
if the angles can make an equilateral triangle, write *equilateral*
if the angles cannot make either type of triangle, write *no*.

1 30°, 30°, 120°   **2** 40°, 50°, 90°
3 60°, 60°, 60°   **4** 70°, 70°, 40°
5 50°, 80°, 50°   **6** 70°, 60°, 50°
7 30°, 75°, 75°   **8** 80°, 20°, 80°

Practice

Ⓟ Find the missing angle in each of the following triangles.

Example

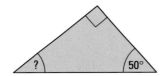

Working   The angles in a triangle add up to 180°.
90° + 50° = 140°
180° − 140° = 40°
Answer   40°

1
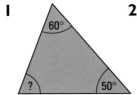

2

3 **4**

5

6
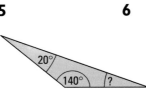

7
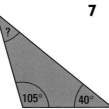

8
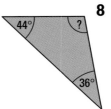

Q Find the missing angles in each of the following triangles.

Example

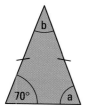

These sides are equal so the triangle is isosceles.

50° ← These angles are equal so a = 50°.

b a

Working The triangle is isosceles so a = 50°.
50° + 50° = 100°
180° − 100° = 80°

Answer a = 50°, b = 80°

1
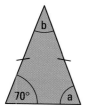
b
70° a

2
a
b
30°

3
a
b
40°

4
45°
b
a

5
b
65° a

6
a
75°
b

7
80°
a b

Hint: The other two angles are equal. Three angles add up to 180°.

8
40°
a b

9
a
50°
b

10
a
c
b

Finished Early?
➡ Go to page 326

Further Practice

(R) Arnie the abstract artist has just finished this painting. Work out the angles shown by letters.

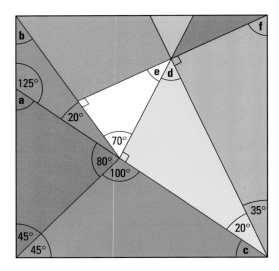

Finished Early?
➡ Go to page 326

T ❹ # Quadrilaterals

Remember?

- Any shape with four straight sides is called a **quadrilateral**.

- There are many sorts of quadrilateral.

Any shape with four sides is a quadrilateral.

Special quadrilaterals have names.

Parallelogram (Opposite sides are parallel. The arrows show parallel lines.)

Trapezium

Kite

Learn About It

When you join opposite corners of a quadrilateral with a straight line, you make two triangles.
The red and the blue angles each add up to 180°.

total = 180°
total = 180°

So the angles in a quadrilateral add up to 360°.

total = 360°

Special quadrilaterals also have other properties.

Parallelograms have opposite sides equal and opposite angles equal.

All the angles of a **rectangle** are 90°.

All the sides of a **rhombus** are equal. Opposite angles are equal.

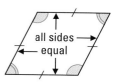

All the sides of a **square** are equal.
All the angles of a square are 90°.

Example   Find the missing angle.

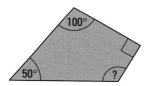

Working   50° + 100° + 90° = 240°
The angles in a quadrilateral add up to 360°.
360° − 240° = 120°

Answer   120°

Try It Out

 Sketch each shape and write its name underneath.

1   2   3   4

5   6

Key Fact

Each shape has all the properties of the shape above.

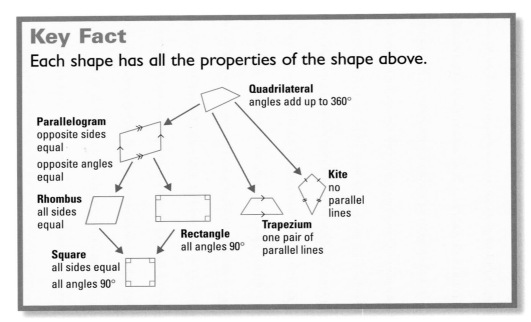

Quadrilateral
angles add up to 360°

Parallelogram
opposite sides
equal
opposite angles
equal

Rhombus
all sides
equal

Kite
no
parallel
lines

Rectangle
all angles 90°

Trapezium
one pair of
parallel lines

Square
all sides equal
all angles 90°

Practice

(T) Some of the shapes below are correctly labelled and some are not.
For each, write *correct* or explain why it is wrong.

Example

122°   57°
58°   123°
Parallelogram

Answer   Incorrect. The opposite angles should be equal.

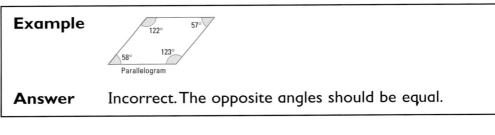

1	2	3	4
Quadrilateral	Rhombus	Parallelogram	Kite

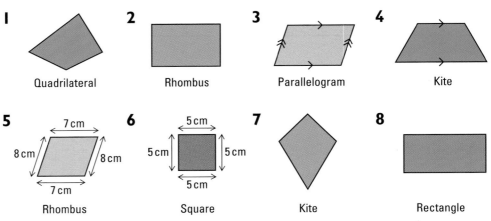

5
7 cm
8 cm   8 cm
7 cm
Rhombus

6
5 cm
5 cm   5 cm
5 cm
Square

7
Kite

8
Rectangle

U Find the missing angle in each of the following quadrilaterals.

1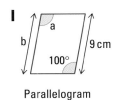
2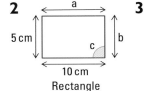
3
4

V Find the missing sides and angles (shown by letters) in each of the following quadrilaterals.

1
Parallelogram

2
Rectangle

3
Square

4
Rhombus

5
Parallelogram

6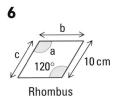
Rhombus

7
Parallelogram

8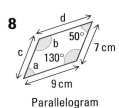
Parallelogram

> **Finished Early?**
> ➡ Go to page 327

Further Practice

W Sketch the shapes below. Your diagrams need not be accurate.
Mark in the sizes of as many sides and angles as you can.

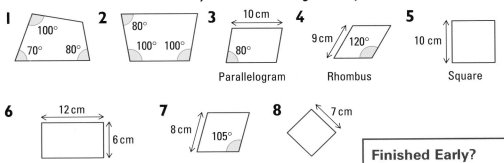

1 100° 70° 80°

2 80° 100° 100°

3 10 cm 80° Parallelogram

4 9 cm 120° Rhombus

5 10 cm Square

6 12 cm 6 cm Rectangle

7 8 cm 105° Rhombus

8 7 cm Square

> **Finished Early?**
> ➡ Go to page 327

4 Symmetry

In this chapter you will learn about ...
1. line symmetry
2. rotational symmetry

T 1 Line Symmetry

Remember?

- A shape has **line symmetry** if you can fold one half exactly on to the other. The dotted line is a **line of symmetry** for this face.
  One half folds exactly on to the other. One half is a **mirror image** or **reflection** of the other.

- A shape can have more than one line of symmetry. This pattern has eight lines of symmetry.

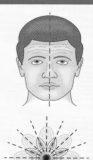

 Squared paper

Try It Out

A Copy these shapes and draw the lines of symmetry, if any.

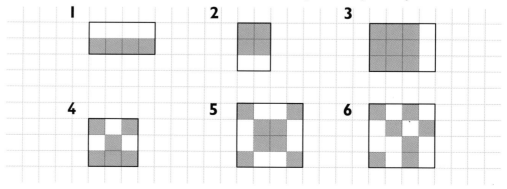

1 2 3

4 5 6

Learn About It

These shapes are drawn on coordinate axes. The line of symmetry for the triangle is a vertical line. The rectangle has two lines of symmetry — a vertical line and a horizontal line.

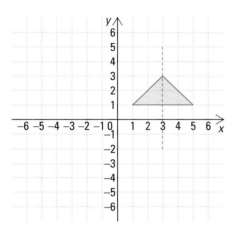
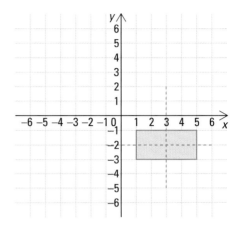

Try It Out

B Draw the following shapes on squared paper. Mark their lines of symmetry.

1
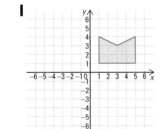

2
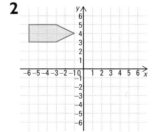

3
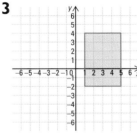

4
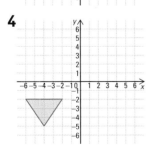

5
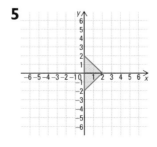

6
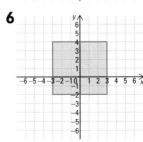

Learn More About It

Suppose you want to make the dotted line a line of symmetry.

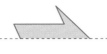

You complete the figure by drawing a mirror image. A point below the line matches the point the **same distance** above the line.

points the same distance above and below

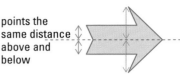

This triangle is drawn on axes:

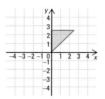

Symmetrical about the *x*-axis:

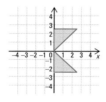

Symmetrical about the *y*-axis:

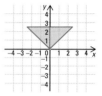

Try It Out

C Draw these diagrams on squared paper. Make them symmetrical about the *x*-axis.

1

2

3

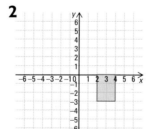

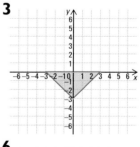

4

5

6

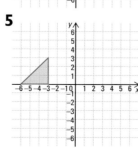

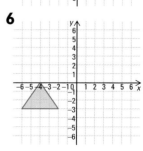

Word Check
....
line symmetry one half of a shape is a mirror image of the other
line of symmetry line that divides a shape into mirror images

Practice

D Copy the following diagrams and mark the lines of symmetry.

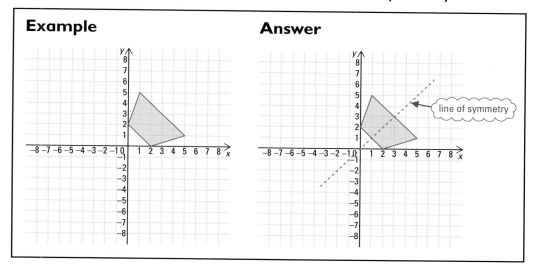

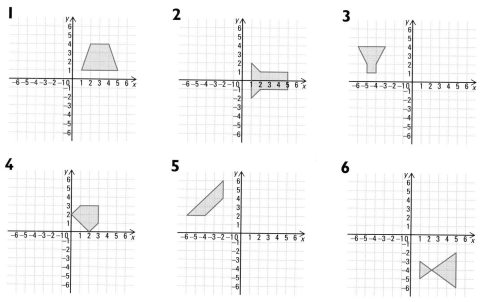

E Copy the following shapes. Make them symmetrical about both the lines of symmetry shown.

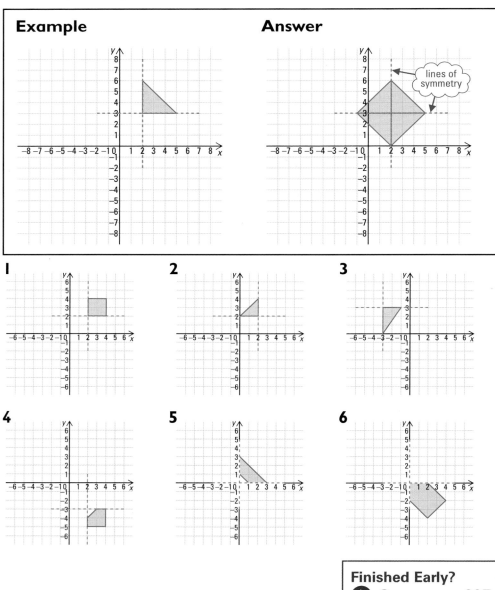

Finished Early?

➡ Go to page 327

Further Practice

F Copy these shapes and mark their lines of symmetry.

1
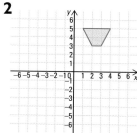

2
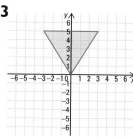

3

4

5
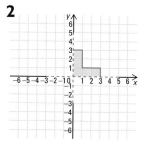

6
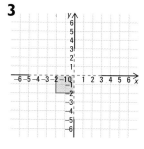

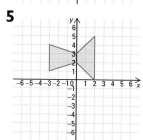

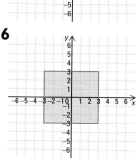

G Copy these diagrams. Make the shapes symmetrical about the *x*- and *y*-axes.

1

2

3

4

5

6

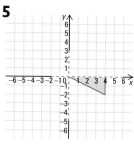

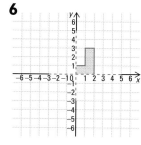

> **Finished Early?**
> ➡ Go to page 327

T ② Rotational Symmetry

Remember?

The letter S has **rotational symmetry** because it looks the same in two different positions.
S has rotational symmetry of **order 2**.
To have rotational symmetry, the order must be 2 or more.

The shape is rotated about the **centre of the rotation**.

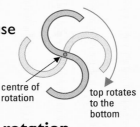

centre of rotation

top rotates to the bottom

 Tracing paper, squared paper, protractor

Try It Out

Ⓗ Do these shapes have rotational symmetry? Give the order of the symmetry.

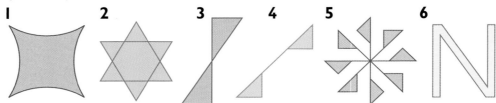

1 2 3 4 5 6

Learn About It

This equilateral triangle has rotational symmetry of order 3.

$360° \div 3 = 120°$. If you turn it through $120°$, it looks the same.

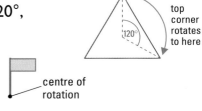

top corner rotates to here

To make this shape have symmetry of order 3, turn it through $120°$ then through $120°$ again.

centre of rotation

Tracing paper helps with rotations. Trace the green shape and press the point of your pencil at the centre of rotation.

Then keep the pencil still as you turn the tracing paper and draw the new shapes.

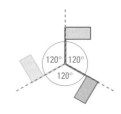

Try It Out

1 Copy these shapes and rotate them to make a pattern with the order of symmetry shown.
(a) Find the angle through which you need to turn the shape.
(b) Draw the completed shape.

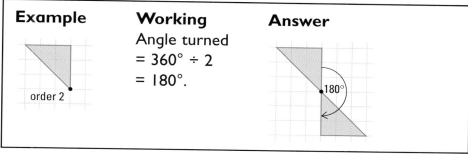

1 order 2　**2** order 2　**3** order 4　**4** order 4

Word Check

rotate turn about a point

rotational symmetry a shape looks the same in more than one position when rotated about a point

centre of rotation the point about which a shape is turned

Key Fact

To calculate the angle turned so that the final shape has rotational symmetry of a given order, divide 360° by the order of rotation.

Practice

J Copy each of the following shapes. Rotate it to form a pattern with rotational symmetry of order 4 about the centre of rotation shown.

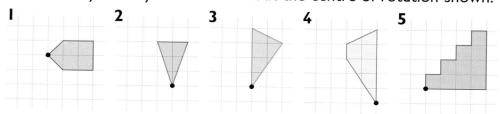

1　**2**　**3**　**4**　**5**

K Copy the following shapes. Rotate each of them about the origin to form a pattern with the rotational symmetry shown.

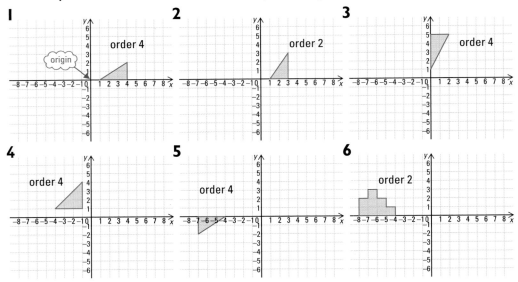

Further Practice

L Copy each shape below. Rotate it through the angle shown, and repeat until it returns to its original position. Write down the order of the symmetry of the final diagram.

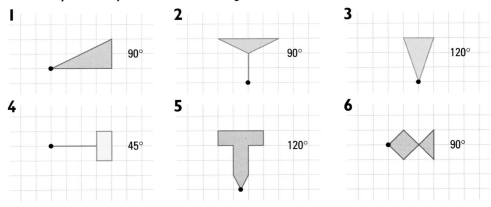

> **Finished Early?**
> ➡ Go to page 328

5 Three Dimensions

In this chapter you will learn about ...
1. solids
2. drawing solids
3. nets

1 Solids

> **Remember?**
>
> A solid takes up space; it is not flat.
>
> A solid has **faces**, **edges** and **corners**.
>
> This cuboid has 6 faces, 8 corners and 12 edges.
>
>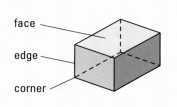
>
> face
> edge
> corner

Try It Out

A Copy and complete this table. The diagrams below will help you.

Solid	Faces	Corners	Edges
Cube	6	8	12
Triangular prism			
Triangular pyramid			
Cuboid			

Cube

Triangular prism

Cuboid

Triangular pyramid

Word Check

face surface of a solid shape

edge where two faces meet

corner where three or more edges meet

Learn About It

Here are the names for some different sorts of solids.

A **polyhedron** has straight edges and flat faces. The red shapes are polyhedra.

The others are not, as they have curved faces.

A slice through a **prism** always gives the same cross-section.

A cross-section
is a slice like this

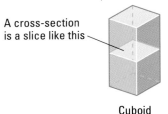

| Cuboid | Triangular prism | Hexagonal prism | Cylinder |

Pyramids have flat bases, but come to a point at the top.

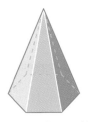

| Square-based pyramid | Triangular pyramid | Hexagonal pyramid | Cone |

Here are some other shapes.

| Octahedron | Sphere | Hemisphere |

Try It Out

B For each of the objects below:

(a) write the name of its shape

(b) write down whether it is a prism or a
pyramid or neither

(c) write down whether it is a polyhedron.

Example

Nut Flake Biscuits

Answer   **(a)** cylinder   **(b)** prism   **(c)** not a polyhedron

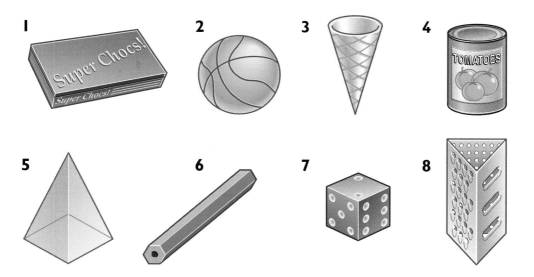

1

2

3

4   TOMATOES

5

6

7

8

Word Check

prism solid with the same cross-section
all the way through

pyramid solid that comes to a point

polyhedron solid with straight edges
and flat sides

Practice

C Copy and complete the table to include information about all the solids below.

Name	Faces	Corners	Edges
I Cuboid	6	8	12

1 **2** **3** **4**

5 **6** **7** **8**

D Write down the name of any shape with ...

1 6 faces	**2** 8 corners	**3** 5 faces	**4** 12 corners
5 4 faces	**6** 8 faces	**7** 12 edges	**8** 9 edges.

Further Practice

E Copy and complete the table to include information about all the prisms below. Draw the cross-section in the first column.

Cross-section	Faces	Corners	Edges
	8	12	18

1 **2** **3** **4**

5 **6** **7** **8**

Finished Early?
➡ Go to page 328

❷ Drawing Solids

Triangular dotted paper

Learn About It

You can draw a cube on squared paper but the sides will be different lengths.

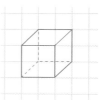

1 Use triangular dotted paper to draw this cube. The dots on the paper must be in clear vertical lines.

Draw the top first.   Then draw the sides.   Complete the cube.

Measure and mark the lengths of the sides of the cube. Use dotted lines to show the hidden edges.

2 Draw the cubes on the right and measure their sides. Write the lengths on your diagram.

3 Write down what you notice about the sides of the cubes.

4 Draw this cuboid in the same way. Write the lengths of the sides on your diagram.

Try It Out

F Draw these shapes and mark the lengths of the sides.

1   **2**   **3**   **4**   **5**

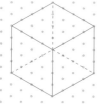

> ## Key Fact
> Cuboids drawn on triangular dotted paper have their sides in the correct proportion.

Practice

  Cubes

Make these shapes from cubes. Draw them on triangular dotted paper.

1   **2**   **3**   **4**   **5**   **6**

H Draw these shapes the correct size on triangular dotted paper.

1 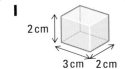 **2**   **3**   **4**

5 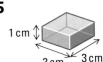 **6**   **7** 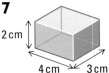 **8**

> **Finished Early?**
> ➡ Go to page 329

Further Practice

I Draw cuboids with these sides.

1 3 cm, 2 cm, 4 cm

2 4 cm, 5 cm, 2 cm

3 2 cm, 4 cm, 6 cm

4 5 cm, 7 cm, 2 cm

5 6 cm, 6 cm, 6 cm

Cubes

Each of these shapes is shown in two different positions. Make each shape with cubes and draw it in both positions.

1 (a) **(b)** **2 (a)** **(b)**

3 (a) **(b)** **4 (a)** **(b)**

Finished Early?
➡ Go to page 329

❸ Nets

Learn About It

Here is a cuboid folded out, making a flat surface. This is called the **net** of the cuboid.

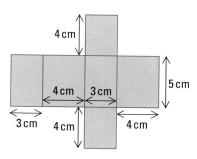

Try It Out

Squared paper

Ⓚ Draw the nets of these cuboids.

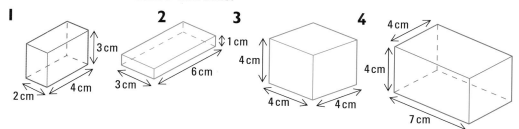

Learn More About It

Starting with a net, you can make a 3D shape. Each side must be the same length as the side it will be joined to. Here, the sides of 4 cm must be put together.

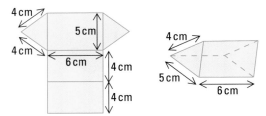

> ### Key Fact
> A net represents the surface of a solid, drawn flat.

To make a shape, you usually have to include flaps to attach the edges. They are not part of the net.

Try It Out

Triangular dotted paper

L Draw the 3D shape that could be made from each of these nets.

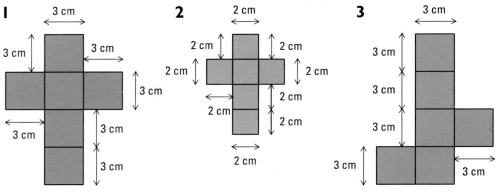

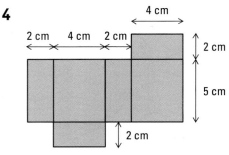

Practice

Squared paper

Ⓜ Draw the nets of these 3D shapes.

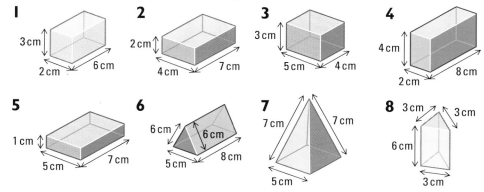

1 3 cm, 2 cm, 6 cm

2 2 cm, 4 cm, 7 cm

3 3 cm, 5 cm, 4 cm

4 4 cm, 2 cm, 8 cm

5 1 cm, 5 cm, 7 cm

6 6 cm, 6 cm, 5 cm, 8 cm

7 7 cm, 7 cm, 5 cm

8 3 cm, 3 cm, 6 cm, 3 cm

Ⓝ Sketch the solid shape each net would make.

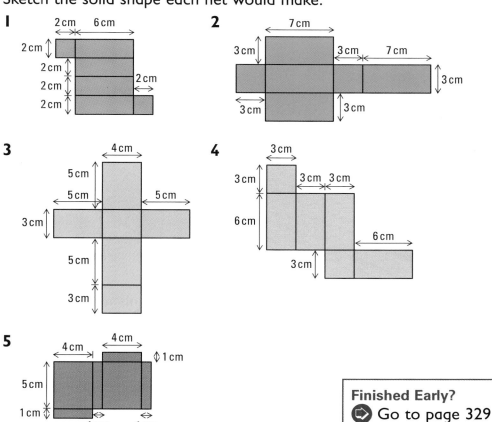

1 2 cm, 6 cm, 2 cm, 2 cm, 2 cm, 2 cm, 2 cm

2 7 cm, 3 cm, 3 cm, 7 cm, 3 cm, 3 cm, 3 cm

3 4 cm, 5 cm, 5 cm, 5 cm, 3 cm, 5 cm, 3 cm

4 3 cm, 3 cm, 3 cm, 3 cm, 6 cm, 6 cm, 3 cm

5 4 cm, 4 cm, 1 cm, 5 cm, 1 cm, 1 cm, 1 cm

Finished Early?
➡ Go to page 329

Further Practice

Card, squared paper, glue, scissors

⊚ On card, draw the net for each of the following shapes. Add flaps to each net so that you can stick the sides together. Cut out the net. Fold and stick the net to make the 3D shape.

Example

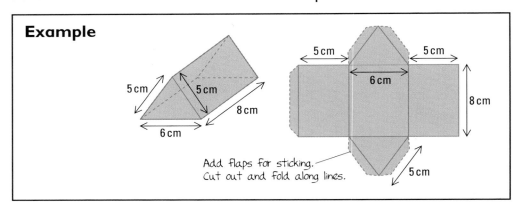

Add flaps for sticking.
Cut out and fold along lines.

I

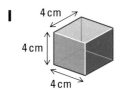

2

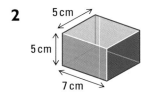

3

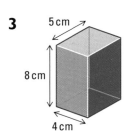

4

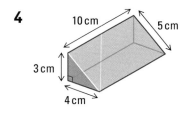

Finished Early?
⇨ Go to page 329

Unit 3 *Angles and Shapes*
Summary of Chapters 3, 4 and 5

Angles

- Angles on a **straight line** add up to 180°.

Angles add up to 180°.

- Angles **at a point** add up to 360°.

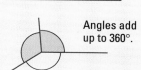

Angles add up to 360°.

- Angles in a **triangle** add up to 180°.

Angles add up to 180°.

Quadrilaterals

Any shape with four straight sides is called a **quadrilateral**.

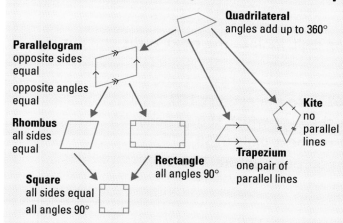

Quadrilateral angles add up to 360°

Parallelogram opposite sides equal
opposite angles equal

Rhombus all sides equal

Kite no parallel lines

Trapezium one pair of parallel lines

Rectangle all angles 90°

Square all sides equal all angles 90°

Symmetry

- A shape has **line symmetry** if one half is a mirror image of the other.

- A shape has **rotational symmetry** if it looks the same in different positions when it is rotated about a point.

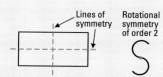

Lines of symmetry
Rotational symmetry of order 2

Brush Up Your Number 4

Rounding Whole Numbers

Learn About It

A number line can help you to round a number. 2456 rounded ...
to the nearest 10 is 2460.

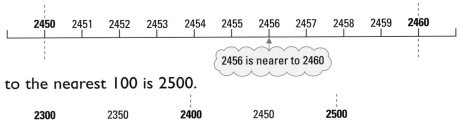

to the nearest 100 is 2500.

to the nearest 1000 is 2000.

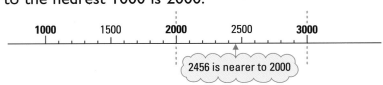

To round to a particular digit, look at the **next digit** and if it is
5, 6, 7, 8 or 9, round up.

Example	Round 6250 to the nearest 100.
Working	The 2 is the digit which shows hundreds.
	Look at the next digit. 62<u>5</u>0.
	As this is 5, round up the 2 to a 3.
Answer	6300

Try It Out

 1 Round these numbers to the nearest 10.

    (a) 234   **(b)** 1548   **(c)** 74   **(d)** 329

    (e) 7682   **(f)** 385   **(g)** 7775   **(h)** 864

2 Round these numbers to the nearest 100.

    (a) 844   **(b)** 7654   **(c)** 351   **(d)** 8650

    (e) 2385   **(f)** 3400   **(g)** 2540   **(h)** 972

3 Round these numbers to the nearest 1000.
(a) 3499   (b) 2527   (c) 12 672   (d) 9329
(e) 18 276   (f) 19 574   (g) 9673   (h) 8885

Practice

B The table below shows the weekly sales of some magazines. For each magazine, round the sales to (a) the nearest 100, (b) the nearest 1000, (c) the nearest 10 000.

	Magazine	Sales
1	Good Games	131 245
2	Stargazing	15 356
3	Sport Weekly	23 892
4	Mega Sounds	98 450
5	Travel Tales	33 420
6	Puzzle Fun	142 367
7	Perfect Pets	100 548
8	Cookery Tips	89 535
9	Top Computers	117 389
10	Super Planes	43 244

C The table below shows a survey of the number of cars using different roads in a day.

Copy and complete the table.

Road	Number of cars	Nearest 10	Nearest 100	Nearest 1000
A	3 477			
B	27 869			
C	35 276			
D	2 456			
E	687			
F	32 450			
G	134 351			
H	455			

> **Finished Early?**
> ➡ Go to page 329

6 Decimals

In this chapter you will learn about ...
1. decimals
2. rounding decimals
3. adding and subtracting decimals
4. place value calculations
5. multiplying and dividing decimals

 1 Decimals

Remember?

In a decimal number, the decimal point separates the whole number from the decimal fraction.

The **first decimal place** shows tenths.

The **second decimal place** shows hundredths.

To find which is the larger of two or more decimal numbers, look at the digits in order, from left to right.

2·37	2·37	2·37	2.37 is bigger
2·365	2·365	2·365	than 2.365
the same	the same	7 is larger than 6	

Try It Out

A Write each set of numbers in order, with the smallest first.

1. 2.45, 2.38, 2.39
2. 3.64, 3.72, 3.55
3. 41.75, 41.71, 41.69
4. 12.5, 12.49, 12.45
5. 2.08, 2.07, 2.14
6. 4.72, 4.81, 4.73
7. 14.82, 14.87, 14.86
8. 9.65, 9.64, 9.63

NUMBER SKILLS Use place value of digits

Learn About It

I After the decimal point, the first place shows tenths, the second hundredths, etc.

Continue the pattern to show the first five places in this table.

1st place	2nd place	3rd place	4th place	5th place
$\frac{1}{10}$	$\frac{1}{100}$			

2 The 5 in the number 2.42**5**4 is in the third decimal place.

Its value is $\frac{5}{1000}$.

Write down the values of the digits shown in red.

(a) 2.3**5**   **(b)** 14.3**3**4   **(c)** 5.4**7**6

The **scale** on a ruler is used to measure lengths. The length of this leaf is 5.6 cm.

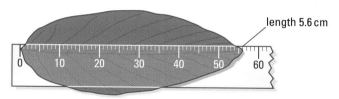

length 5.6 cm

3 The scale on a microscope measures to more decimal places.
Write down the lengths of these objects.

(a)   **(b)**   **(c)**

a hair
3.251 3.252 3.253

a crystal
2.8 2.81 2.82 2.83

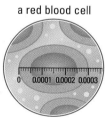
a red blood cell
0 0.0001 0.0002 0.0003

Try It Out

B Write down the value of the digits shown in red.

Example	14.5**3**4
Answer	$\frac{3}{100}$

I 2.3**4**5   **2** **1**.7   **3** 12.3**1**2   **4** 4.2**2**3

5 6.554 **1**5   **6** 0.02**6**   **7** 0.0**3**5   **8** 30.3**6**2

C Write down the values marked by arrows on this scale.

D Write down each set of numbers in order, with the smallest first.

1 2.35, 2.34, 2.36
2 0.725, 0.741, 0.739
3 1.813, 1.812, 1.821
4 3.2501, 3.254, 3.249
5 7.227, 7.226, 7.229
6 8.104, 8.003, 8.103
7 6.276, 6.274, 6.275
8 5.455, 5.554, 5.544

Key Fact

Starting at the decimal point, the place value of each digit is 10 times smaller than the place value of the digit to its left, e.g. tenths, hundredths, thousandths, etc.

Practice

E Write down the values marked by arrows on these scales.

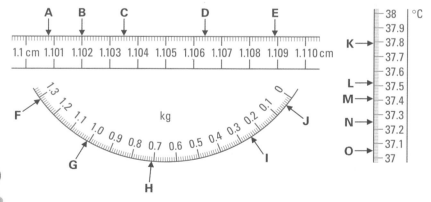

F Squared paper

Copy this scale and mark the following values, using arrows.

0   0.1   0.2   0.3   0.4   0.5   0.6   0.7   0.8

1 0.2
2 0.02
3 0.45
4 0.63
5 0.79
6 0.33
7 0.12
8 0.55

Write each set of numbers in order, with the smallest first.

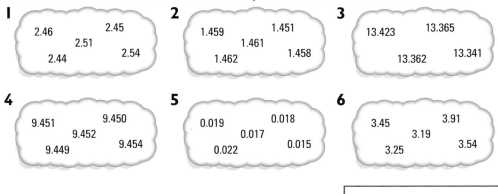

1
2.46   2.45   2.51   2.44   2.54

2
1.459   1.451   1.461   1.462   1.458

3
13.423   13.365   13.362   13.341

4
9.451   9.450   9.452   9.454   9.449

5
0.019   0.018   0.017   0.022   0.015

6
3.45   3.91   3.19   3.25   3.54

> **Finished Early?**
> ➡ Go to page 330

Further Practice

A scientist measures the time it takes cars to cover 100 m.

She times each car five times.

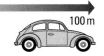

1 The times for the first car are shown on this scale.

6.8 6.9 7.0 7.1 7.2 7.3 7.4 7.5 7.6 7.7 7.8 7.9 8.0 8.1
seconds

Write down the times in order, with the shortest time first.

2 The times for the second car are, in seconds, 6.91, 7.05, 7.43, 7.59, 7.75. Write these on a scale like that used in question 1.

3 The times for the third car are, in seconds, 8.05, 7.71, 7.04, 6.88, 7.53. Write these in order, with the shortest time first.

4 The times for the fourth car are, in seconds, 7.543, 6.925, 8.04, 7.125, 7.555. Write these in order, with the shortest time first.

5 Which car travelled the distance in the shortest time?

6 Which car travelled the distance in the longest time?

> **Finished Early?**
> ➡ Go to page 330

T ❷ Rounding Decimals

Remember?

Whole numbers can be **rounded** to the nearest 10, 100, etc.

2453 rounded to the nearest 10 is 2450.

2453   becomes   2450   rounded to the nearest 10
this is the↗   ↖the next digit
10s digit   is less than 5

2453 rounded to the nearest 100 is 2500.

2453   becomes   2500   rounded to the nearest 100
this is the↗   ↖the next digit is   ↖increase the digit by 1 because
100s digit   5, 6, 7, 8 or 9   the next digit is 5, 6, 7, 8 or 9

2453 rounded to the nearest 1000 is 2000.

Try It Out

❶ Round these numbers to **(a)** the nearest 10, **(b)** the nearest 100.

1 274   **2** 134   **3** 267   **4** 585

5 2359   **6** 125 746 **7** 812   **8** 795

Learn About It

You can round a number to the nearest **whole number**.

You can also round to a certain number of **decimal places, d.p.** for short.

0.5641 rounded:

to the nearest whole number is 1

to 1 decimal place is 0.6

to 2 decimal places is 0.56

to 3 decimal places is 0.564

Try It Out

J **1** Round these numbers to the nearest whole number.

    (a) 2.34   **(b)** 12.57   **(c)** 10.8   **(d)** 239.59

2 Round these numbers to 1 decimal place.

    (a) 2.34   **(b)** 15.47   **(c)** 2.02   **(d)** 4.99

3 Round these numbers to 2 decimal places.

    (a) 0.344   **(b)** 15.225   **(c)** 0.008   **(d)** 2.503

4 Round these numbers to 3 decimal places.

    (a) 5.6432   **(b)** 0.0025   **(c)** 0.3157   **(d)** 12.0005

> ## Key Fact
> When using decimal places (d.p.), round to a given number of places after the decimal point. Round up if the next digit is 5, 6, 7, 8 or 9.

Practice

K A scientist measured the masses of chemicals, using electronic scales.

Copy and complete the table.

Chemical	Mass (g)	Rounded to nearest whole number	1 d.p.	2 d.p.
Carbon	2.256			
Sodium	4.5345			
Mercury	5.2472			
Strontium	4.952			
Argon	0.435			

L Calculate the following and round your answers to 2 d.p.

1 13.56 − 4.273

2 7.853 + 6.237

3 12.563 + 11.238

4 6.356 + 17.37 + 2.211

5 2.54 × 6.27

6 13.58 × 4.57

7 34.57 ÷ 4.56

8 0.675 ÷ 0.265

Finished Early?
➡ Go to page 330

Further Practice

 Copy and complete this table.

| Mass (g) | Rounded to | | |
	nearest whole number	1 d.p.	2 d.p.
2.347			
0.0585			
230.235			
11.957			
21.075			
112.507			
0.4756			
3.3472			

Finished Early?
➡ Go to page 330

❸ Adding and Subtracting Decimals

Remember?

To add or subtract whole numbers, make sure they are lined up in columns with the units on the right.

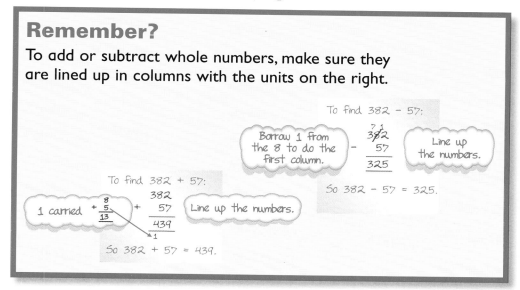

To find 382 − 57:

Borrow 1 from the 8 to do the first column.

$$\begin{array}{r} {}^{7\ 1}\\ 3\cancel{8}\cancel{2}\\ -\ \ 57\\ \hline 325 \end{array}$$

Line up the numbers.

So 382 − 57 = 325.

To find 382 + 57:

1 carried

$$\begin{array}{r} {}^{8}\\ +\ \frac{5}{13} \end{array}$$

$$\begin{array}{r} 382\\ +\ \ 57\\ \hline 439\\ {}_{1} \end{array}$$

Line up the numbers.

So 382 + 57 = 439.

Try It Out

Ⓝ Work out the following.

I 12 + 43   **2** 123 + 26   **3** 334 + 121   **4** 235 + 48

5 145 − 23   **6** 356 − 122   **7** 428 − 142   **8** 345 − 216

Learn About It

To add or subtract decimals, first line up the decimal points. Then work out as for whole numbers.

The number of decimal places does not have to be the same.

36·25 + 5·1

$$\begin{array}{r} 36\cdot25\\ +\ \ 5\cdot1\\ \hline 41\cdot35\\ {}_{1} \end{array}$$

Line up the decimal points and add.

12·5 − 4·23

$$\begin{array}{r} {}^{0\ 1\ 4\ 1}\\ \cancel{12}\cdot\cancel{5}\cancel{0}\\ -\ \ 4\cdot23\\ \hline 8\cdot27 \end{array}$$

Adding a zero at the end of a decimal fraction does not alter the value of the number.

Try It Out

Ⓞ Work out the following.

I 12.5 + 6.2   **2** 23.4 + 9.3   **3** 6.25 + 3.4   **4** 5.5 + 7.45

5 12.5 − 6.3   **6** 23.44 − 11.22   **7** 25.7 − 12.8   **8** 34.25 − 14.3

Practice

P A shop sells these items.

Old record £2.55

Earphones £9.64

CD cleaner £3.36

Personal stereo £38.49

CDs £8.85

Tape £1.56

CD storage box £8.65

What is the total cost of ...

I a personal stereo and a CD?   **2** a CD and an old record?

3 a tape and earphones?   **4** a CD and a CD box?

5 earphones and a CD box?   **6** a CD and a CD cleaner?

7 a personal stereo and earphones? **8** a tape and an old record?

9 a tape and a CD cleaner?   **10** an old record and earphones?

Q Find the difference in price between each pair of items in Exercise **P**.

> **Finished Early?**
> ➡ Go to page 331

Further Practice

R These items are on sale on a toy stall.

Talking doll £11.25

Bicycle £89.65

Model racing car £9.79

Roller skates £27.50

Video game £31.28

Dressmaking kit £13.49

I What is the total cost of ...
  (a) the roller skates and the racing car?
  (b) the doll and the dressmaking kit?
  (c) the bicycle and the video game?
  (d) the roller skates and the bicycle?
  (e) the dressmaking kit and the racing car?

2 What is the difference between the costs of ...
   (a) the roller skates and the dressmaking kit?
   (b) the racing car and the video game?
   (c) the bicycle and the dressmaking kit?
   (d) the video game and the roller skates?
   (e) the roller skates and the doll?

> **Finished Early?**
> ➡ Go to page 331

❹ Place Value Calculations

Learn About It

When you multiply by 10, 100, 1000 ... the answer is larger.
The digits move to the left.

To multiply by 10, move the digits one place to the left.

To work out 2.35×10, you can multiply each digit by 10.

Place value	10	1	$\frac{1}{10}$	$\frac{1}{100}$
		2	3	5
	$\times 10$	$\times 10$	$\times 10$	
	2	3	5	

So $2.35 \times 10 = 23.5$.
$12.76 \times 10 = 127.6$
$34 \times 10 = 340$

> **Word Check**
> **place value** the value of a column in the decimal system, e.g. hundreds column

When you divide by 10, 100, 1000 ... the answer is smaller.
The digits move to the right.

To divide by 10, move the digits one place to the right.
$23.5 \div 10 = 2.35$

Place value	10	1	$\frac{1}{10}$	$\frac{1}{100}$
	2	3	5	
		$\div 10$	$\div 10$	$\div 10$
		2	3	5

Try It Out

S Work out the following.

1 2.3 × 10	**2** 2.3 × 100	**3** 3.25 × 100	**4** 12.4 × 10
5 67 ÷ 10	**6** 67 ÷ 100	**7** 92.5 ÷ 10	**8** 623 ÷ 100

Practice

T A shop buys these goods in bulk.

Jumper £23.42

Coat £23.52

Trainers £13.25

Shoes £21.59

Trousers £19.24

Hat £3.62

1 Find the cost of the following.

   (a) 10 coats   **(b)** 100 pairs of trousers

   (c) 10 hats   **(d)** 100 pairs of trainers

   (e) 10 pairs of shoes   **(f)** 10 jumpers

   (g) 1000 hats   **(h)** 1000 coats

   (i) 1000 pairs of trousers   **(j)** 1000 jumpers.

2 Find the cost of one item if ...

   (a) 100 raincoats cost £4350

   (b) 10 scarves cost £47.50

   (c) 1000 pairs of socks cost £3250

   (d) 10 skirts cost £137.50

   (e) 1000 waterproof jackets cost £23 450

   (f) 1000 straw hats cost £2330.

> **Finished Early?**
>  Go to page 332

Further Practice

U Multiply each of the following amounts by **(a)** 10, **(b)** 100, **(c)** 1000.

1 £2.37	**2** £12.50	**3** £0.63	**4** £3.45
5 2.64 m	**6** 5.25 m	**7** 12.3 g	**8** 64.254 kg

> **Finished Early?**
> Go to page 332

⑤ Multiplying and Dividing Decimals

Learn About It

$12 \times 13 = 156$

You can work these multiplications from the first calculation:

$12 \times 1.3 = 15.6$ (move the digits one place, $156 \div 10$)

$1.2 \times 1.3 = 1.56$ (move the digits two places, $156 \div 100$)

$1.2 \times 0.13 = 0.156$ (move the digits three places, $156 \div 1000$).

The total number of decimal places in the question equals the number of decimal places in the answer.

Example	17.2×3.25	There are 3 decimal places in question.

$$\begin{array}{r} 172 \\ \times \quad 325 \\ \hline 860 \\ 3440 \\ 51600 \\ \hline 55900 \end{array}$$

First calculate without the decimal points.

$\leftarrow 172 \times 5$
$\leftarrow 172 \times 20$
$\leftarrow 172 \times 300$

Now put 3 d.p. in the answer.

Answer $55.900 = 55.9$

Try It Out

Ⓥ Work out the following.

1 3.5×2.4 **2** 2.5×1.2 **3** 2.4×0.6 **4** 3.6×1.1

5 2.5×0.7 **6** 0.26×0.5 **7** 0.36×0.3 **8** 0.28×0.6

Learn More About It

When dividing decimals, multiply both numbers by 10, 100, etc. until the number you are dividing by is a whole number.

$156 \div 12 = 13$

To work out $156 \div 1.2$, multiply **both** numbers by 10.

$156 \div 1.2 = 1560 \div 12 = 130$

To work out $1.56 \div 0.12$, multiply **both** numbers by 100.

$1.56 \div 0.12 = 156 \div 12 = 13$

When you divide by a number which is less than 1, the answer is larger than the number divided.

Try It Out

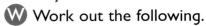 Work out the following.

1 6.48 ÷ 1.2	**2** 6.48 ÷ 0.12	**3** 0.648 ÷ 1.2	**4** 27.5 ÷ 1.1
5 2.43 ÷ 0.9	**6** 6.44 ÷ 0.8	**7** 3.64 ÷ 0.4	**8** 12.1 ÷ 0.25

Key Fact

When **multiplying** decimals, there are the same number of decimal places in the answer as in the question.

When **dividing** decimals, multiply both numbers by 10, 100, … until you can divide by a whole number.

Practice

X Copy and complete this table.

Length (m)	2.5	6.2		4.24	5.75	4.3
Width (m)	1.4	1.75	2.5		3.2	
Area (m²)			6.25	14.84		14.19

> **Finished Early?**
> ➡ Go to page 332

Further Practice

Y The calculations in the boxes are correct. Use them to answer the questions below.

23 × 355 = 8165	18 × 38 = 684	27 × 137 = 3699
36 × 166 = 5976	756 ÷ 42 = 18	493 ÷ 17 = 29

1 0.18 × 3.8	**2** 1.66 × 3.6	**3** 0.23 × 3.55
4 7.56 ÷ 4.2	**5** 0.27 × 13.7	**6** 49.3 ÷ 0.17

> **Finished Early?**
> ➡ Go to page 332

Unit 4 *Decimals*

Summary of Chapter 6

- In a decimal number, the **decimal point** separates the whole number from the decimal fraction.

Decimal places

The **first decimal place** shows tenths.

The **second decimal place** shows hundredths.

The **third decimal place** shows thousandths.

- To find which is the larger of two or more decimal numbers, look at the digits in order, from left to right.

2.135**5**9   2.1360 is the larger number
2.136**6**0   because 5 is less than 6

- You can round to a certain number of **decimal places, d.p.** for short.

Rounding to **one decimal place (1 d.p.)** is the same as rounding to the nearest tenth.

If the next digit is 5, 6, 7, 8 or 9, round up

12.43¦5 rounded to 2 d.p. = 2.44

Calculating with decimals

- When you multiply a number by 10, the digits move one place to the left.

When you multiply a number by 100, the digits move two places to the left.

When you divide by 10, 100 ... the digits move to the right.

- To **add** and **subtract** decimals, line up the decimal points. Then work out as for whole numbers.

- When you **multiply** decimals, you should have the same number of decimal places in the answer as in the question.

When you **divide** decimals, multiply both numbers by a power of 10 (10, 100, 1000, etc.) until you can divide by a whole number.

Brush Up Your Number 5

T Multiplying Whole Numbers

Learn About It

To be able to multiply numbers, you need to know your **multiplication tables**.

To multiply by 10, 100 or 1000, move the digits to the **left** 1, 2 or 3 places. Fill empty columns with zeros.

$23 \times 10 = 230$
$410 \times 100 = 41\,000$

To multiply 1 s.f. numbers, use tables **and** move digits.

$40 \times 2 = 4 \times 10 \times 2$
$\qquad\quad = 8 \times 10$ (*You know that 4 × 2 = 8.*)
$\qquad\quad = 80$
$600 \times 30 = 6 \times 100 \times 3 \times 10$
$\qquad\qquad = 18 \times 1000$ (*You know that 6 × 3 = 18.*)
$\qquad\qquad = 18\,000$

To multiply by a two-digit number, use the box method or set out the calculation in columns.

Example 435×37

Working (box method):

×	400	30	5
30	12 000	900	150
7	2 800	210	35

Totals   14 800   1110   185

14 800 + 1110 = 15 910
15 910 + 185 = 16 095

Working (column method):

$$
\begin{array}{r}
4\ 3\ 5 \\
\times\quad 3\ 7 \\
\hline
3\ 0_2 4_3 5 \\
1\ 3_1 0_1 5\ 0 \\
\hline
1\ 6\ 0\ 9\ 5 \\
\end{array}
$$

Answer   16 095

Try It Out

A Work out the following.

1 31 × 7	**2** 256 × 4	**3** 975 × 6
4 1447 × 2	**5** 42 628 × 8	**6** 41 × 10
7 12 × 100	**8** 235 × 10	**9** 703 × 100
10 250 × 1000	**11** 60 × 7	**12** 400 × 6
13 30 × 50	**14** 9 × 200	**15** 300 × 40
16 55 × 25	**17** 2605 × 42	**18** 5038 × 77

Practice

B **1** Copy and complete the Mallinson's Cakes production sheet for this week. Write your working underneath.

Type of cake	Number per box	Number of boxes	Number of cakes
Cherry bakewell	5	690	
Choc sponge roll	6	1235	
Mini battenburg	8	562	
Jam tarts	6	348	
Strawberry tarts	4	744	

Their target is to make 20 000 cakes a week. Have they met their target this week?

2 Calculate the following.

(a) 12 × 16 × 23   **(b)** 104 × 16 × 5

(c) 29 × 28 × 26 × 27   **(d)** 300 × 9 × 5 × 17

(e) 15 × 11 × 12 × 14 × 13   **(f)** 2 × 100 × 19 × 50 × 3 × 29

> **Finished Early?**
> Go to page 333

7 Formulae and Expressions

In this chapter you will learn about ...
1. substitution
2. making formulae
3. simplifying expressions

Ⓣ① Substitution

> ### Remember?
>
> - In a formula or expression, you can use letters to stand for numbers, e.g. you could use **M** to stand for Michael's age.
>
> - Michael's age plus 4 can be written as **M** + 4.
>
> - Miss out the multiplication sign (×) when using letters. For example, 3 times Michael's age is 3 × **M**, which you write as 3**M**. Write numbers before letters, e.g. 3**M** not **M**3.
>
> - Don't use the division sign (÷) when using letters. For example, if you divide Michael's age by 4, you get **M** ÷ 4. Write it as $\frac{M}{4}$.
>
> - To square a number, multiply it by itself. For example, the square of 7 is 7 × 7 = 49. Write the square of 7 like this: 7^2. You say '7 squared'. So, $7^2 = 7 \times 7 = 49$.

Try It Out

Ⓐ 1 Write each of the following as an expression, using the red letter.
   (a) **D**elia's age plus 6
   (b) **T**ahir's age divided by 2
   (c) **R**oger's age minus 1
   (d) 4 times **B**arbara's age

2 Write these the correct way.

(a) $m5$ (b) $p \div 6$ (c) $8 \times q$

3 Calculate the following.

(a) 4^2 (b) the square of 3   (c) nine squared   (d) 10^2

Learn About It

Jenny and her friends go to a fast-food restaurant.

Three burgers, please.

	Burger	90p
	Fries	60p
	Cola	70p
	Doughnut	40p

The assistant presses $3b$ on the cash register. $3b$ means $3 \times b$.
The cash register replaces b by 90p to calculate the cost.
This is called **substituting**.

expression   **value** of the expression

$3b = 3 \times 90p = 270p$

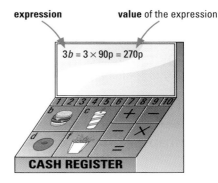

CASH REGISTER

The cash register calculated more costs for customers:

A burger and a cola: Cost $= b + c = 90p + 70p = 180p$

Three colas and two doughnuts: Cost $= 3c + 2d$

$$= 3 \times 70p + 2 \times 40p$$

$$= 210p + 80p = 290p$$

Half a portion of fries: Cost $= \dfrac{f}{2} = \dfrac{60}{2} = 30p$

Word Check

expression a mixture of numbers, letters and symbols that does not include the $=$ symbol

substitute put in place of

value the answer you get after substituting numbers for letters in an expression

Try It Out

B Calculate the values of these expressions when $f = 30$ and $t = 10$.

Example	**(a)** $4f$ **(b)** $\frac{f}{6}$ **(c)** $2f + 4t$
Working	Replace f by 30 and t by 10 in the expressions.
	(a) $4f = 4 \times 30 = 120$
	(b) $\frac{f}{6} = \frac{30}{6} = 5$
	(c) $2f + 4t = 2 \times 30 + 4 \times 10 = 60 + 40 = 100$
	(Remember: Multiply first, then add or subtract.)
Answers	**(a)** 120 **(b)** 5 **(c)** 100

1 $t + f$	**2** $f - t$	**3** $2f$	**4** $3t$
5 $\frac{f}{5}$	**6** $\frac{t}{2}$	**7** $f + 5t$	**8** $2f - t$
9 $f - 3t$	**10** $2f + 3t$	**11** $4f + 2t$	**12** $7t - 2f$

Learn More About It

Example	Calculate the values of these expressions when $m = 4$ and $n = 8$.
	(a) mn **(b)** $\frac{n}{m}$ **(c)** n^2 **(d)** $m^2 + n$
Working	Replace m by 4 and n by 8 in the expressions.
	(a) $mn = m \times n = 4 \times 5 = 20$
	(b) $\frac{n}{m} = \frac{8}{4} = 2$
	(c) $n^2 = n \times n = 8 \times 8 = 64$
	(d) $m^2 + n = 4^2 + 8 = 4 \times 4 + 8 = 16 + 8 = 24$
Answers	**(a)** 20 **(b)** 2 **(c)** 64 **(d)** 24

Try It Out

C Calculate the values of these expressions when $p = 4$ and $q = 3$.

1 pq 2 qp 3 p^2 4 q^2
5 $q^2 + 6$ 6 $p^2 - 10$ 7 $20 - p^2$ 8 $p + q^2$
9 $q^2 - q$ 10 $p^2 + q^2$

> Remember: multiply and divide before adding and subtracting.

Practice

D Calculate the value of each expression below when $f = 4$, $g = 8$ and $h = 2$.

1 $g - 3h$ 2 $2f + 2g$ 3 $5h - g$ 4 $5f + 2h$
5 $20h - 5g$ 6 $3g + 3h$ 7 $\frac{g}{2} + h$ 8 $f - \frac{g}{8}$
9 $fh + g$ 10 $hf - h$ 11 $gh + \frac{f}{2}$ 12 $gf - f$
13 $fg - fh$

> **Key Fact**
> Work out one part of an expression at a time.

E Calculate the value of each expression below when $c = 3$, $d = 6$ and $e = 2$.

Example	$\frac{d}{c} + e^2$
Working	$\frac{d}{c} = \frac{6}{3} = 2$ and $e^2 = 2^2 = 2 \times 2 = 4$
	$\frac{d}{c} + e^2 = 2 + 4 = 6$
Answer	6

1 $dc - 5e$ 2 $ed + ec$ 3 $cd - ce$ 4 $c^2 + e^2$
5 $d^2 - c^2$ 6 $e^2 + de$ 7 $\frac{d}{c} + 2e$ 8 $ce - \frac{d}{e}$
9 $c^2 + \frac{d}{c}$ 10 $\frac{d}{e} - \frac{c}{3}$

> **Finished Early?**
> Go to page 333

Further Practice

F Calculate the value of each expression when $x = 5, y = 10$ and $t = 2$.

1 (a) $2 + x$ (b) $y - 7$ (c) $x + y$ (d) $x - t$

  (e) $3x$ (f) xt (g) $\frac{y}{2}$ (h) $\frac{y}{x}$

2 (a) $2x - 4$ (b) $3y + 2$ (c) $20 - 4t$ (d) $2x - y$

  (e) $2t + 2y$ (f) $3y - 4x$

G Find the value of each expression below when $p = 3, q = 4$ and $r = 6$. In each question, two of the expressions have the same value. Find the odd one out in each case.

1 (a) $p + 1 + r$ (b) $p + qr$ (c) $p^2 + 3r$

2 (a) $2p + q - r$ (b) $r^2 - 8p$ (c) $p + \frac{6}{r}$

3 (a) $pr - q^2$ (b) $r^2 - 5q + p$ (c) $4p - q - r$

> **Finished Early?**
> ➡ Go to page 333

2 Making Formulae

Learn About It

Stella bought 3 stamps at 20 pence each. She calculated the total cost, C, like this:
$C = 3 \times 20$ pence $= 60$ pence.

Stella used this formula to calculate the cost:
$C =$ number of stamps $\times$ cost of a stamp.

1 Write down the cost, C, of 6 stamps at 25 pence each.

Stella needs 3 stamps costing s pence each.
$C = 3 \times s$ pence $= 3s$ pence

2 Write a formula for the cost, C, of 5 stamps at t pence each.

Stella posts a parcel using n stamps at 20 pence each.
$C = n \times 20$ pence $= 20n$ pence

> *Remember: $n \times 20$ is the same as $20 \times n$.*

3 Write a formula for the cost, C, of m stamps at 20 pence each.

Stella needs n stamps at s pence each to send a parcel.
$C = n \times s$ pence $= ns$ pence

4 Write a formula for the cost, C, of m stamps at t pence each.

Stella has 90 pence to buy stamps costing 15 pence each.
The number, N, she can buy is:
$N = \dfrac{90}{15} = 90 \div 15 = 6$

She used this formula:
$N = \dfrac{\text{money to spend}}{\text{price of a stamp}}$.

5 Write formulae for the number, N, of stamps she can buy if she has …
  (a) 80 pence to buy 20-pence stamps
  (b) x pence to buy 20-pence stamps
  (c) 80 pence to buy m-pence stamps
  (d) x pence to buy m-pence stamps.

6 Stella buys a first-class stamp and a second-class stamp.
  Write formulae for the total cost, C, when …
  (a) first-class stamps cost 30 pence and second-class stamps cost 20 pence
  (b) first-class stamps cost f pence and second-class stamps cost 20 pence
  (c) first-class stamps cost 30 pence and second-class stamps cost s pence
  (d) first-class stamps cost f pence and second-class stamps cost s pence.

Try It Out

(H) Write formulae for the total cost, C, of …

1 3 dice at 40 pence each
2 3 dice at a pence each
3 n dice at 40 pence each
4 n dice at s pence each
5 a sticker costing 15 pence and a sticker costing 10 pence
6 a sticker costing a pence and one costing b pence.

Practice

(I) 1 The following TV programmes are going to be recorded on video. Write a formula for the total recording time, T for …

(a) four chat shows lasting 20 minutes each and 15 minutes of the news
(b) two cartoons lasting c minutes each and a soap lasting 25 minutes
(c) three soaps lasting s minutes each and two films lasting f minutes each
(d) three documentaries lasting d minutes each and half a film lasting f minutes
(e) four episodes of a comedy lasting S minutes each and n cartoons lasting c minutes each
(f) m minutes of the news and a quarter of a quiz show lasting q minutes
(g) m adverts lasting a minutes each and n cartoons lasting c minutes each.

2 (a) Brenda spent 80 pence buying green pencils costing 10 pence each. Write a formula for the number, N, she bought.
(b) Charles spent 60 pence on red pencils costing r pence each. Write a formula for the number, N, that he bought.
(c) Kelly spent 50 pence on red pencils costing r pence each. She also bought three blue pencils. Write a formula for the total number, N, of pencils that she bought.
(d) Prakesh spent 90 pence on red pencils costing r pence each and 60 pence on blue pencils costing b pence each. Write a formula for the number, N, of pencils he bought.

J Find the formulae made by the machines below.

> **Example** b ⟩÷3⟩ ⟩+c⟩ a
> **Working** $b \div 3 + c$ gives the answer a
> **Answer** $a = \dfrac{b}{3} + c$

1 b ⟩+5⟩ a 2 x ⟩×10⟩ y 3 n ⟩−3k⟩ m

4 B ⟩×B⟩ A 5 5 ⟩−h²⟩ T 6 x^2 ⟩+y²⟩ l

7 b ⟩+3⟩→⟩−c⟩ a 8 5 ⟩÷n⟩→⟩−p⟩ s 9 m ⟩×n⟩→⟩+r⟩ d

10 e ⟩×f⟩→⟩×g⟩ h

Finished Early?
⮕ Go to page 334

Further Practice

1 Write formulae for the volume, V, remaining in a 50 cl bottle of juice after filling …
   (a) a glass with 10 cl of juice
   (b) a glass with s cl of juice
   (c) 4 glasses with 10 cl of juice each
   (d) 4 glasses with s cl of juice each
   (e) n glasses with 10 cl of juice each
   (f) n glasses with s cl of juice each.

2 Write a formula for each of the following.
   (a) A book costs b pence. A pen costs n pence. What is the total cost, C?
   (b) There are 20 biscuits in a box. Mrs Jones buys m boxes. What number, N, of biscuits does she buy?
   (c) £30 is divided among n children. What amount, A, does each child receive?
   (d) A ribbon r metres long is cut into n pieces. What is the length, l, of each piece?
   (e) Packets contain s wine gums. Lotti buys m packets. What number, W, of wine gums does she buy?
   (f) A spoon holds 5 g of sugar. n spoons are taken from a 500 g packet. What weight, W, of sugar is left in the packet?
   (g) A train engine is t metres long. It has n carriages, each c metres long. What is the total length, L?

Finished Early?
⮕ Go to page 334

T ❸ Simplifying Expressions

Learn About It

Packets of crisps cost c pence each.
Mrs Purvis buys three packets for $3c$ pence.

Then she buys another two packets for $2c$ pence.

Altogether she spends $2c + 3c$ pence.
This simplifies to $5c$ pence.
Look at this expression: $3a + 4a - 2a$.

The $+$ and $-$ signs break up the expression into **terms**: $3a + 4a - 2a$.
All the terms have the same letter (a), so they are called **like terms**.
Like terms can be **simplified**:
$3a + 4a - 2a = 5a$ (because $3 + 4 - 2 = 5$).

> ### Key Fact
> The $+$ and $-$ signs belong to
> the terms that follow them.
> Like terms can be simplified.

The terms of $4mn + 3mn$ have exactly the same letters (m and n).
They are like terms and can be simplified:
$4mn + 3mn = 7mn$ (because $4 + 3 = 7$).

Word Check

terms parts of an expression,
   separated by $+$ and $-$ signs
like terms terms that have
   exactly the same letters
simplify combine several like
   terms into one term

Try It Out

Simplify the following expressions.

Example	$7m - 2m$
Working	$7 - 2 = 5$
Answer	$5m$

1 **(a)** $t + t + t$ **(b)** $n + n + n + n + n + n$ **(c)** $F + F$
   (d) $2q + 9q$ **(e)** $8p - 5p$ **(f)** $3f + f$
   (g) $10x - 5x$ **(h)** $25K + 25K$ **(i)** $5k - k$

Example	$5b + 3b - 2b$
Working	$5 + 3 - 2 = 6$
Answer	$6b$

2 **(a)** $2s + 8s - 4s$ **(b)** $8k - 3k + 2k$ **(c)** $9r - 2r + 3r$

Example	$4rs + 3rs$
Working	$4 + 3 = 7$
Answer	$7rs$

3 **(a)** $2mn + 10mn$ **(b)** $4xy + 8xy$ **(c)** $20de - 6de$

Example	$4d - d$
Working	$4d - d = 4d - 1d$ (d is the same as 1d.)
	$4 - 1 = 3$
Answer	$3d$

4 **(a)** $9t - t$ **(b)** $7m - m$ **(c)** $5r + r$
   (d) $3k - k + 2k$ **(e)** $6i - 5i$ **(f)** $5rt - 4rt$

Learn More About It

Mrs Purvis buys three packets of crisps and two cans of cola for $3c + 2d$ pence.

Mr Purvis buys four packets of crisps and one can of cola for $4c + d$ pence.

Altogether, they spend $3c + 2d + 4c + d$ pence.

Put the like terms together:
$3c + 4c + 2d + d$.

This simplifies to $7c + 3d$.

 You cannot simplify $7c + 3d$ because $7c$ and $3d$ have different letters, so they are *not* like terms.

The like terms in this expression are mixed up:
$5x - 2y - 3x + 6y$.

Put the like terms together:
$$5x - 2y - 3x + 6y$$
$$= 5x - 3x + 6y - 2y$$
$$= 2x + 4y.$$

Key Fact

When terms are rearranged, each sign stays with the term that follows it.

Try It Out

 I Simplify the following.
  (a) $4d + 5d + 5e - 2e$
  (b) $5m - 2m + 4n - 3n$
  (c) $4w - 2w + 3x - x$
  (d) $9r - r + 8v - v$

2 In each of the following expressions, put the like terms next to each other, then simplify.
  (a) $2a + 3b + 5a + 2b$
  (b) $4k + 9l + 2l + 5k$
  (c) $6p + 4q + 2q + 3p$
  (d) $2t + 7s + 8t - 2s$
  (e) $2u + 3v - v + 7u$
  (f) $5w + 7q - 2w + 3q$

Practice

N Simplify the following expressions.

Example	$2ab + 3ba$
Working	ba is the same as ab, so
	$2ab + 3ba = 2ab + 3ab = 5ab$
Answer	$5ab$

1 $5pr + 2rp$ 2 $12mt - 9tm$ 3 $4tv - vt$

4 $5xy + 2yx + 3xy$ 5 $9ba - 2ab - 4ab$ 6 $8pq - 2pq + 3qp$

D Simplify these expressions.

1 $3a + 4a + 3 + 5$ | *Hint: 3 and 5 are like terms.* |

2 $5p + 3 + 4p + 9$

3 $6d + 7 - 4d - 2$ 4 $6pq + 2ab + 5ab - 2pq$

5 $4jk + 3mn + 6jk - 2mn$ 6 $8wd + 5 - 3wd - 2$

Finished Early?
➡ Go to page 334

Further Practice

1 In each question, two of the three terms are like terms.
Write down the odd one out in each question.

  (a) $5r, 2s, 4r$ **(b)** $2bc, 4ac, 8ac$ **(c)** $2pq, 6qp, 3pr$

  (d) $5d, 2de, 4de$ **(e)** $2vw, 8w, wv$

2 Simplify the following expressions.

  (a) $3H + 5K + 2H$ **(b)** $6u + 4d - d$ **(c)** $3sf + 5st - 3st$

  (d) $10k + 4kn - 6k$ **(e)** $9m + 2d - 2m + 3e$ **(f)** $7 + 3f + 2$

D Simplify the following expressions. In each question, two of the three expressions have the same value. Write down the odd one out in each question.

1 **(a)** $2d + 3d$ **(b)** $8d - 3d$ **(c)** $10d - 6d$

2 **(a)** $6m - 2m + 3m$ **(b)** $2m + 4m - m$ **(c)** $6m + 3m - 2m$

3 **(a)** $9pq - 3pq$ **(b)** $4pq + 2qp$

  (c) $8pq - pq$ | Finished Early? |
| | ➡ Go to page 334 |

8 Equations

In this chapter you will learn about ...
1. making equations
2. solving equations
3. equations with two operations

1 Making Equations

Learn About It

Tara's weight plus 10 kg of potatoes is 60 kg.

You can write this **equation** using words:
Tara's weight plus 10 kg equals 60 kg.

It's shorter to use *w* for Tara's weight,
and the + and = symbols.

You don't need to write the units (kg)
in the equation as they are all the same.

$$w + 10 = 60$$

Word Check

equation two expressions joined by an
= sign to show they have the same value

Try It Out

Write an equation using the red letter in each of the following statements.

Example	Stephen's weight went down by 5 kg. Now he weighs 60 kg.
Working	Stephen's weight less 5 kg equals 60 kg.
Answer	$w - 5 = 60$

1 Chris's weight plus 3 kg is 45 kg.
2 Karen's weight went down by 4 kg. Now she weighs 62 kg.
3 San Wan's weight went up 2 kg. Now he weighs 80 kg.
4 Scott's weight went down 1 kg. Now he weighs 63 kg.

Learn More About It

Three bags of sweets contain 27 sweets altogether.

You can write the equation using words:
3 bags equals 27 sweets.

If you use b to stand for the number of sweets in a bag, then there are $3 \times b$ sweets in 3 bags.
$3 \times b = 27$
You don't need to write the $\times$ sign, so $3b = 27$.

A bag of sweets is divided among 3 children.
They each get 5 sweets.
In words, the equation is:
bag divided by 3 equals 5 sweets.
b divided by 3 is written as $\frac{b}{3}$, so the equation is $\frac{b}{3} = 5$.

Try It Out

Write an equation for each question below, using the red letter.

1 Together, 2 bags of sweets contain 16 sweets.
2 A bag of sweets is divided among 4 children. Each child gets 6 sweets.
3 10 bags of crisps contain 250 crisps altogether.
4 Half a bag of nuts contains 25 nuts.

Hint: to find half of something, divide by 2.

Practice

C Write the following statements as equations.

Example	I think of a number, add 5 and get 7.
Working	number add 5 equals 7
Answer	$n + 5 = 7$

1 **(a)** I think of a number, subtract 5 and get 7.
  (b) I think of a number, add 10 and get 25.
  (c) My number plus 4 is 18.
  (d) If you add 1 to my number, you get 7.

2 **(a)** I think of a number, divide by 6 and get 2.
  (b) Twice my number is 16.
  (c) A quarter of my number is 3.
  (d) A third of my number is 10.

Hint: to find a quarter of something, divide by 4.

D Write the following statements as equations.
  1 Toby added 5 stamps to his collection. Now he has 60 stamps.
  2 Maria cut a ribbon into five pieces. Each part was 10 cm long.
  3 Jerry took £25 from his bank account. He had £120 left.
  4 The temperature went up by 4 °C. It is now 25 °C.

Finished Early?
➡ Go to page 335

Further Practice

E Write the following statements as equations.
  1 **(a)** My age plus 4 equals 19.
    (b) In 6 years' time, Kate's age will be 20.
    (c) Isha's age 30 years ago was 25.

  2 **(a)** If you multiply Dominic's age by 2, you get 24.
    (b) Three times Jason's age is 36.
    (c) Half Sara's age is 6.

Write these as equations.

1 Class 8G added £8 to the school computer fund. Now there is £450 altogether.

2 3 cans contain 900 ml of cola.

3 Sonia picked 20 apples from the tree. There are 65 left.

4 Rob has used a third of his exercise book. That's 20 pages.

5 2 people get on a bus. Now there are 12 passengers.

6 I bought 4 Twinky bars for 80p.

Finished Early?
➡ Go to page 335

Solving Equations

Remember?

- The **operations** of arithmetic are: addition (+), subtraction (−), multiplication (×), division (÷).

- An **inverse** is the opposite of an operation:
  addition and subtraction are inverse operations, for example: + 2 is the inverse of − 2.
  multiplication and division are inverse operations, for example: ÷ 4 is the inverse of × 4.

- You can write calculations using number machines, for example:
  20 $\boxed{÷4}$ ▷ 5 means 20 ÷ 4 = 5.

- You can reverse number machines to write the inverse operation, for example:
  20 ◁ $\boxed{×4}$ 5 means 5 × 4 = 20.

- You can reverse number machines to find missing numbers.

Example	? $\boxed{+2}$ ▷ 7
Working	? ◁ $\boxed{-2}$ 7 (*The inverse of + 2 is − 2.*)
	7 − 2 = 5
Answer	? = 5

Try It Out

 1 Write down the inverses of these.

(a) − 4　　(b) ÷ 3　　(c) + 6　　(d) × 5

2 Work out the missing numbers in these calculations.

(a) 3 [+5] ?　(b) 12 [÷3] ?　(c) 4 [+10] ?　(d) 3 [×4] ?

(e) ? [÷2] 6　(f) ? [+3] 5　(g) ? [×3] 4　(h) ? [−4] 10

3 Work out the missing numbers in these calculations.

(a) ? [−2] 8　　　(b) ? [+3] 4　　　(c) ? [÷5] 10

(d) ? [×2] 6　　　(e) ? [+10] 20　　(f) ? [×6] 30

Learn About It

Francis sets Maria this problem.

I'm thinking of a number, *n*.

I add 2.

The answer is 7. Can you find *n*?

Maria works backwards, to find *n*.

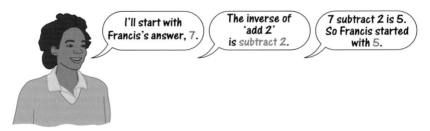

I'll start with Francis's answer, 7.

The inverse of 'add 2' is subtract 2.

7 subtract 2 is 5. So Francis started with 5.

Maria solved Francis's problem.

She found the solution, $n = 5$.

> **Word Check**
> **solve** find the answer to a problem
> **solution** answer

Try It Out

1 Work backwards to find *n* in each case.

1 (a)

| Start with *n*. | Multiply by 2. | The answer is 12. |

(b)

| Start with *n*. | Subtract 5. | The answer is 6. |

(c)

| Start with *n*. | Add 10. | The answer is 30. |

(d)

| Start with *n*. | Divide by 3. | The answer is 5. |

2 (a) I think of a number, *n*. If I add 6, I get 14.
   (b) I think of a number, *n*. If I multiply by 3, I get 15.
   (c) I think of a number, *n*. If I subtract 1, I get 6.
   (d) I think of a number, *n*. If I divide by 4, I get 2.

Learn More About It

Maria sets Francis this problem.

| I'm thinking of a number, *n*. | I subtract 3. | The answer is 6. Can you find *n*? |

She wrote her problem as an equation:
$n - 3 = 6$.

Francis works backwards, to find *n*.

| I'll start with Maria's answer, 6. | The inverse of 'subtract 3' is add 3. | Maria started with 9. |

Francis writes down his calculation and answer: $n = 6 + 3$
$n = 9$.

Francis **solved** Maria's equation.

Word Check
solve an equation find the number a letter stands for

Try It Out

I Arun wrote the following equations to show his mental calculations.
For each equation:
(a) What did he do to n: add, subtract, multiply or divide?
(b) What is the inverse (opposite) operation?
(c) Work backwards to find n.

Example	$\frac{n}{3} = 2$
Working	(a) Arun divided n by 3.
	(b) The inverse of ÷ 3 is × 3.
	(c) Start with the answer, 2.
	Multiply by 3 to get $2 \times 3 = 6$.
Answer	$n = 6$

I $2n = 18$ **2** $n - 3 = 8$ **3** $\frac{n}{5} = 2$

4 $n + 10 = 15$ **5** $3n = 21$ **6** $n + 5 = 20$

7 $\frac{n}{3} = 6$ **8** $n - 7 = 7$

Practice

J Solve these equations by working backwards. Show your working.

I $x - 2 = 7$ **2** $2x = 12$ **3** $\frac{y}{5} = 8$

4 $y + 7 = 20$ **5** $\frac{t}{3} = 4$ **6** $m - 5 = 5$

7 $\frac{a}{10} = 6$ **8** $2b = 24$ **9** $f - 20 = 30$

10 $10x = 70$

K Write an equation for each of the following questions, using the red letter.
Solve the equation. Answer the question.

Example	5 stamps cost 60p. How much does one stamp cost?
Working	$5s = 60$ (5 times the cost of a stamp, s, equals 60p.)
	$s = \dfrac{60}{5}$ (The inverse of × 5 is ÷ 5.)
	$s = 12$
Answer	12p

1 Julie's savings plus £7 total £20. What are Julie's savings?

2 A piece of liquorice rope is divided among 3 children. Each child gets 8 cm. How long is the rope?

3 William unloads 4 boxes, leaving 23 boxes on his lorry. How many boxes were on the lorry to start with?

4 Half Sam's age is 9. How old is he?

5 Nasreen gave Barry 30p of her pocket money. She had 60p left. How much was her pocket money?

6 Hamid swam 8 lengths of the swimming pool. He swam 240 m altogether. How long is the swimming pool?

> **Finished Early?**
> ➡ Go to page 336

Further Practice

1 Solve these equations by adding or subtracting.
(a) $p + 2 = 5$ (b) $v - 6 = 3$ (c) $a - 5 = 8$
(d) $b + 1 = 4$ (e) $t - 3 = 3$ (f) $h + 15 = 20$

2 Solve these equations by multiplying or dividing.
(a) $4k = 20$ (b) $\frac{d}{2} = 8$ (c) $3m = 33$
(d) $\frac{r}{8} = 2$ (e) $9f = 27$ (f) $\frac{g}{5} = 7$

> **Finished Early?**
> ➡ Go to page 336

❸ Equations with Two Operations

> **Remember?**
> Calculate using this order of operations:
> **1** division and multiplication (work from left to right)
> **2** addition and subtraction (work from left to right).

Try It Out

Calculate the following.
1 $2 \times 6 - 10$ **2** $4 + 2 \times 3$ **3** $4 \times 3 - 5$ **4** $12 - 2 \times 5$
5 $2 \times 10 - 9$ **6** $1 + 2 \times 4$ **7** $6 \div 2 - 1$ **8** $5 + 8 \div 2$

NUMBER SKILLS Four operations with TU, order of operations, inverse of an operation   **107**

Learn About It

Darren sets Zoe this problem.

I'm thinking of a number, *n*.

If I multiply by 2,

and then add 3,

the answer is 11. Can you find *n*?

Zoe works backwards, to find *n*.

I'll start with Darren's answer, 11.

The inverse of 'add 3' is subtract 3.

That gives me 8.

The inverse of 'multiply by 2' is divide by 2.

Darren started with 4.

Try It Out

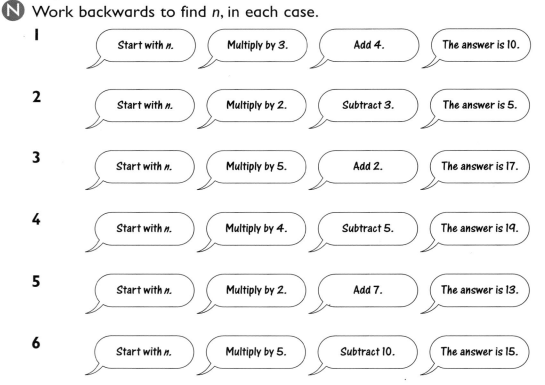

Work backwards to find *n*, in each case.

1. Start with *n*. | Multiply by 3. | Add 4. | The answer is 10.

2. Start with *n*. | Multiply by 2. | Subtract 3. | The answer is 5.

3. Start with *n*. | Multiply by 5. | Add 2. | The answer is 17.

4. Start with *n*. | Multiply by 4. | Subtract 5. | The answer is 19.

5. Start with *n*. | Multiply by 2. | Add 7. | The answer is 13.

6. Start with *n*. | Multiply by 5. | Subtract 10. | The answer is 15.

Learn More About It

Zoe sets Darren this problem.

She writes down her problem as an equation: $3n - 2 = 13$.
Darren works backwards, to find n.

Darren writes down his calculation and answer:

$13 + 2 = 15$
$15 \div 3 = 5$
$n = 5$

Try It Out

Kevin wrote the following equations to show his mental calculations. For each equation, work backwards to find n.

Example	$3n - 5 = 7$
Working	Start with the answer, 7.
	Change $- 5$ to $+ 5$.
	Add 5: $\qquad$ $7 + 5 = 12$.
	Change $\times 3$ to $\div 3$.
	Divide by 3: $12 \div 3 = 4$.
Answer	$n = 4$

1 $4n - 2 = 8$ $\qquad$ **2** $5n + 10 = 30$ $\qquad$ **3** $9n - 3 = 15$
4 $2n + 3 = 19$ $\qquad$ **5** $6n - 10 = 26$ $\qquad$ **6** $7n + 3 = 45$

Practice

Solve these equations by working backwards. Show your working.

1 $2n + 4 = 10$ $\qquad$ **2** $5m - 3 = 7$ $\qquad$ **3** $6a + 2 = 20$
4 $2d + 1 = 15$ $\qquad$ **5** $3s - 5 = 10$ $\qquad$ **6** $8f + 3 = 43$
7 $2r - 11 = 11$ $\qquad$ **8** $10t + 15 = 45$ $\qquad$ **9** $7k - 13 = 29$

Q For each question below, write an equation, solve the equation and answer the question.

Example	A waitress fills 6 **b**owls with sugar lumps. Customers use 48 lumps. There are 42 sugar lumps left. How many sugar lumps are there in a full bowl?
Working	6 **b**owls less 48 sugar lumps leaves 42 lumps.
	$6b - 48 = 42$
	$6b = 42 + 48$ (+ 48 is the inverse of − 48.)
	$6b = 90$
	$b = 90 \div 6b$ (÷ 6 is the inverse of × 6.)
	$b = 15$
Answer	There are 15 sugar lumps in a full bowl.

1 Howard has 5 stamps. He buys 4 **b**ooks of stamps. Now he has 29 stamps. How many stamps are in a book?

2 Wai Mun filled her flask with 5 **c**ups of coffee. She drank 20 cl. There was 70 cl left in the flask. How much coffee does a cup hold?

3 There are 5 full **t**ables in a classroom. 6 children leave the class. There are 24 children left. How many children sit at a table?

4 Sharon buys 3 **r**olls of sticky tape. She uses 5 m of tape and has 22 m left. How long is one new roll of tape?

5 Two **h**istory lessons and a 10-minute break last 80 minutes. How long is a history lesson?

Finished Early?
➡ Go to page 336

Further Practice

R Solve these equations by working backwards. Show your working.

1 $2x - 1 = 7$	**2** $5y + 2 = 27$	**3** $3d + 5 = 14$
4 $4p - 3 = 17$	**5** $2g - 5 = 7$	**6** $4w + 10 = 30$
7 $5t + 25 = 65$	**8** $8f + 13 = 45$	**9** $6s - 27 = 21$

Finished Early?
 Go to page 336

Unit 5 *Algebra*

Summary of Chapters 7 and 8

- An algebraic **expression** is a mixture of numbers, letters and signs, without an = sign.

  To calculate the **value** of an expression, **substitute** numbers for the letters in the expression.

- Remember to multiply and divide *before* adding and subtracting.

Example	Find the value of $b^2 - ab$ when $a = 3$ and $b = 4$.
Working	$4^2 - 3 \times 4 = 16 - 12 = 4$
Answer	4

- **Like terms** have the same letters, e.g. $4a$ and $3a$.

  Like terms can be **simplified**, for example: $4a + 3a = 7a$ and $5ab - 3ab = 2ab$.

  Unlike terms cannot be simplified, for example, $2a + 3b$ cannot be simplified.

- The terms of an expression can be rearranged. For example: $9m + 3n - 5m + 4n = 9m - 5m + 3n + 4n = 4m + 7n$.

  Remember: if a term moves, so must the sign in front of it.

- **Equations** show that one expression is equal to another. Use them to solve problems.

Example	I think of a number, n, and add 3. The answer is 7. What is n?
Working	$n + 3 = 7$
	The inverse of $+ 3$ is $- 3$.
	Start with the answer, 7.
	Subtract 3: $7 - 3 = 4$
Answer	$n = 4$

Brush Up Your Number 6

T Dividing Whole Numbers

Learn About It

Dividing is the opposite or **inverse** of multiplying. You can divide if you know how to multiply.

For example: $24 \div 3 = 8$ because $8 \times 3 = 24$

$25 \div 3 = 8$ remainder 1 (or $8\frac{1}{3}$).

To **divide** by 10, 100 or 1000, move the digits to the **right** 1, 2 or 3 places. Put in a decimal point if you have to.

$140 \div 10 = 14$

$14 \div 10 = 1.4$

$140 \div 100 = 1.4$

$14 \div 100 = 0.14$

To divide by 1 s.f. numbers, use tables **and** move digits.

For example: $60 \div 3 = 20$ because $6 \div 3 = 2$ and $60 = 6 \times 10$

$2400 \div 40 = 60$ because $24 \div 4 = 6$ and

$2400 = 24 \times 100$ and $40 = 4 \times 10$.

To divide larger numbers, use short or long division.

For example:

$714 \div 3$

$$\begin{array}{r} 2\ 3\ 8 \\ 3\overline{)7\,^1 1\,^2 4} \end{array}$$

$714 \div 3 = 238$

$1288 \div 23$

$$\begin{array}{r} 56 \\ 23\overline{)1288} \\ 115\downarrow \\ \hline 138 \\ 138 \\ \hline 0 \end{array}$$

$1288 \div 23 = 56$

Try It Out

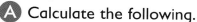 Calculate the following.

1 **(a)** 35 ÷ 7   **(b)** 256 ÷ 4   **(c)** 972 ÷ 6
  (d) 1447 ÷ 5   **(e)** 42 624 ÷ 8

2 **(a)** 510 ÷ 10   **(b)** 1200 ÷ 100   **(c)** 23 500 ÷ 10
  (d) 703 000 ÷ 100   **(e)** 2 500 000 ÷ 1000

3 **(a)** 420 ÷ 6   **(b)** 400 ÷ 8   **(c)** 3000 ÷ 50
  (d) 8000 ÷ 200   **(e)** 36 000 ÷ 40

4 **(a)** 480 ÷ 16   **(b)** 1958 ÷ 22   **(c)** 4598 ÷ 38
  (d) 399 ÷ 57   **(e)** 18 952 ÷ 92

Practice

B 1 Jamal's keyboard can play 512 different sounds, which are divided into banks. There are 16 sounds in each bank. How many banks of sounds are there?

2 A CD lasts for an average of 70 minutes.
Mandy has 132 CDs.
  (a) How many minutes of music is
this altogether?
  (b) How many hours of music is this?
  (c) Mandy decides to listen to **all** her CDs.
She spends 8 hours each day listening.
How many days does it take her?

> *Hint: divide answer
> (a) by 60*

3 Copy and complete this diagram.

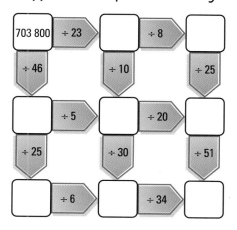

> **Finished Early?**
> Go to page 337

9 Computation

In this chapter you will learn about ...

1 mixed operations and brackets

2 powers

3 square roots

P **1** Mixed Operations and Brackets

Remember?

- Use a number line to help you to add and subtract numbers.

Example	$3 - 7$	
Working	The number line shows the answer is negative.	subtract 7 
Answer	-4	

Example	$(-2) - 4$	
Working	The number line shows the answer is negative.	subtract 4 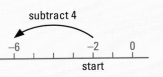
Answer	-6	

- Use these rules to combine + and − signs:

Same signs give +	**Example**	$(-8) - (-2)$
+ + gives +	**Working**	$(-8) + 2$ (− − *gives* +.)
− − gives +	**Answer**	-6

Different signs give −	**Example**	$3 + (-7)$
+ − gives −	**Working**	$3 - 7$ (+ − *gives* −.)
− + gives −	**Answer**	-4

- Write negative numbers in brackets, e.g. write −3 as (−3).

NUMBER SKILLS **Add/subtract U**

Try It Out

 Calculate the following.

1 (a) $(-3) + 7$ (b) $5 - 9$ (c) $(-5) - 5$
  (d) $(-6) + 13$ (e) $32 - 50$ (f) $(-29) + 14$

2 (a) $(-3) + 5 - 1$ (b) $3 - 5 + 8$
  (c) $(-2) - 4 - 6$ (d) $7 - 9 - 8$
  (e) $2 - 3 + 4 - 5 + 6 - 7$ (f) $20 - 40 - 60 + 80$

3 (a) $2 - (-5)$ (b) $6 - 5$ (c) $4 + (-9)$
  (d) $(-3) - (-5)$ (e) $1 + (-7)$ (f) $(-9) + (-7)$

Learn About It

1 Joanne and Marcel both calculated $5 + 2 \times 3$.
  They got different answers.

$$5 + 2 \times 3$$
$$= 5 + 6$$
$$= 11$$

$$5 + 2 \times 3$$
$$= 7 \times 3$$
$$= 21$$

Who is correct? Why?

 2 Use your calculator to calculate $5 + 2 \times 3$.
  Did you get the same answer as Joanne or Marcel?

Your calculator uses the correct order of **operations**:
division and multiplication (from left to right) before addition and
subtraction (from left to right).

3 Work out the following calculations. Show your working.
  Check your answers using a calculator.

Example	$5 \times 3 + 10 \div 2$
Working	$5 \times 3 = 15$
	$10 \div 2 = 5$ *(Multiplication and division before addition.)*
	$15 + 5 = 20$
Answer	20

(a) $10 - 2 \times 4$ (b) $8 \div 2 + 2$ (c) $2 + 8 \times 3$
(d) $3 \times 4 - 10$ (e) $7 + 1 - 2 \times 3$ (f) $2 \times 6 + 8 \div 4$
(g) $6 - 1 \times 3 - 2$ (h) $20 \div 2 - 3 \times 2$ (i) $9 \times 2 - 18 \div 3$

Try It Out

B Calculate the following. Show your working.

1 $7 - 2 \times 3$
2 $8 \times 2 + 4$
3 $9 - 12 \div 3$
4 $3 \times 2 + 4 \times 3$
5 $1 + 3 \times 5 - 2$
6 $20 \div 4 + 1$
7 $3 + 12 \div 3 + 1$
8 $30 \div 3 - 2 \times 4$
9 $4 \times 2 - 1 + 10 \div 5$

Learn More About It

1 This calculation has brackets: $(3 + 4) \times 2$. Joanne and Marcel got different answers again.

$(3 + 4) \times 2$
$= 3 + 8$
$= 11$

$(3 + 4) \times 2$
$= 7 \times 2$
$= 14$

Who is correct? Why?

2 Use your calculator to calculate $(3 + 4) \times 2$.

Press (3 + 4) × 2 = .

Your calculator works out **brackets first**.

Key Fact

Work out calculations in the following order.
Remember it as **BoDMAS**:

Brackets
Division and **M**ultiplication (left to right)
Addition and **S**ubtraction (left to right)

---

3 Work out the following calculations. Remember to work out the brackets first. Check your answers using your calculator.

(a) $10 - (8 - 5)$
(b) $(6 + 2) \div 4$
(c) $12 \div (9 - 3)$
(d) $5 \times (3 - 1)$
(e) $24 \div (3 \times 2)$
(f) $(5 - 2) \times (3 + 4)$

Try It Out

C Calculate the following. Show your working. Check your answers using your calculator.

1 (a) $5 \times (3 + 6)$ **(b)** $12 - (8 - 2)$ **(c)** $(10 + 3) \times 2$
   (d) $36 \div (4 \times 3)$ **(e)** $(5 + 2) \times (4 + 1)$ **(f)** $(6 + 2) \div (5 - 3)$

2

Example	$6 + (5 - 2) \times 4$
Working	$= 6 + 3 \times 4$ *(Brackets first.)*
	$= 6 + 12$ *(Multiplication before addition.)*
Answer	18

(a) $5 \times (6 - 2) + 4$ **(b)** $(4 + 8) \div 3 + 1$ **(c)** $2 \times 7 - (5 - 2)$
(d) $9 - (4 - 1) \times 2$ **(e)** $20 - 3 \times (5 - 2)$ **(f)** $6 + 12 \div (2 + 4)$

Practice

D **1** Calculate the following. Some of the answers are negative.

Example	$10 - (4 - 6)$
Working	$= 10 - (-2)$ *(Brackets first.)*
	$= 10 + 2$ *(− − gives +.)*
	$= 12$
Answer	12

Example	$2 - 3 \times 4$
Working	$= 2 - 12$ *(Multiplication before subtraction.)*
	$= -10$
Answer	-10

(a) $5 - 6 \times 2$ **(b)** $(-3) + 8 \div 4$
(c) $12 \div 3 - 7$ **(d)** $8 - (3 - 6)$
(e) $30 \div 10 - 20 \times 4$ **(f)** $(5 - 8) + (9 - 7)$
(g) $3 - 2 \times (5 + 1)$ **(h)** $(-2) + 4 \times 3 - 8$
(i) $2 \times 5 - (10 - 15)$

2 Calculate the following. Do not use a calculator.

Example	$5.7 - (6.5 - 1.2)$
Working	$= 5.7 - 5.3$ *(Brackets first.)*
	$= 0.4$
Answer	0.4

Example	$15 - 10 \times 0.85$
Working	$15 - 8.5$ *(Multiplication before subtraction.)*
	$= 6.5$
Answer	6.5

(a) $5 + 10 \times 1.8$
(b) $0.9 - (0.8 - 0.5)$
(c) $3.6 + 6 \div 3$
(d) $4 \times 0.6 + 3$
(e) $10 \times (1.2 + 3.5)$
(f) $4.8 \div 2 + 1.3$
(g) $6.9 - (2.4 + 3.3)$
(h) $4.9 - 2 \times 1.4$

Finished Early?
➡ Go to page 338

Further Practice

E Calculate the following. Some calculations involve negative numbers.

1 $10 - (4 \times 2)$
2 $4 \times (6 - 1)$
3 $4 \div (4 - 2)$
4 $(-2) + (5 \times 3)$
5 $15 \div (3 + 2)$
6 $2 + 3 \times (5 - 1)$
7 $13 - (14 - 6)$
8 $5 - (3 - 7)$
9 $5 + 2 \times (3 - 5)$
10 $6 \times 2 - (10 - 20)$
11 $20 - 3 - (5 \times 2)$
12 $0 - (5 - 8)$
13 $(14 \div 7) + (3 \times 6)$
14 $(-10) + (6 \div 2)$
15 $(4 + 2) \times 3$
16 $2 \times 3 - (5 \times 2)$
17 $(9 - 2) \times (6 - 4)$
18 $(10 - 15) + (6 - 7)$

Finished Early?
 Go to page 338

❷ Powers

> ## Remember?
> To square a number, multiply it by itself.
> For example: 3 squared = 3^2 = 3 × 3 = 9.

Try It Out

F Calculate the following.

1 5^2 **2** 9^2 **3** the square of 7

4 4 squared   **5** 10^2 **6** 12^2

Learn About It

When you multiply a number by itself, you get a **power** of that number.

Here are some powers of 2:

2 × 2 = 4
2 × 2 × 2 = 8
2 × 2 × 2 × 2 = 16
2 × 2 × 2 × 2 × 2 = 32

The more times you multiply the number by itself, the higher the power.

> ### Word Check
> **power** a number multiplied by itself a given number of times
> **base** the number being multiplied in a power
> **index** the number of numbers being multiplied in a power

1 Work out the next power of 2.

2 × 2 × 2 × 2 × 2 is the **fifth power of 2** because five numbers are multiplied together. This is also known as **2 raised to the fifth power** or simply **2 to the fifth**. 2 is the base and 5 is the index. We write 2^5.

 2^5 does not mean 2 × 5.

2 Write each power in a shorter way, using a base and index, e.g. 7 × 7 × 7 = 7^3.

  (a) 5 × 5 × 5   **(b)** 10 × 10 × 10 × 10 × 10 × 10

  (c) 6 × 6 × 6 × 6   **(d)** 3 × 3

  (e) 4 × 4 × 4 × 4 × 4   **(f)** 1 × 1 × 1 × 1 × 1 × 1 × 1

Here are some more powers:
$4^3 = 4 \times 4 \times 4 = 64$ The third power of 4.
$6^5 = 6 \times 6 \times 6 \times 6 \times 6 = 7776$ The fifth power of 6.

3 Write these powers the longer way (e.g. $5 \times 5 \times 5$) and calculate them.

(a) 2^7 (b) 3^3 (c) the third power of 5
(d) 4^4 (e) 10^5 (f) 1^9

The **cube** of a number is another name for the third power.
For example, the cube of 2 is $2^3 = 2 \times 2 \times 2 = 8$.

4 Calculate:
(a) the cube of 4   (b) 3 cubed
(c) 10^3 (d) the cube of 5.

Word Check
cube third power

Key Fact
The **o** in BoDMAS stands for **Power**. Work out calculations in this order:

Brackets
Powers
Division and **M**ultiplication (left to right)
Addition and **S**ubtraction (left to right).

5 Calculate the following.

Example $3^4 - 4^3$
Working $3^4 - 4^3$
$= 3 \times 3 \times 3 \times 3 - 4 \times 4 \times 4$ (Calculate powers before
$= 81 - 64$ subtracting.)
$= 17$
Answer 17

(a) $5^2 + 3^2$ (b) $9^2 - 4^2$ (c) $4^2 + 2^3$
(d) $5^3 - 10^2$ (e) 3×2^4 (f) $4^2 \times 5$
(g) $3^2 \times 2^3$ (h) $\frac{4^3}{8}$ (i) $\frac{8^2}{4^2}$

Try It Out

G **I** Write these powers the short way, using a base and index.
   (a) $7 \times 7 \times 7 \times 7$
   (b) $10 \times 10 \times 10 \times 10 \times 10 \times 10 \times 10$
   (c) $6 \times 6 \times 6$
   (d) $9 \times 9 \times 9 \times 9 \times 9$
   (e) $1 \times 1 \times 1 \times 1 \times 1 \times 1 \times 1 \times 1 \times 1 \times 1$

2 Calculate the following. Show your working.
   (a) the fifth power of 2 **(b)** 10^4 **(c)** 1^6
   (d) $2^4 - 4^2$ **(e)** 3×10^2 **(f)** $\dfrac{10^4}{10^3}$

Practice

H Calculate the following. Remember to use BoDMAS.

I $30 - 4^2$ **2** $8^2 + 3^2$ **3** $7^2 - 5^2$

4 $3^3 + 6$ **5** $21 \div 3 + 2^3$ **6** $3^2 \times (8 - 2)$

7 $\dfrac{4^3}{2^3}$ **8** $6^2 - (12 - 5)$ **9** $5^2 - 4^2 - 3^2$

10 $4^3 + 20 - 3^4$ **11** $10^2 \div (30 - 25)$ **12** $3 \times (2^3 - 3)$

I Calculate the values of the following expressions.
Do not use a calculator.

Example	$a^3 + b^4$ when $a = 2$ and $b = 3$
Working	$a^3 + b^4 = 2^3 + 3^4$
	$= 2 \times 2 \times 2 + 3 \times 3 \times 3 \times 3$
	$= 8 + 81 = 89$
Answer	89

I a^5 when $a = 2$ **2** x^3 when $x = 5$

3 m^3 when $m = 3$ **4** r^7 when $r = 10$

5 $p^3 + 10$ when $p = 2$ **6** $\dfrac{b^3}{4}$ when $b = 2$

7 $3 \times t^4$ when $t = 2$ **8** $c^4 - d^3$ when $c = 3$ and $d = 4$

9 $a^3 \times b^3$ when $a = 4$ and $b = 10$

Finished Early?
Go to page 339

Further Practice

J Write these calculations the long way, then work them out.
Show your working.

1 2^4	**2** 4^3	**3** 10^5	**4** 12^2
5 $5^2 + 6^2$	**6** $3^2 - 2^3$	**7** $6^2 + 2^5$	**8** $3^3 + 2^4$
9 $4^3 - 2^5$	**10** 4×2^4	**11** 2×3^2	**12** $3^2 \times 2^3$
13 $2^3 \times 2^2$	**14** $\dfrac{3^4}{3^2}$	**15** $\dfrac{4^3}{2^4}$	

> **Finished Early?**
> ➡ Go to page 339

T ③ Square Roots

Learn About It

Squaring 3 gives 9. The square of $3 = 3^2 = 3 \times 3 = 9$.

Finding the **square root** ($\sqrt{\ }$) of 9 gives 3.

The square root of $9 = \sqrt{9} = 3$.

Finding the square root is the inverse (opposite) operation to finding the square. $4^2 = 16$, so $\sqrt{16} = 4$.

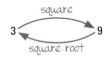

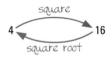

You have to use a calculator to find $\sqrt{12}$.

You can see the answer is a decimal number between 3 and 4.

On the calculator: 🔘√ 🔘1 🔘2 🔘= ⎨3.464101615⎬

Round the answer to 2 decimal places.
$\sqrt{12} = 3.46$ correct to 2 d.p.

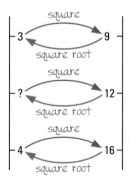

Word Check

square root ($\sqrt{\ }$) inverse (opposite) of square

Try It Out

K **1** Copy the diagrams. Fill in the missing numbers.

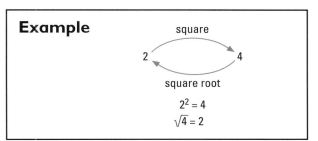

Example

square

2 ⟶ 4

square root

$2^2 = 4$

$\sqrt{4} = 2$

(a)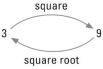

square

3 ⟶ 9

square root

$3^2 = ?$

$\sqrt{9} = ?$

(b)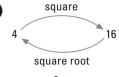

square

4 ⟶ 16

square root

$4^2 = ?$

$\sqrt{16} = ?$

(c)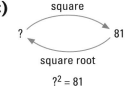

square

? ⟶ 81

square root

$?^2 = 81$

$\sqrt{81} = ?$

(d)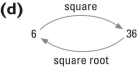

square

6 ⟶ 36

square root

$?^2 = 36$

$\sqrt{?} = 6$

(e)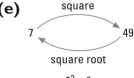

square

7 ⟶ 49

square root

$?^2 = ?$

$\sqrt{?} = ?$

(f)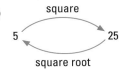

square

5 ⟶ 25

square root

$?^2 = 25$

$\sqrt{?} = 5$

(g)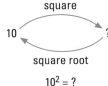

square

10 ⟶ ?

square root

$10^2 = ?$

$\sqrt{?} = 10$

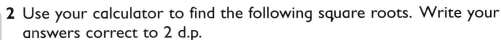

2 Use your calculator to find the following square roots. Write your answers correct to 2 d.p.

   (a) $\sqrt{17}$ **(b)** $\sqrt{250}$ **(c)** $\sqrt{1000}$

   (d) $\sqrt{2}$ **(e)** $\sqrt{60}$ **(f)** $\sqrt{2300}$

Learn More About It

The $\sqrt{\ }$ on Helen's calculator has broken.
She wants to calculate $\sqrt{14}$.
She has to guess.

First she guesses 3.
She checks by squaring: $3^2 = 9$ (less than 14). 3 is too small.
Next she guesses 4.
She checks by squaring: $4^2 = 16$ (more than 14). 4 is too big.
So $\sqrt{14}$ is in between 3 and 4.
It must be a decimal number.
Helen guesses 3.5 next.

?
3 3.1 3.2 3.3 3.4 3.5 3.6 3.7 3.8 3.9 4

She checks by squaring: $3.5^2 = 12.25$ (less than 14). 3.5 is too small.
Next she guesses 3.8.
She checks by squaring: $3.8^2 = 14.44$ (more than 14). 3.8 is too big.
Next she guesses 3.7.
She checks by squaring: $3.7^2 = 13.69$ (less than 14). 3.7 is too small.
So $\sqrt{14}$ is in between 3.7 and 3.8.

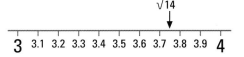

$\sqrt{14}$
3 3.1 3.2 3.3 3.4 3.5 3.6 3.7 3.8 3.9 4

Helen made this table to show her guesses.

Guess	Square	Comment
3	$3^2 = 9$	Too small. $\sqrt{14}$ is bigger than 3.
4	$4^2 = 16$	Too big. $\sqrt{14}$ is smaller than 4.
3.5	$3.5^2 = 12.25$	Too small. $\sqrt{14}$ is bigger than 3.5.
3.8	$3.8^2 = 14.44$	Too big. $\sqrt{14}$ is smaller than 3.8.
3.7	$3.7^2 = 13.89$	Too small. $\sqrt{14}$ is bigger than 3.7.

$\sqrt{14}$ is between 3.7 and 3.8.

Try It Out

L Find $\sqrt{39}$ by:

- copying this table

Guess	Square	Comment
7	7^2 $= 7 \times 7 =$	
6	6^2 $=$	
6.5	$6.5^2 =$	
6.2	$6.2^2 =$	
6.3	$6.3^2 =$	

- trying the guesses
- writing a comment for each guess
- deciding which two of the decimal numbers $\sqrt{39}$ lies between.

Practice

M Here is a page of square roots from Mario's exercise book.

(a) $\sqrt{9} = 3$ (b) $\sqrt{1000} = 100$ (c) $\sqrt{49} = 7$

(d) $\sqrt{1} = 1$ (e) $\sqrt{12} = 6$ (f) $\sqrt{10\,000} = 100$

(g) $\sqrt{0} = 0$ (h) $\sqrt{50} = 25$ (i) $\sqrt{900} = 30$

1 Copy Mario's answers. Check his calculations by squaring. Do not use your calculator. Put a tick beside each correct answer and a cross beside each incorrect one. Show your working.

> **Example** $\sqrt{10} = 5$
> **Working** $5^2 = 5 \times 5 = 25$, not 10.
> **Answer** $\sqrt{10} = 5$ ✗

2 Correct Mario's mistakes. Use the ☐ key of your calculator. Write your answers correct to 2 d.p.

Copy and continue these tables to guess the square roots.

 I Guess $\sqrt{8}$.

Guess	Square	Comment
2	2^2 = 2 × 2 = 4	Too small. $\sqrt{8}$ is bigger than 2.
3	3^2 = 3 × 3 =	
2.7	2.7^2 =	

$\sqrt{8}$ lies between ? and ?

2 Guess $\sqrt{70}$.

Guess	Square	Comment	
9	9^2 =		

$\sqrt{70}$ lies between ? and ?

Finished Early?
 Go to page 339

Further Practice

 Copy these statements and fill in the missing numbers.

I $5^2 = ?$
$\sqrt{?} = 5$

2 $1^2 = ?$
$\sqrt{?} = 1$

3 $?^2 = 36$
$\sqrt{36} = ?$

4 $?^2 = 100$
$\sqrt{100} = ?$

5 $?^2 = 16$
$\sqrt{16} = ?$

6 $?^2 = 64$
$\sqrt{64} = ?$

 I Calculate the areas of these squares.

(a) ?
4 cm

(b) ?
7 m

(c) ?
10 mm

(d) ?
23 m

2 Calculate the length of the sides of each of these squares.

(a) 36 cm²
?

(b) 81 m²
?

(c) 20 m²
?

(d) 500 cm²
?

Finished Early?
 Go to page 339

Unit 6 *Computation*

Summary of Chapter 9

- Work out calculations in this order. Remember it as **BoDMAS**:
  Brackets
  Powers
  Division and **M**ultiplication (work from left to right)
  Addition and **S**ubtraction (work from left to right).

- Multiplying the same number by itself a number of times gives a power of the number, e.g. $2 \times 2 \times 2$.

- Powers are written using an index and a base.
  $$\underset{\text{base}}{2}\overset{\text{index}}{^3} = 2 \times 2 \times 2$$

- The third power of a number is called its **cube**.

- Finding the **square root** ($\sqrt{\ }$) is the inverse (opposite) of finding the square. For example:
  the square root of $9 = \sqrt{9} = 3$
  the square of $3 = 3^2 = 3 \times 3 = 9$.

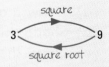

- You can find the square root of a number by guessing. For example, to find $\sqrt{20}$, you might guess 4. $4^2 = 16$; too small. You might guess 5. $5^2 = 25$; too big, so $\sqrt{20}$ is between 4 and 5.

Brush Up Your Number 7

 Fraction Diagrams

Learn About It

You can show the fraction $\frac{2}{5}$ using different diagrams.
Here are some:

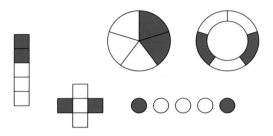

$\frac{2}{5}$ means '2 parts out of 5'. The diagrams all have 5 parts.
2 parts are coloured in.

> *Remember: the bottom number (denominator) of a fraction tells you how many parts there are in a whole. The top number (numerator) tells you how many of the parts are needed.*

Try It Out

Squared paper

 1 (a) Draw a grid like this on squared paper.
    (b) Shade the fraction $\frac{4}{9}$.
    (c) Draw the grid five more times and shade $\frac{4}{9}$ in a different way on each.

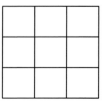

2 Copy each of the following shapes. Shade the fraction shown.

(a)   **(b)**   **(c)**   **(d)**

     $\frac{3}{5}$ $\frac{11}{12}$ $\frac{4}{5}$ $\frac{2}{9}$

Practice

Squared paper and triangular grid paper

B For each shape below ...
  (a) write down the fraction that is shaded
  (b) copy the shape and shade the fraction a different way.

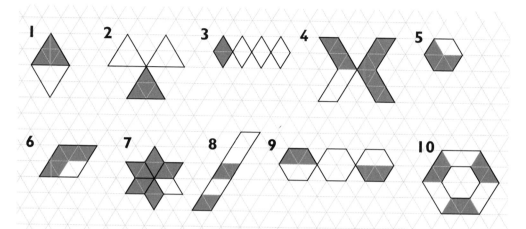

C Draw a diagram of any shape to represent each of the
following fractions.

1 $\frac{1}{2}$	2 $\frac{1}{8}$	3 $\frac{3}{8}$	4 $\frac{3}{10}$
5 $\frac{2}{3}$	6 $\frac{1}{6}$	7 $\frac{5}{12}$	8 $\frac{2}{7}$
9 $\frac{4}{5}$	10 $\frac{13}{15}$	11 $\frac{11}{20}$	12 $\frac{7}{25}$

> **Finished Early?**
> ➡ Go to page 340

10 Fractions

In this chapter you will learn about ...
1. equivalent fractions
2. mixed numbers
3. decimals and fractions

P 1 Equivalent Fractions

Learn About It

Half this cake has pink icing.
Spencer cut the cake in half and then into quarters.

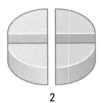

$$\frac{1}{2} \quad = \quad \frac{2}{4}$$

The pink fractions are the same.
They are **equivalent fractions**.

You can make equivalent fractions by multiplying.
Multiply the **numerator** (top number) and **denominator** (bottom number) by the *same* number.

$$\frac{1}{2} \overset{\times 2}{\underset{\times 2}{=}} \frac{2}{4}$$

Word Check

numerator top number of a fraction
denominator bottom number of a fraction

1 Spencer cut this cake differently.
Write down the equivalent fraction.

$$\frac{1}{2} \quad = \quad \frac{?}{?}$$

You can change $\frac{1}{2}$ into $\frac{3}{6}$ by multiplying both the
numerator and denominator by the *same* number, 3.

2 Find **?** for these equivalent fractions.

(a)

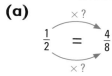

$$\frac{1}{2} = \frac{4}{8}$$

(b)

$$\frac{1}{2} = \frac{10}{20}$$

(c)

$$\frac{2}{3} = \frac{6}{9}$$

(d)

$$\frac{5}{6} = \frac{25}{30}$$

3 Find **?** first. Then complete the equivalent fraction.

(a)

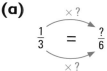

$$\frac{1}{3} = \frac{?}{6}$$

(b)

$$\frac{2}{5} = \frac{6}{?}$$

(c)

$$\frac{3}{4} = \frac{?}{20}$$

(d)

$$\frac{7}{10} = \frac{21}{?}$$

Key Fact

You can make equivalent fractions by multiplying. Multiply both
the numerator and the denominator by the *same* number.

Try It Out

 1 Copy and complete these diagrams to make equivalent fractions.

(a)

$$\frac{1}{4} = \frac{?}{?}$$
$\times 5$

(b) $\times 3$

$$\frac{4}{5} = \frac{?}{?}$$

(c)

$$\frac{1}{6} = \frac{?}{?}$$
$\times 10$

(d) $\times 4$

$$\frac{2}{9} = \frac{?}{?}$$

(e)

$$\frac{7}{10} = \frac{?}{?}$$
$\times 10$

(f) $\times 4$

$$\frac{2}{3} = \frac{8}{?}$$
$\times 4$

2 Find the equivalent fractions.

(a) $\times ?$

$$\frac{1}{5} = \frac{?}{10}$$
$\times ?$

(b) $\times ?$

$$\frac{3}{8} = \frac{15}{?}$$
$\times ?$

(c)

$$\frac{9}{10} = \frac{?}{30}$$
$\times ?$

(d) $\times ?$

$$\frac{2}{7} = \frac{20}{?}$$

(e) $\frac{3}{4} = \frac{?}{36}$ **(f)** $\frac{1}{2} = \frac{100}{?}$ **(g)** $\frac{5}{6} = \frac{?}{24}$ **(h)** $\frac{3}{10} = \frac{18}{?}$

Learn More About It

You can make equivalent fractions by dividing, too.
This is called **cancelling**. You need to find a number which is a factor of both the numerator *and* the denominator. Then divide both the numerator and denominator by this number.
Look at this fraction. 2 is a factor of both 2 and 4.

 =

$$\div 2$$
$$\frac{2}{4} = \frac{1}{2}$$
$$\div 2$$

Word Check

cancel divide the numerator and the denominator of a fraction by the same number

Cancel these fractions.

(a) $\div 3$

$$\frac{6}{9} = \frac{2}{}$$
$\div 3$

(b) $\div 2$

$$\frac{8}{10} = \frac{}{5}$$
$\div 2$

(c) $\div 5$

$$\frac{15}{20} = \frac{3}{}$$
$\div 5$

(d) $\div 10$

$$\frac{60}{70} = \frac{}{}$$
$\div 10$

Key Fact

You can make equivalent fractions by dividing. Divide both the numerator and the denominator by the *same* number. This is called **cancelling**.

Try It Out

B Cancel these fractions.

1

$$\frac{6}{10} = \frac{3}{?}$$
÷2 ... ÷2

2
$$\frac{9}{12} = \frac{?}{?}$$
÷3 ... ÷3

3
$$\frac{5}{15} = \frac{?}{?}$$
÷5 ... ÷5

4

$$\frac{8}{14} = \frac{4}{?}$$
÷? ... ÷?

5

$$\frac{30}{40} = \frac{?}{4}$$
÷? ... ÷?

6

$$\frac{15}{18} = \frac{5}{?}$$
÷? ... ÷?

Learn More About It

Sometimes you can divide several times.

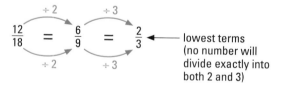
$$\frac{12}{18} = \frac{6}{9} = \frac{2}{3}$$
÷2 ... ÷3 ← lowest terms (no number will divide exactly into both 2 and 3)
÷2 ... ÷3

When you cannot divide any more, the fraction is in its **lowest terms**.

1 Cancel these fractions to their lowest terms.

(a)
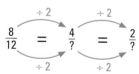
$$\frac{8}{12} = \frac{4}{?} = \frac{2}{?}$$
÷2 ... ÷2
÷2 ... ÷2

(b)
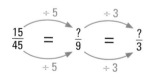
$$\frac{15}{45} = \frac{?}{9} = \frac{?}{3}$$
÷5 ... ÷3
÷5 ... ÷3

(c)
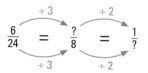
$$\frac{6}{24} = \frac{?}{8} = \frac{1}{?}$$
÷3 ... ÷2
÷3 ... ÷2

(d)
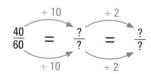
$$\frac{40}{60} = \frac{?}{?} = \frac{?}{?}$$
÷10 ... ÷2
÷10 ... ÷2

You can cancel like this:

$\dfrac{\cancel{6}^2}{\cancel{9}_3} = \dfrac{2}{3}$
$\qquad \dfrac{\cancel{12}^{\cancel{6}^2}}{\cancel{18}_{\cancel{9}_3}} = \dfrac{2}{3}$

Cross off each number as you
divide it. Write the answer next to it.

2 Cancel these fractions to their lowest terms.

(a) $\frac{8}{10}$ (b) $\frac{9}{12}$ (c) $\frac{10}{15}$ (d) $\frac{6}{12}$ (e) $\frac{16}{28}$ (f) $\frac{24}{36}$

Try It Out

C **1** Cancel these fractions.

(a)
$$\frac{5}{20} = \frac{?}{?}$$
÷ ?   ÷ ?

(b)
$$\frac{9}{15} = \frac{?}{?}$$
÷ ?   ÷ ?

(c)
$$\frac{8}{12} = \frac{?}{?}$$
÷ ?   ÷ ?

(d)
$$\frac{10}{18} = \frac{?}{?}$$
÷ ?   ÷ ?

(e)
$$\frac{7}{14} = \frac{?}{?}$$
÷ ?   ÷ ?

(f)
$$\frac{60}{80} = \frac{?}{?}$$
÷ ?   ÷ ?

2 Cancel these fractions to their lowest terms.

(a) $\frac{9}{15}$ (b) $\frac{15}{25}$ (c) $\frac{8}{20}$ (d) $\frac{22}{33}$ (e) $\frac{20}{28}$ (f) $\frac{18}{27}$

Practice

D Fill in the missing numbers to make equivalent fractions.

1 $\frac{9}{10} = \frac{?}{30}$ **2** $\frac{1}{4} = \frac{?}{40}$ **3** $\frac{1}{6} = \frac{5}{?}$ **4** $\frac{3}{4} = \frac{300}{?}$

5 $\frac{3}{8} = \frac{9}{?}$ **6** $\frac{5}{12} = \frac{15}{?}$ **7** $\frac{3}{20} = \frac{?}{60}$ **8** $\frac{1}{6} = \frac{100}{?}$

9 $\frac{5}{8} = \frac{55}{?}$ **10** $\frac{9}{10} = \frac{45}{?}$ **11** $\frac{7}{8} = \frac{21}{?}$ **12** $\frac{11}{12} = \frac{?}{60}$

E Write the following facts as fractions and cancel them to their
lowest terms.

Example	12 out of 30 school children bring sandwiches for lunch.
Working	12 out of 30 $= \dfrac{\cancel{12}^{\cancel{4}^2}}{\cancel{30}_{\cancel{10}_5}} = \dfrac{2}{5}$
Answer	$\frac{2}{5}$

1 8 marbles out of a bag of 12 are red.
2 9 out of a class of 24 children wear glasses.
3 15 out of 50 draw tickets won a prize.
4 14 out of 20 people said they use semi-skimmed milk.
5 60 of the 90 football supporters wore a scarf at the match.
6 14 miles of the 21-mile journey was by motorway.
7 200 out of 250 letters were delivered the next day.
8 18 days in April were sunny.

> **Finished Early?**
> ➡ Go to page 341

Further Practice

F Change the outer ring of fractions to equivalent fractions with the same denominator as the fraction in the centre circle.

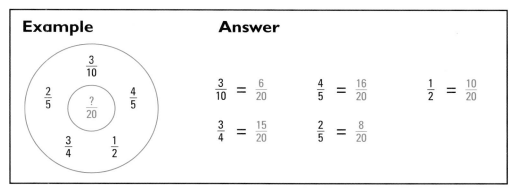

Example

Answer

$$\frac{3}{10} = \frac{6}{20} \qquad \frac{4}{5} = \frac{16}{20} \qquad \frac{1}{2} = \frac{10}{20}$$

$$\frac{3}{4} = \frac{15}{20} \qquad \frac{2}{5} = \frac{8}{20}$$

1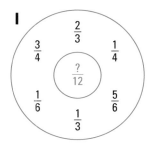

2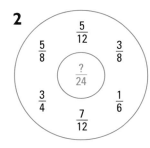

3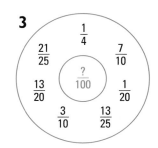

> **Finished Early?**
> ➡ Go to page 341

T ② Mixed Numbers

Learn About It

Darren has cut some pizzas into quarters.

1 quarter	2 quarters	3 quarters	1 whole = 4 quarters
$\frac{1}{4}$	$\frac{2}{4}$	$\frac{3}{4}$	$1 = \frac{4}{4}$

Each whole pizza has 4 quarters.
So 2 whole pizzas have $2 \times 4 = 8$ quarters.

$$2 \ = \ \frac{8}{4}$$

    =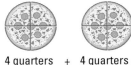

2 wholes and 3 quarters = 4 quarters + 4 quarters + 3 quarters

= 11 quarters altogether

$$2\frac{3}{4} \ = \ \frac{11}{4}$$

Mixed number   **Improper (top-heavy) fraction**

These three pizzas haven't been cut up yet.

They have 1 part each. So you can write 3 wholes as the improper fraction $\frac{3}{1}$.

Word Check

improper fraction a fraction in which the numerator is bigger (or the same as) the denominator

top-heavy fraction an improper fraction

mixed number a whole number and a fraction

Try It Out

G **1** In each question below ...
  (i) write a mixed number to describe the shaded area
  (ii) write an improper (top-heavy) fraction to describe the shaded area.

Example	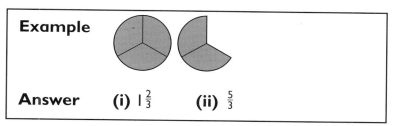
Answer	**(i)** $1\frac{2}{3}$ **(ii)** $\frac{5}{3}$

(a)    **(b)**    **(c)**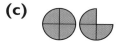

(d)    **(e)**    **(f)**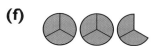

(g) 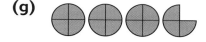   **(h)**

(i) 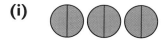   **(j)**

2 Convert these mixed numbers to improper fractions.

Example	$4\frac{1}{3}$
Working	$4\frac{1}{3}$ = 4 wholes + 1 third
	1 whole = 3 thirds
	So 4 wholes = 4 × 3 = 12 thirds
	12 third + 1 third = 13 thirds altogether
Answer	$\frac{13}{3}$

(a) $1\frac{3}{4}$ **(b)** $1\frac{3}{5}$ **(c)** $2\frac{1}{3}$ **(d)** $3\frac{1}{2}$

(e) $2\frac{5}{6}$ **(f)** $3\frac{5}{8}$ **(g)** $9\frac{1}{2}$

Learn More About It

You can change improper fractions to mixed numbers like this:

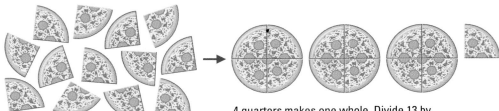

Here are 13 quarters of pizza. You can write this as the improper fraction $\frac{13}{4}$.

4 quarters makes one whole. Divide 13 by 4 to see how many whole pizzas there are.
$13 \div 4 = 3$ remainder 1.
There are 3 whole pizzas and 1 quarter left over. That can be written as the mixed number $3\frac{1}{4}$.
So $\frac{13}{4} = 3\frac{1}{4}$.

Try It Out

H Convert these improper (top-heavy) fractions to mixed numbers.

Example	$\frac{17}{3}$
Working	$17 \div 3 = 5$ remainder 2
Answer	$5\frac{2}{3}$

1 $\frac{5}{3}$ **2** $\frac{9}{2}$ **3** $\frac{9}{4}$ **4** $\frac{8}{4}$ **5** $\frac{12}{5}$ **6** $\frac{13}{6}$ **7** $\frac{19}{5}$

8 $\frac{15}{4}$ **9** $\frac{15}{5}$ **10** $\frac{27}{10}$ **11** $\frac{25}{11}$ **12** $\frac{15}{13}$ **13** $\frac{8}{1}$ **14** $\frac{15}{3}$

Practice

I For each improper fraction below, **(a)** cancel it to its lowest terms, **(b)** convert it to a mixed number.

1 $\frac{10}{4}$ **2** $\frac{12}{9}$ **3** $\frac{14}{8}$ **4** $\frac{24}{10}$ **5** $\frac{70}{20}$ **6** $\frac{55}{25}$ **7** $\frac{800}{500}$

J **1** Convert the pink mixed numbers to improper fractions.
2 Cancel the blue improper fractions to their lowest terms.
3 Match each blue fraction with the equivalent pink mixed number.

$1\frac{3}{5}$ $\frac{22}{12}$ $\frac{27}{12}$

$\frac{80}{30}$ $2\frac{1}{4}$ $2\frac{2}{3}$

$4\frac{1}{2}$ $\frac{24}{15}$ $1\frac{5}{6}$ $\frac{45}{10}$

Finished Early?
➡ Go to page 342

NUMBER SKILLS Multiply/divide HTU by TU, with remainder

Further Practice

Convert these mixed numbers to improper fractions.

1 $3\frac{1}{3}$　　**2** $2\frac{4}{5}$　　**3** $3\frac{4}{7}$　　**4** $2\frac{9}{10}$　　**5** $3\frac{7}{20}$　　**6** $2\frac{47}{100}$　　**7** 5

1 Write an improper fraction to describe each shaded area.
Make sure your answers are cancelled to their lowest terms.

(a) 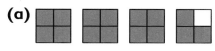　　**(b)**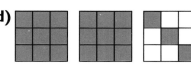

(c) 　　**(d)**

(e) 　　**(f)**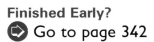

2 Convert your answers to question 1 to mixed numbers.

> **Finished Early?**
> ➡ Go to page 342

Decimals and Fractions

Remember?

The decimalizer shows the
columns used for decimals.

This number has 3 tenths ($\frac{3}{10}$) and 4 hundredths ($\frac{4}{100}$).

Units	Tenths	Hundredths	Thousands
0	3	4	

Try It Out

A decimalizer

Write down the fractions that make up each of the following numbers.
Use your decimalizer to help you.

1 0 . 2 9　　　　**2** 0 . 5 7　　　　**3** 0 . 0 9
4 0 . 4　　　　　**5** 0 . 2 0　　　　**6** 0 . 2 4 8
7 0 . 0 0 6　　　**8** 0 . 3 0 7　　　**9** 0 . 0 8 5
10 0 . 0 3 0

Learn About It

This square is divided into 10 equal strips.

Each strip is 1 tenth ($\frac{1}{10}$) of the square.

3 tenths ($\frac{3}{10}$) are shaded red.

You can write 3 tenths ($\frac{3}{10}$)
as the decimal 0.3.

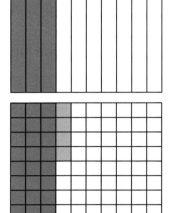

The square is now divided into 100
small squares.

4 hundredths ($\frac{4}{100}$) are shaded blue.

So 3 tenths ($\frac{3}{10}$) and 4 hundredths ($\frac{4}{100}$)
are shaded altogether.

You can write this as the
decimal 0.34.

34 hundredths ($\frac{34}{100}$) are shaded altogether.

0.34 means $\frac{34}{100}$.

In the top diagram above, $\frac{3}{10}$ (0.3) are shaded red.

In the second diagram above, $\frac{30}{100}$ (0.30) are shaded red.

So 0.30 is the same as 0.3 in the same way that $\frac{3}{10}$ and $\frac{30}{100}$ are
equal (equivalent).

Try It Out

 1 Write the following decimals as fractions. Do not cancel your answers.

Example	0.245
Working	Look at the last digit. It is in the thousandths column, so the denominator is 1000. So 0.245 = 245 thousandths.
Answer	$\frac{245}{1000}$

(a) 0.7　　　　(b) 0.03　　　(c) 0.2　　　(d) 0.93

(e) 0.491　　(f) 0.6　　　　(g) 0.009　　(h) 0.017

(i) 0.302　　(j) 0.1　　　　(k) 0.06　　　(l) 0.18

(m) 0.403　　(n) 0.90　　　(o) 0.030　　(p) 0.400

2 Write these fractions as decimals.

Example $\frac{29}{1000}$

Working   The last column will be thousandths.

Answer   0.029

tenths
hundredths
thousandths
0.0 2 9

(a) $\frac{9}{10}$ **(b)** $\frac{1}{10}$ **(c)** $\frac{23}{100}$ **(d)** $\frac{70}{100}$

(e) $\frac{924}{1000}$ **(f)** $\frac{607}{1000}$ **(g)** $\frac{3}{1000}$ **(h)** $\frac{58}{1000}$

Learn More About It

Fractions that don't have the denominator 10, 100, 1000, etc. can be changed to decimals too. Change their denominators to 10, 100 or 1000.

Example   Change $\frac{2}{5}$ to a decimal.

Working

$$\frac{2}{5} \xlongequal{\times 2} \frac{4}{10} = 4 \text{ tenths} = 0.4$$

Answer   0.4

Example   Change $\frac{4}{25}$ to a decimal.

Working

$$\frac{4}{25} \xlongequal{\times 4} \frac{16}{100} = 16 \text{ hundredths} = 0.16$$

Answer   0.16

Another way is to divide the numerator by the denominator.

$\frac{19}{4}$ means $19 \div 4 = 4.75$.

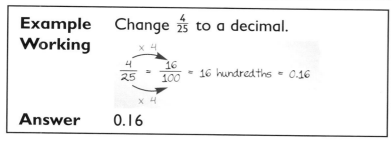

$$\begin{array}{r} 4.\,7\,5 \\ 4\overline{)19.^30^20} \end{array}$$

You can also use your calculator.

Example   Change $\frac{2}{5}$ to a decimal.

Working $\frac{2}{5}$ means $2 \div 5$.

     [2] [÷] [5] [=]   ⟦   0.4 ⟧

Answer   0.4

Try It Out

 I Convert each fraction to an equivalent fraction with the denominator 10, 100 or 1000. Then write the fraction as a decimal. Do not use your calculator.

(a) $\frac{3}{5}$ **(b)** $\frac{1}{5}$ **(c)** $\frac{4}{5}$ **(d)** $\frac{32}{50}$

(e) $\frac{3}{50}$ **(f)** $\frac{7}{50}$ **(g)** $\frac{1}{2}$ **(h)** $\frac{7}{20}$

(i) $\frac{3}{20}$ **(j)** $\frac{18}{20}$ **(k)** $\frac{9}{25}$ **(l)** $\frac{2}{25}$

(m) $\frac{24}{25}$ **(n)** $\frac{4}{500}$ **(o)** $\frac{31}{500}$ **(p)** $\frac{422}{500}$

(q) $\frac{1}{200}$ **(r)** $\frac{7}{200}$ **(s)** $\frac{26}{200}$

2 Use short division to convert these fractions to decimals.

(a) $\frac{1}{5}$ **(b)** $\frac{1}{8}$ **(c)** $\frac{5}{8}$ **(d)** $\frac{12}{5}$

(e) $\frac{21}{4}$ **(f)** $\frac{22}{5}$ **(g)** $\frac{7}{20}$ **(h)** $\frac{51}{20}$

 3 Use your calculator to convert these fractions to decimals.

(a) $\frac{3}{8}$ **(b)** $\frac{7}{25}$ **(c)** $\frac{13}{20}$ **(d)** $\frac{37}{40}$

(e) $3\frac{1}{4}$ **(f)** $2\frac{5}{8}$ **(g)** $10\frac{3}{4}$ **(h)** $14\frac{3}{5}$

(i) $12\frac{7}{8}$ **(j)** $8\frac{9}{20}$

Practice

 Convert the following decimals to fractions then cancel them to their lowest terms.

Example	0.625	**Working**
		thousandths
		$0.625 = \dfrac{625}{1000} = \dfrac{5}{8}$
Answer	$\frac{5}{8}$	

I 0.8   **2** 0.60   **3** 0.05   **4** 0.45

5 0.36   **6** 0.15   **7** 0.62   **8** 0.005

9 0.025   **10** 0.040   **11** 0.225   **12** 0.650

Write the numbers in the following groups in order, from smallest to largest. Use a calculator to convert the fractions to decimals first.

Example $\frac{3}{5}$ $\frac{5}{8}$ 0.45

Working   Convert the fractions to decimals:

$\frac{3}{5} = 3 \div 5 = 0.6$

$\frac{5}{8} = 5 \div 8 = 0.625$

Put the decimals in order: 0.45   0.6   0.625

Write the original numbers in order.

Answer   0.45 $\frac{3}{5}$ $\frac{5}{8}$

---

1 $\frac{3}{8}$ $\frac{2}{5}$ 0.35   **2** $\frac{9}{4}$ 2.33 $\frac{43}{20}$

3 $\frac{29}{8}$ 3.7 $\frac{69}{20}$ **4** $5\frac{4}{5}$ $\frac{23}{4}$ 5.64

5   0.09 $\frac{2}{25}$ $\frac{17}{200}$

6   2.853 $\frac{231}{80}$ $\frac{714}{250}$

Finished Early?
➡ Go to page 343

Further Practice

 Copy and complete these tables. Write the fractions in their lowest terms.

Fraction	Decimal	Fraction	Decimal	Fraction	Decimal
$\frac{1}{2}$		$\frac{3}{8}$		$\frac{3}{16}$	
	0.25		0.625		0.3125
$\frac{3}{4}$		$\frac{7}{8}$		$\frac{3}{100}$	
	0.2		0.1		0.23
$\frac{2}{5}$		$\frac{3}{10}$		$\frac{1}{200}$	
	0.6		0.7		0.004
$\frac{4}{5}$		$\frac{9}{10}$		$\frac{34}{1000}$	
	0.125		0.0625		0.234
$\frac{80}{100}$		$\frac{74}{1000}$		$\frac{400}{1000}$	
	0.90		0.570		0.070

Finished Early?
➡ Go to page 343

NUMBER SKILLS Know the columns of the decimal system.
Multiply/divide 4 digits by TU

11 Calculating with Fractions

In this chapter you will learn about ...
1. adding and subtracting fractions
2. multiplying and dividing fractions
3. fractions of an amount

T 1 Adding and Subtracting Fractions

Learn About It

To add fractions with the same denominator, just add their numerators (top numbers).

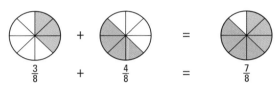

$$\frac{3}{8} + \frac{4}{8} = \frac{7}{8}$$

Sometimes the denominators are different. You have to make them the same. Find equivalent fractions so that the denominators are the same. When fractions have the same denominator, it is called the **common denominator**.

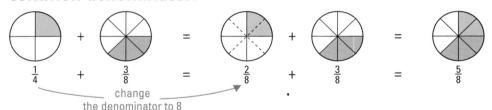

$$\frac{1}{4} + \frac{3}{8} = \frac{2}{8} + \frac{3}{8} = \frac{5}{8}$$

change the denominator to 8

Sometimes you have to change both denominators. Multiply them together to find the common denominator.

> **Word Check**
> ....
> **common denominator**
>   same denominator

$$\frac{1}{3} + \frac{1}{2} = \frac{2}{6} + \frac{3}{6} = \frac{5}{6}$$

common denominator is 3 × 2 = 6

> ## Key Fact
> To add or subtract fractions when the denominators are the same, simply add or subtract the numerators. When the denominators are different, find equivalent fractions that have the same denominator.

Try It Out

 I Work out the following calculations. Add or subtract the numerators. If possible, cancel your answers to their lowest terms.

(a) $\frac{2}{5} + \frac{1}{5}$ (b) $\frac{4}{7} - \frac{1}{7}$ (c) $\frac{6}{9} + \frac{2}{9}$ (d) $\frac{5}{8} - \frac{3}{8}$

(e) $\frac{5}{6} - \frac{1}{6}$ (f) $\frac{3}{10} + \frac{1}{10}$ (g) $\frac{11}{12} - \frac{5}{12}$ (h) $\frac{7}{20} + \frac{8}{20}$

(i) $\frac{31}{50} - \frac{11}{50}$ (j) $\frac{3}{10} + \frac{7}{10}$

2 Work out the following calculations. Multiply the top and bottom of the fraction that has the smaller denominator so that it has the same denominator as the other fraction. Cancel your answers, if possible.

Example	$\frac{1}{3} + \frac{1}{6}$
Working	$= \frac{2}{6} + \frac{1}{6}$ (*Change $\frac{1}{3}$ into sixths $\frac{2}{6}$.*) $\times 2$
	$= \frac{2+1}{6}$
	$= \frac{3^{1}}{6_{2}}$ (*Cancel to lowest terms.*)
	$= \frac{1}{2}$
Answer	$\frac{1}{2}$

(a) $\frac{1}{2} + \frac{1}{6}$ (b) $\frac{1}{4} + \frac{3}{8}$ (c) $\frac{3}{5} - \frac{3}{10}$ (d) $\frac{2}{5} - \frac{3}{10}$

(e) $\frac{2}{3} - \frac{2}{9}$ (f) $\frac{1}{16} + \frac{3}{4}$ (g) $\frac{7}{10} - \frac{9}{20}$ (h) $\frac{13}{20} + \frac{7}{40}$

(i) $\frac{3}{10} + \frac{13}{50}$ (j) $\frac{6}{7} - \frac{10}{21}$

3 Work out the following calculations. Multiply the denominators to find the common denominator. Cancel your answers if possible.

Example $\frac{2}{3} - \frac{1}{5}$

Working Common denominator = $3 \times 5 = 15$.

$\frac{2}{3} = \frac{10}{15}$ $\qquad$ $\frac{1}{5} = \frac{3}{15}$ $\qquad$ *(Change to equivalent fractions.)*

$= \frac{10}{15} - \frac{3}{15} = \frac{10-3}{15} = \frac{7}{15}$

Answer $\frac{7}{15}$

(a) $\frac{3}{4} - \frac{2}{5}$ $\qquad$ **(b)** $\frac{2}{3} + \frac{1}{5}$ $\qquad$ **(c)** $\frac{3}{10} + \frac{1}{4}$ $\qquad$ **(d)** $\frac{1}{4} + \frac{1}{5}$

(e) $\frac{1}{3} + \frac{2}{7}$ $\qquad$ **(f)** $\frac{2}{5} - \frac{1}{3}$ $\qquad$ **(g)** $\frac{4}{9} + \frac{1}{2}$ $\qquad$ **(h)** $\frac{5}{6} + \frac{1}{7}$

(i) $\frac{1}{2} - \frac{4}{9}$ $\qquad$ **(j)** $\frac{5}{6} - \frac{1}{7}$

Learn More About It

To add or subtract mixed numbers, change them to improper (top-heavy) fractions. Convert your answer to a mixed number, if necessary.

Example $3\frac{1}{4} - 1\frac{3}{8}$

Working $= \frac{13}{4} - \frac{11}{8}$ $\qquad$ *(Convert to improper fractions.)*

$= \frac{26}{8} - \frac{11}{8}$ $\qquad$ *(Change to the same denominator.)*

$= \frac{26-11}{8}$ $\qquad$ *(Subtract the fractions.)*

$= \frac{15}{8} = 1\frac{7}{8}$ $\qquad$ *(Convert the answer back to a mixed number.)*

Answer $1\frac{7}{8}$

Sometimes you need to subtract a fraction from a whole number. Change the whole number into an improper fraction before calculating.

Example John drinks $\frac{3}{8}$ of a can of drink. What fraction does he have left?

Working A whole can is $\frac{8}{8}$.

$\frac{8}{8} - \frac{3}{8} = \frac{8-3}{8} = \frac{5}{8}$

Answer $\frac{5}{8}$

NUMBER SKILLS Equivalent fractions, add/subtract TU

Key Fact

Change mixed numbers and whole numbers to improper fractions before adding or subtracting fractions.
Change your answer back to a mixed number if your answer is an improper fraction.

Try It Out

B **1** Calculate the following. Convert mixed numbers to improper fractions first. Then add or subtract.

(a) $2\frac{4}{5} + 1\frac{2}{5}$ (b) $3\frac{1}{4} - 1\frac{3}{4}$ (c) $1\frac{2}{3} + 4\frac{2}{3}$ (d) $3\frac{2}{5} - 1\frac{3}{5}$

(e) $2\frac{3}{8} + 1\frac{5}{8}$ (f) $1\frac{1}{6} - \frac{5}{6}$ (g) $4\frac{3}{10} + 2\frac{9}{10}$ (h) $2\frac{5}{8} - 1\frac{7}{8}$

2 Calculate the following. Convert mixed numbers to improper fractions first. Then make the denominators the same.

(a) $2\frac{1}{4} - \frac{3}{8}$ (b) $1\frac{3}{5} + 2\frac{3}{10}$ (c) $2\frac{1}{6} - 1\frac{2}{3}$ (d) $3\frac{1}{5} - 1\frac{3}{10}$

(e) $2\frac{3}{8} + 1\frac{3}{4}$ (f) $2\frac{1}{3} - 1\frac{3}{4}$ (g) $2\frac{1}{4} + 1\frac{4}{5}$ (h) $4\frac{1}{2} - 2\frac{3}{4}$

3 Calculate the following. Convert whole numbers and mixed numbers to improper fractions first. Give each of them the same denominator as the other fraction in the calculation.

(a) $1 - \frac{3}{5}$ (b) $1 - \frac{7}{8}$ (c) $1 - \frac{1}{10}$ (d) $3 - 1\frac{2}{3}$

(e) $2 + 1\frac{4}{5}$ (f) $4\frac{3}{4} - 2$ (g) $5 - 2\frac{5}{8}$ (h) $3\frac{1}{6} - 1$

Practice

C Calculate the following. Cancel your answers if possible. In each question, two of the three answers are the same. Find the odd one out.

1 (a) $\frac{7}{8} - \frac{1}{8}$ (b) $\frac{5}{6} - \frac{1}{6}$ (c) $\frac{2}{12} + \frac{7}{12}$

2 (a) $\frac{7}{10} + \frac{1}{10}$ (b) $\frac{2}{5} + \frac{2}{5}$ (c) $\frac{9}{10} - \frac{3}{10}$

3 (a) $\frac{1}{3} + \frac{1}{6}$ (b) $\frac{3}{4} - \frac{1}{3}$ (c) $\frac{7}{8} - \frac{3}{8}$

4 (a) $\frac{5}{6} - \frac{1}{3}$ (b) $\frac{2}{3} - \frac{1}{4}$ (c) $\frac{1}{4} + \frac{1}{6}$

5 (a) $1\frac{3}{8} + \frac{5}{8}$ (b) $2\frac{1}{8} - \frac{3}{8}$ (c) $2\frac{7}{8} - 1\frac{1}{8}$

6 (a) $1\frac{1}{3} + 1\frac{1}{2}$ (b) $3\frac{2}{3} - 1\frac{5}{6}$ (c) $1\frac{5}{6} + \frac{2}{3}$

D Add or subtract fractions to answer the questions below. Write your answers as cancelled fractions or mixed numbers.

Example	Isabel bought some chocolate. She gave $\frac{3}{4}$ of a bar to Sara and $\frac{2}{3}$ of a bar to Tarun. How much chocolate did she give away altogether?
Working	$\frac{3}{4} + \frac{2}{3} = \frac{9}{12} + \frac{8}{12} = \frac{9+8}{12} = \frac{17}{12} = 1\frac{5}{12}$
Answer	Isabel gave away $1\frac{5}{12}$ bar.

1 $\frac{2}{5}$ of a new candle burned down one evening and $\frac{1}{3}$ the next evening. What fraction of the candle burned down altogether?

2 In morning break-time, Nazir drank $\frac{3}{4}$ litre of water. At lunch he drank $\frac{1}{3}$ litre. How much more did he drink at break-time?

3 $\frac{1}{10}$ of people use skimmed milk. $\frac{3}{5}$ use semi-skimmed milk. $\frac{3}{10}$ use full-cream milk.
   (a) What fraction of people use skimmed or full-cream milk?
   (b) What fraction use skimmed or semi-skimmed milk?
   (c) What fraction use semi-skimmed or full-cream milk?

4 There were 4 hours recording time on Jabbar's video tape. He recorded a film lasting $1\frac{2}{3}$ hours and a documentary lasting $\frac{1}{2}$ hour.
   (a) How much of the video tape was used up?
   (b) How much recording time was left on the tape?

5 $\frac{2}{5}$ of a class got a grade A in a test. What fraction did not?

6 Douglas wrote $2\frac{1}{2}$ pages of history and $1\frac{2}{3}$ pages of French.
   (a) How many pages did he write altogether?
   (b) How many more pages of history than French did he write?

> **Finished Early?**
> ➡ Go to page 343

Further Practice

E 1 Calculate the following. Add or subtract the numerators. Cancel your answers, where possible.
   (a) $\frac{1}{5} + \frac{2}{5}$ **(b)** $\frac{5}{7} - \frac{2}{7}$ **(c)** $\frac{1}{6} + \frac{3}{6}$ **(d)** $\frac{1}{12} + \frac{5}{12}$

2 Calculate the following. Change the smaller denominator to match the bigger denominator.

(a) $\frac{1}{3} + \frac{1}{6}$ **(b)** $\frac{7}{8} - \frac{1}{2}$ **(c)** $\frac{3}{10} + \frac{2}{5}$

(d) $\frac{3}{4} - \frac{3}{8}$ **(e)** $\frac{5}{6} - \frac{2}{3}$ **(f)** $\frac{4}{15} + \frac{2}{5}$

3 Calculate the following. First, multiply the denominators to find the common denominator.

(a) $\frac{1}{4} + \frac{1}{3}$ **(b)** $\frac{2}{3} - \frac{1}{5}$ **(c)** $\frac{2}{5} - \frac{1}{6}$

(d) $\frac{1}{2} + \frac{2}{3}$ **(e)** $\frac{7}{8} - \frac{2}{5}$ **(f)** $\frac{5}{7} + \frac{1}{2}$

4 Calculate the following. First, convert mixed numbers to improper fractions.

(a) $1\frac{3}{4} + \frac{3}{4}$ **(b)** $2\frac{1}{3} - 1\frac{2}{3}$ **(c)** $2\frac{1}{2} + 2\frac{3}{4}$

(d) $2\frac{3}{5} - 1\frac{7}{10}$ **(e)** $1\frac{3}{4} + 2\frac{1}{3}$ **(f)** $3\frac{1}{5} - 1\frac{1}{2}$

5 Calculate the following. First, change the whole numbers and mixed numbers to improper fractions.

(a) $1 - \frac{7}{10}$ **(b)** $1 - \frac{4}{9}$ **(c)** $\frac{4}{5} + 2$

(d) $3 - 1\frac{5}{6}$ **(e)** $5\frac{2}{5} - 2$

> **Finished Early?**
> ➡ Go to page 343

❷ Multiplying and Dividing Fractions

Learn About It

$\frac{6}{8}$ of the cheese portions are left in this box.

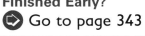

The remaining cheese portions have been divided in half.

Each half has $\frac{3}{8}$. So $\frac{1}{2}$ of $\frac{6}{8}$ is $\frac{3}{8}$.

In maths, **of** means ×. So $\frac{1}{2}$ of $\frac{6}{8} = \frac{1}{2} \times \frac{6}{8} = \frac{3}{8}$.

You can work this out another way:

$\frac{1}{2} \times \frac{6}{8} = \frac{1 \times 6}{2 \times 8}$ Multiply the numerators.
Multiply the denominators.

$= \frac{6^{\,3}}{16_{\,8}}$ Cancel.

$= \frac{3}{8}$

You can cancel first to make the numbers smaller to multiply:

$\frac{1}{2} \times \frac{\overset{3}{\cancel{6}}}{\underset{4}{\cancel{8}}} = \frac{1}{2} \times \frac{3}{4} = \frac{1 \times 3}{2 \times 4} = \frac{3}{8}$

Here is another way of cancelling. Divide any numerator and any denominator by a common factor.

$\frac{1}{\underset{1}{\cancel{2}}} \times \frac{\overset{3}{\cancel{6}}}{8} = \frac{1}{1} \times \frac{3}{8} = \frac{1 \times 3}{1 \times 8} = \frac{3}{8}$

Change mixed numbers to improper fractions, then cancel, before multiplying:

$1\frac{3}{5} \times 3\frac{1}{3} = \frac{8}{\underset{1}{\cancel{5}}} \times \frac{\overset{2}{\cancel{10}}}{3} = \frac{8 \times 2}{1 \times 3} = \frac{16}{3} = 5\frac{1}{3}$

Change whole numbers to improper fractions before cancelling and multiplying:

$3 \times \frac{6}{8} = \frac{3}{1} \times \frac{3}{4} = \frac{3 \times 3}{1 \times 4} = \frac{9}{4} = 2\frac{1}{4}$

write 3 as
a fraction

Key Fact

To multiply fractions:
- change mixed numbers to improper fractions
- change whole numbers to improper fractions
- cancel any numerator with any denominator
- multiply the numerators
- multiply the denominators
- change the answer to a mixed number, if necessary.

Try It Out

F 1 Multiply the following fractions. Cancel your answers to their lowest terms.

(a) $\frac{2}{3} \times \frac{1}{4}$ (b) $\frac{3}{5} \times \frac{1}{6}$ (c) $\frac{3}{4} \times \frac{4}{5}$

(d) $\frac{2}{5} \times \frac{10}{3}$ (e) $\frac{5}{8} \times \frac{4}{5}$ (f) $\frac{3}{10} \times \frac{4}{9}$

2 Cancel these fractions first, then multiply them.

(a) $\frac{6}{8} \times \frac{1}{5}$ (b) $\frac{3}{7} \times \frac{5}{10}$ (c) $\frac{2}{3} \times \frac{6}{7}$

(d) $\frac{5}{6} \times \frac{3}{10}$ (e) $\frac{4}{6} \times \frac{12}{16}$ (f) $\frac{5}{4} \times \frac{8}{15}$

3 Change the mixed numbers to improper fractions, then multiply. Write your answers as mixed numbers.

(a) $2\frac{2}{3} \times \frac{5}{6}$ (b) $\frac{3}{4} \times 1\frac{3}{5}$ (c) $2\frac{1}{2} \times 1\frac{3}{10}$ (d) $3\frac{1}{5} \times 1\frac{1}{8}$

4 Change the whole numbers to improper fractions, then multiply. Write your answers as mixed numbers in their lowest terms.

(a) $\frac{5}{7} \times 2$ (b) $3 \times \frac{2}{5}$ (c) $\frac{2}{3} \times 6$

(d) $5 \times \frac{3}{4}$ (e) $\frac{5}{14} \times 8$

Learn More About It

You can divide fractions by changing $\div$ to $\times$ and turning the second fraction upside down.

$$\frac{6}{8} \div \frac{3}{8} = \frac{6}{8} \times \frac{8}{3} = \frac{\cancel{6}^{2}}{\cancel{8}_{1}} \times \frac{\cancel{8}^{1}}{\cancel{3}_{1}} = \frac{2 \times 1}{1 \times 1} = \frac{2}{1} = 2$$

Change mixed numbers to improper fractions before dividing:

$$2\frac{5}{8} \div 2\frac{1}{3} = \frac{21}{8} \div \frac{7}{3} = \frac{\cancel{21}^{3}}{8} \times \frac{3}{\cancel{7}_{1}} = \frac{3 \times 3}{8 \times 1} = \frac{9}{8} = 1\frac{1}{8}$$

Change whole numbers to fractions before dividing:

$$\frac{6}{7} \div 3 = \frac{6}{7} \div \frac{3}{1} = \frac{\cancel{6}^{2}}{7} \times \frac{1}{\cancel{3}_{1}} = \frac{2 \times 1}{7 \times 1} = \frac{2}{7}$$

Key Fact

To divide one fraction by another fraction:
- change mixed numbers to improper fractions
- change whole numbers to improper fractions
- change $\div$ to $\times$ and turn the second fraction upside down
- multiply the fractions
- cancel the answer to its lowest terms, if necessary
- change the answer to a mixed number, if necessary.

Try It Out

 G Work these out. Change your answers to mixed numbers, if necessary.

1 (a) $\frac{2}{3} \div \frac{5}{6}$ (b) $\frac{3}{4} \div \frac{1}{6}$ (c) $\frac{1}{8} \div \frac{3}{4}$ (d) $\frac{5}{6} \div \frac{1}{2}$

(e) $\frac{3}{10} \div \frac{4}{5}$

2 (a) $2\frac{1}{4} \div \frac{3}{4}$ (b) $1\frac{3}{5} \div 2\frac{4}{5}$ (c) $3\frac{1}{3} \div 1\frac{1}{5}$ (d) $2\frac{5}{8} \div 1\frac{3}{4}$

3 (a) $3 \div \frac{4}{5}$ (b) $\frac{3}{8} \div 2$ (c) $2 \div \frac{2}{3}$ (d) $5 \div \frac{3}{4}$

(e) $2\frac{2}{3} \div 8$

Practice

 H 1 Choose six pairs of these fractions for your partner to multiply.
Check each other's answers.

2 Choose six pairs of fractions from above. In each pair, choose one red and one blue fraction.
Ask your partner to divide the blue fraction by the red fraction.
Check each other's answers.

I Answer the following questions by dividing fractions. Show your working.

Example	Judy's dog eats $\frac{2}{3}$ of a can of Doggydins each day. How many days will 4 cans last?
Working	Find how many lots of $\frac{2}{3}$ there are in 4.
	$4 \div \frac{2}{3} = \frac{4}{1} \div \frac{2}{3}$ *(Change 4 to $\frac{4}{1}$.)*
	$= \frac{4}{1} \times \frac{3}{2}$ *(Change $\div$ to $\times$ and turn $\frac{2}{3}$ upside down.)*
	$= \frac{4 \times 3}{1 \times 2}$
	$= \frac{12}{2}$
	$= 6$
Answer	4 cans will last 6 days.

1 A TV serial lasts $\frac{2}{3}$ of an hour. How many episodes can be recorded on a 3-hour video tape?

2 How many $2\frac{1}{4}$-minute messages will fit on a 15-minute answering machine tape?

3 Barney is making shelves $1\frac{3}{5}$ m long. How many shelves can he make from a 12 m plank of wood?

4 $6\frac{2}{5}$ kg of oats fill 4 bags. How much does each bag contain?

5 $2\frac{4}{5}$ litres of orangeade is shared between 7 children. How much does each child get?

6 Dennis is 15 years old. Kelly is $3\frac{3}{4}$ years old. How many times older than Kelly is Dennis?

> **Finished Early?**
> ➡ Go to page 344

Further Practice

J
1 Multiply the fractions. Cancel your answers to their lowest terms.

  (a) $\frac{2}{5} \times \frac{1}{3}$ **(b)** $\frac{3}{8} \times \frac{4}{5}$ **(c)** $\frac{4}{9} \times \frac{6}{7}$ **(d)** $\frac{5}{12} \times \frac{9}{10}$

2 Cancel the fractions first, then multiply.

  (a) $\frac{2}{4} \times \frac{3}{5}$ **(b)** $\frac{1}{5} \times \frac{6}{9}$ **(c)** $\frac{10}{15} \times \frac{8}{12}$ **(d)** $\frac{4}{9} \times \frac{6}{5}$

3 Change the mixed numbers to improper fractions, then multiply. Write your answers as mixed numbers.

  (a) $1\frac{1}{2} \times \frac{3}{4}$ **(b)** $\frac{5}{6} \times 2\frac{2}{3}$ **(c)** $2\frac{2}{5} \times 1\frac{1}{9}$ **(d)** $1\frac{2}{3} \times 4\frac{1}{2}$

4 Change the whole numbers to improper fractions, then multiply. Write your answers as mixed numbers.

  (a) $\frac{2}{5} \times 3$ **(b)** $\frac{3}{8} \times 4$ **(c)** $9 \times \frac{5}{6}$ **(d)** $\frac{3}{10} \times 15$

K Calculate the following. Change your answers to mixed numbers if necessary.

1 (a) $\frac{3}{5} \div \frac{1}{6}$ **(b)** $\frac{2}{3} \div \frac{5}{6}$ **(c)** $\frac{1}{8} \div \frac{3}{4}$ **(d)** $\frac{3}{10} \div \frac{4}{15}$

2 (a) $1\frac{1}{3} \div 1\frac{1}{9}$ **(b)** $2\frac{1}{4} \div 2\frac{2}{3}$ **(c)** $1\frac{3}{5} \div 2\frac{2}{5}$ **(d)** $3\frac{1}{3} \div 4\frac{1}{6}$

3 (a) $\frac{3}{8} \div 2$ **(b)** $3 \div \frac{2}{5}$

  (c) $\frac{8}{11} \div 4$ **(d)** $2\frac{2}{9} \div 8$

> **Finished Early?**
> ➡ Go to page 344

T ③ Fractions of an Amount

> **Remember?**
> To find $\frac{1}{*}$ of an amount, divide by *.
>
> | | |
> |---|---|
> | **Example** | Find $\frac{1}{3}$ of £54. |
> | **Working** | $54 \div 3 = 18$ |
> | **Answer** | £18 |

Try It Out

Ⓛ Calculate the following.

1 $\frac{1}{2}$ of 16 mm   2 $\frac{1}{5}$ of £10   3 $\frac{1}{8}$ of 24 kg

4 $\frac{1}{10}$ of 60 minutes   5 $\frac{1}{4}$ of 36 cm   6 $\frac{1}{3}$ of 150 km

Learn About It

Owen and Sohal have 15 conkers each. Paula has none. They decide to give Paula $\frac{2}{5}$ of their conkers.

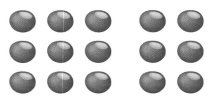

Owen works out $\frac{2}{5}$ of 15 like this.

He divides 15 by the denominator and multiplies his answer by the numerator.

First he finds one fifth ($\frac{1}{5}$) by dividing: $15 \div 5 = 3$

Then he finds two-fifths ($\frac{2}{5}$) by multiplying: $2 \times 3 = 6$

Paula gets 6 conkers from Owen.

Sohal works out $\frac{2}{5}$ of 15 by multiplying fractions.

$\frac{2}{5}$ of $15 = \frac{2}{5} \times 15 = \frac{2}{5} \times \frac{\overset{3}{15}}{1} = \frac{2 \times 3}{1 \times 1} = \frac{6}{1} = 6$

She gets the same answer as Owen.

Try It Out

 1 Calculate the following. Divide first, then multiply.

(a) $\frac{3}{4}$ of £12 (b) $\frac{2}{3}$ of 18 kg (c) $\frac{3}{10}$ of 20 m

(d) $\frac{5}{6}$ of 24 hours (e) $\frac{2}{5}$ of 20 cm (f) $\frac{7}{10}$ of 60 minutes

2 Calculate these amounts by multiplying fractions.

(a) $\frac{3}{7}$ of 21 years (b) $\frac{7}{8}$ of £32 (c) $\frac{9}{10}$ of 30 litres

(d) $\frac{5}{12}$ of 48 mm (e) $\frac{5}{8}$ of 16p (f) $\frac{3}{4}$ of 12 days

Practice

 Calculate the following amounts.

Example	How much is $2\frac{2}{5}$ m of washing line costing 60p a metre?
Working	$2\frac{2}{5} = 2 + \frac{2}{5}$
	2 m costs $2 \times 60p = 120p$.
	$\frac{2}{5}$ m costs $\frac{2}{5}$ of 60p $= \frac{2}{5} \times \frac{60}{1} = \frac{120}{5} = 24p$.
	Total cost $= 120p + 24p = 144p$.
Answer	£1.44

1 $\frac{2}{3}$ of a box of 24 chocolates have soft centres. How many is this?

2 A ladder reaches $\frac{3}{4}$ of the way up a 12 m wall. How long is it?

3 Max's bath holds 90 litres when full. He fills $\frac{5}{6}$ of the bath with water. How much water is in the bath?

4 Sonia has knitted $\frac{3}{8}$ of a 120 cm scarf. What length has she knitted?

5 Errol uses $\frac{7}{10}$ of a 400 g bag of sugar. How many grams is that?

6 Potatoes cost 40p per kg. How much do $4\frac{1}{2}$ kg cost?

7 Harry travels 60 miles in an hour. How far does he travel in $\frac{2}{3}$ hours?

8 A glass can hold 20 cl of wine. How much is $3\frac{3}{4}$ glasses of wine?

9 A full box contains 40 screws. How many screws are in $3\frac{1}{5}$ boxes?

Finished Early?
 Go to page 344

Further Practice

Dr Smelting mixes different amounts of metals. He writes each formula on a strip of paper like this:

$\frac{1}{8}$T	$\frac{1}{4}$C	$\frac{5}{8}$I

T stands for tin, C for copper and I for iron.
Calculate the amount of each metal he uses in the following mixes.

Example 40 kg of

$\frac{1}{8}$T	$\frac{1}{4}$C	$\frac{5}{8}$I

Working Tin $\frac{1}{8}$ of 40 = 40 ÷ 8 = 5 kg

Copper $\frac{1}{4}$ of 40 = 40 ÷ 4 = 10 kg

Iron $\frac{5}{8}$ of 40 = 40 ÷ 8 × 5 = 5 × 5 = 25 kg

Check: 5 kg + 10 kg + 25 kg = 40 kg

Answer   5 kg tin, 10 kg copper, 25 kg iron

---

1 60 kg of

$\frac{1}{6}$T	$\frac{1}{3}$C	$\frac{1}{2}$I

2 50 kg of

$\frac{1}{10}$T	$\frac{3}{10}$C	$\frac{6}{10}$I

3 800 kg of

$\frac{1}{8}$T	$\frac{3}{8}$C	$\frac{1}{2}$I

4 100 kg of

$\frac{3}{20}$T	$\frac{1}{10}$C	$\frac{3}{4}$I

5 54 kg of

$\frac{1}{9}$T	$\frac{2}{9}$C	$\frac{2}{3}$I

6 200 kg of

$\frac{2}{5}$T	$\frac{3}{8}$C	$\frac{9}{40}$I

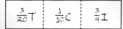

Finished Early?
 Go to page 344

12 Percentages

In this chapter you will learn about ...

① percentages

② percentages of an amount

③ percentage increase and decrease

① Percentages

Remember?

- This rectangle is divided into 100 squares.

  21 out of 100 squares are yellow. That's $\frac{21}{100}$ as a fraction.

- A fraction out of 100 is called a **percentage**.
  21 **per cent** of the rectangle is yellow. This is written 21%.
  The whole rectangle is 100%.

Try It Out

A For each rectangle below ...

(a) write the percentage of the rectangle that is shaded yellow

(b) write the percentage of the rectangle that is shaded red.

1    2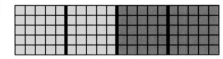

3    4

Learn About It

25 out of 100 squares
are shaded green.

25% is shaded green.

$25\% = \frac{25}{100}$, which cancels to $\frac{1}{4}$.

10 squares are
shaded green.

10% is shaded green.

$10\% = \frac{10}{100} = \frac{1}{10}$

30 squares are
shaded green.

30% is shaded green.

$30\% = \frac{30}{100} = \frac{3}{10}$

For each large square, write down the fraction and percentage that
is shaded green.

1  **2**  **3**  **4**

Try It Out

B Copy and complete this table.

Percentage	10%	20%	25%	30%	40%	50%	60%	70%	75%	80%	90%	100%
Fraction			$\frac{1}{4}$	$\frac{3}{10}$								

Learn More About It

Each slice is 25% of a pizza.
How much pizza is this
altogether?

100% is a whole (1) pizza. 25% is a quarter ($\frac{1}{4}$) pizza.

Altogether there is 125% of a pizza. That's $1\frac{1}{4}$ pizzas.

1 whole pizza
(100%)

$\frac{1}{4}$ pizza
(25%)

> **Key Fact**
> 100% is a whole.
> More than 100% is
> more than a whole.

The pictures below show pizzas and fractions of pizzas.
For each question, write down the amount of pizza as
(a) a percentage of one pizza, **(b)** a mixed number.

1

2

3

4

5

6

Try It Out

Nik Nak chocolate bars are divided into four fingers.
For each question, write down the chocolate bars shown as:
(a) a percentage of one chocolate bar, **(b)** a mixed number.

1

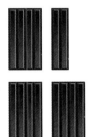

2

3

4

5

6

Practice

1 Write each percentage as a fraction.
   Cancel the fraction to its lowest terms.

Example	85%	
Working	$85\% = \dfrac{85}{100} \; \substack{17 \\ 20}$	
Answer	$\dfrac{17}{20}$	

(a) 70%   **(b)** 25%   **(c)** 40%   **(d)** 90%

(e) 80%   **(f)** 35%   **(g)** 95%   **(h)** 65%

2 Write each of the following percentages as a mixed number.

Example 130%
Working 130% = 100% + 30%
100% is a whole (1)
30% = $\frac{30}{100}$ = $\frac{3}{10}$
So 130% = 1 + $\frac{3}{10}$.
Answer $1\frac{3}{10}$

   (a) 110%   **(b)** 150%   **(c)** 125%   **(d)** 120%
   (e) 175%   **(f)** 200%   **(g)** 300%   **(h)** 450%

E For each picture below ...
   (a) write a mixed number to show how many copies of each
       pattern have been printed
   (b) calculate the total percentage printed.

1   2    3

4   5

Finished Early? ➡ Go to page 345

Further Practice

Squared paper

F **1** For each question below, draw 10 × 10 squares and colour these
    percentages of a square.
    (a) 50%   **(b)** 75%   **(c)** 10%   **(d)** 30%   **(e)** 60%
    (f) 100%   **(g)** 200%   **(h)** 125%   **(i)** 150%   **(j)** 220%

   2 Write each percentage from question 1 as
    a fraction.
    Cancel each fraction to its lowest terms.

Finished Early? ➡ Go to page 345

Percentages of an Amount

> **Remember?**
>
> You can write $\frac{4}{10}$ as the decimal 0.4. 0.4 tenths
>
> You can write $\frac{46}{100}$ as the decimal 0.46. 0.46 tenths hundredths
>
> You can write $\frac{6}{100}$ as the decimal 0.06. 0.06 tenths hundredths
>
> 0.40 is the same as 0.4 – you don't need the zero on the end.

Try It Out

1 Write these fractions as decimals.

(a) $\frac{8}{10}$ (b) $\frac{1}{10}$ (c) $\frac{73}{100}$ (d) $\frac{29}{100}$

(e) $\frac{7}{100}$ (f) $\frac{1}{100}$ (g) $\frac{60}{100}$ (h) $\frac{20}{100}$

2 Write these decimals as fractions with denominators 10 or 100.

(a) 0.2   (b) 0.9   (c) 0.49   (d) 0.81

(e) 0.03   (f) 0.02   (g) 0.30   (h) 0.80

Learn About It

You can write percentages as decimals.

35% means $\frac{35}{100}$ or 35 hundredths. So 35% is the same as the decimal 0.35.

7% means $\frac{7}{100}$ or 7 hundredths. So 7% is the same as the decimal 0.07.

30% means $\frac{30}{100}$ or 30 hundredths. So 30% is the same as the decimal 0.30. Write 0.30 as 0.3.

To change a decimal number less than 1 to a percentage, look at the first two decimal places.

0.45 = 45%.

0.60 = 60%.

Try It Out

 1 Write these percentages as decimals.

(a) 64%   (b) 38%   (c) 75%   (d) 90%
(e) 9%   (f) 6%   (g) 1%   (h) 20%
(i) 50%   (j) 99%

2 Write these decimals as percentages.

(a) 0.25   (b) 0.71   (c) 0.13   (d) 0.08
(e) 0.02   (f) 0.60   (g) 0.20   (h) 0.8
(i) 0.1   (j) 0.01

Learn More About It

This carton contains 40 cl of mixed fruit juice.

You can find the amount of apple juice it contains like this:

You need to find 60% of 40 cl

$= \frac{60}{100} \times 40$ *(60% means $\frac{60}{100}$ and **of** means ×.)*

$= 40 \times \frac{60}{100}$ *(It doesn't matter which way around you multiply.)*

$= 40 \times 60 \div 100$ *($\frac{60}{100}$ means $60 \div 100$.)*

$= 2400 \div 100$

$= 24$ cl

The carton contains 24 cl of apple juice.

> **Word Check**
>
> **of** times (×)

> ### Key Fact
> To work out a percentage of something:
> - multiply it by the number of per cent
> - divide the answer by 100.

Sometimes it is quicker to write a percentage as a fraction.
10% of the drink in the carton is pear juice:
10% of 40 cl

$= \frac{1}{10}$ of 40 cl *(10% is the same as $\frac{1}{10}$.)*

$= 40$ cl $\div 10$

$= 4$ cl

The carton contains 4 cl of pear juice.

If you know 10% you can find 30%.
10% of 40 cl is 4 cl.
30% is 3 × 10%.
So 30% of 40 cl is 3 × 4 cl = 12 cl.
The carton contains 12 cl of orange juice.

Try It Out

Calculate the amount of each type of fruit juice in these cartons.

1

Apple 10%
Orange 50%
Grapefruit 40%
90 cl

2

Mango 25%
Pineapple 20%
Pear 55%
80 cl

3

Raspberry 18%
Blackberry 26%
Strawberry 56%
50 cl

Practice

1 Calculate the following amounts. Change the percentages
to fractions.

(a) 25% of 200 m (b) 60% of £15 (c) 50% of £80
(d) 20% of 75 cl (e) 10% of 60p (f) 1% of 700 g
(g) 80% of 25 litres (h) 6% of 300 g (i) 75% of 16 minutes
(j) 100% of £9.50 (k) 150% of 6 km (l) 120% of 10 mm
(m) 160% of 120 m

2 Calculate the following amounts. Change the percentages to fractions.

(a) 25% of 100 m (b) 10% of 50 litres (c) 50% of £60
(d) 30% of 70 cl (e) 70% of 80 km (f) 90% of £70
(g) 75% of 24 years (h) 20% of 40 g (i) 10% of 40p
(j) 5% of 40p (k) 20% of 15 minutes
(l) 40% of 15 minutes

K The table shows how much four families spend on food each week. The pie chart shows the percentage people in their town spend on each type of food.

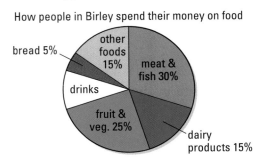

How people in Birley spend their money on food

Amount spent on food each week	
Family	**Amount**
Smith	£48
Yeung	£60
Turner	£52
Patel	£42

Example	How much do the Patel family spend on dairy products each week?
Working	The Patels spend £42 on food each week. They spend 15% on dairy products. 15% of £42 = 15 × 42 ÷ 100 = 630 ÷ 100 = £6.30
Answer	The Patel family spend £6.30 on dairy products.

1 In a week, how much would you expect …
   (a) the Smith family to spend on **(i)** bread, **(ii)** other foods?
   (b) the Yeung family to spend on dairy products?
   (c) the Turner family to spend on fruit and vegetables?
   (d) the Patel family to spend on meat and fish?

2 What percentage do people spend on drinks in Birley?

3 In a week, how much would you expect …
   (a) the Yeung family to spend on **(i)** drinks, **(ii)** dairy products and drinks?
   (b) the Patel family to spend on meat, fish and bread?

4 The Yeung family buy meat and fish for a week. How much of their weekly food money would you expect them to have left?

5 The Turner family spend more on fruit and vegetables than on dairy products. How much more?

6 What is the total amount spent on bread each week by all four families?

Finished Early?
➡ Go to page 346

Further Practice

L Calculate, in grams, the amount of each ingredient in the following foods.

1
OAT BISCUITS
oats 60%
sugar 20%
butter 10%
other 10%   250 g

2
Soy sauce
soya
beans 75%
water 20%
salt 5%
120 ml

3
MARMALADE
sugar 60%
oranges 25%
water 14%
pectin 1%
300 g

4
NUT CRUNCH CEREAL
wheat flakes 32%
barley flakes 20%
nuts 18%
raisins 16%
fruit juice 11%
oil 3%
400 g

Example	Oats in oat biscuits
Working	A packet of oat biscuits weighs 250 g. 60% is oats.
	60% of 250 g = 60 × 250 ÷ 100
	= 15 000 ÷ 100
	= 150 g
Answer	There are 150 g of oats.

M Work out which number is largest in each of the following questions.

Example	20%, $\frac{1}{4}$, 0.21
Working	Change all the fractions and decimals to percentages.
	$\frac{1}{4}$ = 25% 0.21 = 21%
	25% ($\frac{1}{4}$) is biggest.
Answer	$\frac{1}{4}$

1 35%, $\frac{38}{100}$, 0.33   **2** 0.64, $\frac{6}{10}$, 65%   **3** $\frac{8}{10}$, 78%, 0.82

4 9%, $\frac{1}{10}$, 0.12   **5** 4%, $\frac{7}{100}$, 0.06   **6** 140%, $1\frac{1}{2}$, 1.45

Finished Early?
➡ Go to page 346

T ③ Percentage Increase and Decrease

Learn About It

There is 15% off Smash Band's latest CD in a sale.

Dawn works out how much she will save.

15% of £20 $= 15 \times 20 \div 100$
$= 300 \div 100$
$= £3$

Then she takes £3 off the price to work out what she will have to pay.

£20 − £3 = £17

Dawn will have to pay £17 for the CD.

Nathan is buying a personal stereo by mail order.

First, he calculates the charge for postage and packing.

9% of £54 $= 9 \times 54 \div 100$
$= 486 \div 100 = £4.86$

plus **9%** postage and packing

Then he adds this to the price of the stereo:

£54 + £4.86 = £58.86

Nathan has to pay £58.86 altogether.

Try It Out

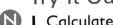 **1** Calculate the following. Do not use a calculator.
  (a) the cost of a £10 book, reduced by 30% in a sale
  (b) the cost of a £200 refrigerator, plus a 10% delivery charge
  (c) Jan drinks 25% of a 300 ml can of cola. How much is left?
  (d) the cost of a £30 dress, plus 5% postage and packing
  (e) the height of a tree that has increased from 600 cm by 2%
  (f) £340 wages after 20% has been taken in income tax
  (g) Jan's savings of £40 increased by 100%
  (h) Graham's weight decreased from 50 kg by 8%.
  (i) the value of a rare stamp, bought for £20 which has increased in value by 110%

2 Use your calculator to calculate the following.
   (a) A standard packet of cereal contains 230 g. A special offer packet contains 15% more. How much does it contain?
   (b) the petrol in a car's tank, having fallen from 40 litres by 65%
   (c) the stretched length of a 30 cm piece of elastic which, when stretched, increases in length by 95%
   (d) a swimming pool's temperature having dropped from 20 °C by 7%
   (e) the taxi fare from Beldon to Swanford having risen by 6% from £5.50
   (f) the price of potatoes after falling from £1.35 by 20%
   (g) Stedmore's population having increased from 61 500 by 4%
   (h) 9% of a 234 000 m² forest was burnt down. How much remained?

Learn More About It

Chris owes £54.23 on his credit card.

27/09/01	**Supermarket** Warwick	£20.21
To reach us by **22/10/01**	Minimum payment 5%	**Present balance** £54.23

He decides to pay 5%.

5% of £54.23 = 5 × 54.23 ÷ 100

   = £2.7115 = £2.71 rounded to the nearest penny.

Chris pays £2.71.

He subtracts £2.71 to find how much he still owes.

£54.23 − £2.71 = £51.52

Try It Out

Calculate the following. Give your answers correct to the nearest penny.
1 Gill's credit card bill of £68.37 plus 2% charges
2 the price of a personal stereo increased from £28.84 by 13%
3 a TV satellite dish costing £104.83 plus 10% installation charge
4 Joe's wages of £248.21 after 6% has been deducted for his pension
5 the London to Paris air fare, increased from £94.73 by 39%
6 the value of €1 (1 euro) decreased from 64p by 3%

Practice

P Calculate the following. Do not use a calculator.

1. 14 mm increased by 50%
2. 30 cl decreased by 20%
3. 12p increased by 25%
4. 40 kg decreased by 30%
5. 28 litres decreased by 75%
6. £500 decreased by 50%
7. 22 cm increased by 100%
8. £4 increased by 150%

Q The map shows how house prices changed from last year to this year. Copy and complete the table.

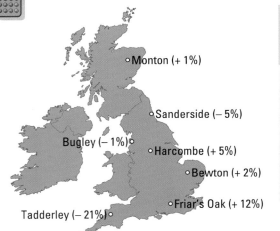

	Last year	This year (to nearest £1000)
Bewton	£93 000	
Bugley	£33 600	
Friar's Oak	£120 000	
Harcombe	£80 000	
Monton	£75 900	
Sanderside	£39 600	
Tadderley	£74 000	

Monton (+ 1%)
Sanderside (− 5%)
Bugley (− 1%)
Harcombe (+ 5%)
Bewton (+ 2%)
Friar's Oak (+ 12%)
Tadderley (− 21%)

Finished Early?
➡ Go to page 346

Further Practice

R The table shows how various prices changed from 2000 to 2001. Calculate the prices in 2001, to the nearest penny.

Price in 2000	% change	Price in 2001
1 Postage stamp 25p	+ 5%	
2 Pack of coffee £1.80	− 2%	
3 Loaf of bread 70p	+ 3%	
4 Bottle of wine £4.60	− 15%	
5 Petrol 74p per litre	+ 65%	
6 Scientific calculator £8.22	− 17%	
7 Rail fare £6.45	− 39%	

Finished Early?
➡ Go to page 346

Unit 7 Fractional Parts

Summary of Chapters 10, 11 and 12

- Multiplying or dividing the numerator and denominator of a fraction by the same number gives an **equivalent fraction**.

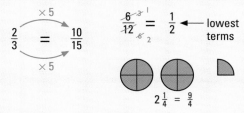

$$2\tfrac{1}{4} = \tfrac{9}{4}$$

- $2\tfrac{1}{4}$ is a mixed number.

- $\tfrac{9}{4}$ is an improper or top-heavy fraction.

- To change a decimal to a fraction, look at the columns.

$$0.3 = \frac{3}{10}$$

- To change a fraction to a decimal:

  divide, e.g. $\tfrac{3}{4} = 3 \div 4 = 0.75$ or

  change the denominator to 10, 100 or 1000, e.g. $\tfrac{2}{5} = \tfrac{4}{10} = 0.4$.

- To add/subtract fractions with different denominators, change them to equivalent fractions with a **common denominator**, e.g. $\tfrac{1}{4} + \tfrac{3}{8} = \tfrac{2}{8} + \tfrac{3}{8} = \tfrac{5}{8}$.

- **Cancel** fractions before multiplying, e.g. $\dfrac{5}{12} \times \dfrac{8}{15} = \dfrac{1 \times 2}{3 \times 3} = \dfrac{2}{9}$

- To divide by a fraction, change $\div$ to $\times$ and turn the fraction upside down, e.g. $\tfrac{5}{8} \div \tfrac{2}{3} = \tfrac{5}{8} \times \tfrac{3}{2} = \tfrac{15}{16}$.

- To find a fraction of an amount, divide by the denominator then multiply by the numerator, e.g. $\tfrac{2}{5}$ of $20\,\text{kg} = 20\,\text{kg} \div 5 \times 2 = 8\,\text{kg}$.

- 25% means $\tfrac{25}{100}$, which cancels to $\tfrac{1}{4}$.

- To calculate a percentage of an amount, multiply the amount by the number of per cent, then divide by 100, e.g. 20% of £30 = $20 \times 30 \div 100 = 600 \div 100 = £6$.

Brush Up Your Number 8

 Calculating with Large Numbers

Learn About It

You add and subtract large numbers the same way you do smaller numbers.

```
      6  3 2 5   0 0 9
  +   3  8 0 8   2 4 3
  ─────────────────────
  1 0  1 3 3   2 5 2
      1      1        1
```

```
      6 13 1      0 1
      7  4 2   6  1 1
  -   2 8 5   4 0 9
  ─────────────────────
      4 5 7   2 0 2
```

Try It Out

 1 Calculate the following.

(a) 426 351 + 266 036   (b) 1 531 402 + 2 270 349
(c) 35 076 999 + 48 742 606 (d) 3 469 043 + 599 950
(e) 261 635 500 + 44 295 000

2 Calculate the following.

(a) 751 348 − 425 244   (b) 5 825 630 − 3 185 798
(c) 58 466 250 − 15 600 500   (d) 2 361 855 − 731 000
(e) 343 000 000 − 7 500 000

Learn More About It

You multiply and divide large numbers the same way you do smaller numbers.

```
        2 7  8 4 8
  ×           2 3
  ───────────────────
        8 3  5 4 4
        2 2  1 2
  +   5 5 6  9 6 0
      1 1    1
  ───────────────────
      6 4 0  5 0 4
      1 1 1    1
```

```
          3 0 9 1  4 8 1
  7) 2 1  6 ⁶4 ¹0  ³3 ⁵6 7
```

Try It Out

Calculate the following.

1 (a) $251\,221 \times 3$ (b) $762\,068 \times 6$ (c) $14\,314\,200 \times 4$
   (d) $5\,990\,900 \times 9$ (e) $660\,066 \times 5$

2 (a) $330\,520 \div 4$ (b) $1\,474\,592 \div 7$ (c) $7\,097\,775 \div 5$
   (d) $21\,031\,839 \div 9$ (e) $2\,000\,004 \div 6$

3 (a) $421\,777 \times 13$ (b) $576\,200 \times 54$ (c) $2\,302\,320 \times 61$
   (d) $1\,535\,328 \div 24$ (e) $10\,674\,895 \div 85$

Practice

1 These are the populations of parts of the UK.

Scotland	4 999 000
Northern Ireland	1 578 000
Wales	2 812 000

   (a) What is the total population of all three parts?

   (b) The population of the whole of the UK is 56 467 000. Use this to work out the population of England.

2 Work out the value of the following expressions if $p = 24\,633$, $q = 12\,644\,021$, $r = 6\,500\,000$, $s = 631\,136$, $w = 4$, $x = 5$, $y = 9$.

> Remember: pw means $p \times w$
> $\frac{p}{w}$ means $p \div w$.

   (a) $p + s$ (b) $q + r$ (c) $r - s$

   (d) pw (e) sy (f) $\frac{p}{y}$

   (g) $\frac{q}{w}$ (h) $\frac{r}{x}$

3 Copy and complete these number machine chains.

   (a) $52\,552$ $\boxed{\times 23}$? $\boxed{+\,1\,208\,604}$? $\boxed{\div 25}$?

   (b) 32 $\boxed{\times 133\,398}$? $\boxed{\div 36}$? $\boxed{-\,87\,005}$?

> **Finished Early?**
> ➡ Go to page 347

13 Using Tables and Charts

In this chapter you will learn about ...
1. tallying and grouping
2. frequency tables, pictograms and bar charts
3. pie charts

1 Tallying and Grouping

Learn About It

A **tally table** helps you to record things you have counted.

This tally table shows the favourite colours of the pupils in class 8F.

Colour	Tally	Frequency
Yellow	|||	3
Red	ЖЖ ЖЖ	10
Blue	ЖЖ ||||	9
Green	||||	4
Pink	||	2
	Total	28

The last column is called **frequency**. It is the total for each colour. You can see that red has the highest frequency, followed by blue.

The tally marks are grouped in **fives**. It makes them easier to count. The last mark in each group of five is drawn across the other four marks in the group.

The **total frequency** is shown at the bottom. This can help you check your counting. If you know there are 28 pupils in 8F, the total frequency should be 28.

Word Check
tally table a table used to record a number of things
frequency how many times something occurs
total frequency all the frequencies added together

Try It Out

1 This tally table shows the favourite colours of class 8G.
Copy and complete it.

Colour	Tally	Frequency
Red	卌 I	
Yellow	III	
Purple	卌	
Green	卌 III	
Orange	II	
	Total	

2 This is a list of the favourite colours of class 8H.

RED	BLUE	BLUE	BLUE	GREEN	ORANGE
ORANGE	RED	BLUE	RED	GREEN	RED
RED	GREEN	PURPLE	BLUE	RED	RED
PURPLE	BLUE	RED	RED	ORANGE	RED
BLUE	RED	RED	GREEN	BLUE	GREEN

Copy and complete this tally table.

Colour	Tally	Frequency
Red		
Blue		
Purple		
Orange		
Green		
	Total	

Learn More About It

Sometimes an ordinary tally table doesn't help, especially if there are lots of values.

This tally table shows you the heights of pupils in class 8F.

Height (cm)	Tally	Frequency	Height (cm)	Tally	Frequency
139	||	2	163	|	1
142	|	1	164	||	2
143	|	1	165	||	2
147	||	2	166	||	2
151	|	1	167	||	2
152	|	1	169	||	2
153	||	2	170	|	1
157	||	2	173	|	1
161	|	1	174	|	1
162	|	1		Total	28

The tally table is much more useful if you put the **data** into **groups**.

The groups mustn't overlap. If you had 130–140 and 140–150, you wouldn't know where to put someone who is 140 cm tall.

Height (cm)	Tally	Frequency
131–140	||	2
141–150	||||	4
151–160	ЖН |	6
161–170	ЖН ЖН ||||	14
171–180	||	2
	Total	28

Word Check

data information or facts

group a range of numbers for a tally table

Try It Out

B **I** Class 8G did a survey of their heights. These are their results.

150 cm	144 cm	154 cm	163 cm	162 cm	161 cm
139 cm	154 cm	136 cm	162 cm	160 cm	144 cm
144 cm	161 cm	148 cm	166 cm	163 cm	159 cm
166 cm	158 cm	167 cm	171 cm	136 cm	150 cm
170 cm	164 cm	164 cm	140 cm	149 cm	159 cm

(a) Copy and complete this tally table using the data above.

Height (cm)	Tally	Frequency
131–140		
141–150		
151–160		
161–170		
171–180		
	Total	

How many pupils are **(b)** taller than 160 cm? **(c)** 150 cm or less?

2 Class 8G also recorded their weights in kilograms.

42 kg	28 kg	45 kg	34 kg	45 kg	50 kg
53 kg	44 kg	38 kg	47 kg	40 kg	32 kg
35 kg	47 kg	45 kg	35 kg	51 kg	41 kg
48 kg	31 kg	40 kg	46 kg	29 kg	29 kg
30 kg	41 kg	28 kg	40 kg	45 kg	35 kg

(a) Copy and complete this tally table.

Weight (kg)	Tally	Frequency
26–30		
31–35		
	Total	

How many pupils weigh …

(b) more than 40 kg?

(c) between 31 kg and 50 kg?

Practice

C **1** Judy did a survey. She asked 20 people about their favourite TV show. These are the results.

DRAMA	COMEDY	SOAP	MUSIC	SOAP
SOAP	DOCUMENTARY	SOAP	SOAP	MUSIC
SOAP	SOAP	COMEDY	DRAMA	COMEDY
MUSIC	DRAMA	COMEDY	DOCUMENTARY	SOAP

Draw a tally table for Judy's survey.

2 Tina looked at the books on her shelf. She checked the number of pages in each one.

The number of pages is printed on each book.

(a) Copy and complete this tally table for Tina's books.

Number of pages	Tally	Frequency
1–100		
101–200		
Total		

(b) How many books have 200 pages or less?

(c) How many books have over 500 pages?

3 Denny asked everybody in his class how they get to school.
These are the answers.

BIKE	WALK	BUS	BIKE	WALK	BUS
BUS	BIKE	BIKE	CAR	BUS	BIKE
WALK	CAR	CAR	BUS	BIKE	BUS
BUS	BUS	WALK	BIKE	BUS	WALK

Draw a tally table for Denny's survey.

4 Mrs Stoner runs a small shop.
Here is a record of what her
customers spent one day.

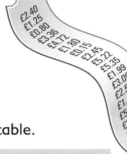

£2.40
£1.25
£0.80
£3.98
£4.72
£1.80
£0.15
£2.45
£5.22
£5.35
£1.99
£3.09
£2.53
£1.40
£5.55
£2.79
£0.36
£3.59
£5.47
£5.51
£4.04
£1.55
£0.60
£1.08
£1.75
£4.25
£5.80

(a) Copy and complete this tally table.

Amount	Tally	Frequency
£1 or less		
£1.01–£2.00		
£2.01–£3.00		
£3.01–£4.00		
£4.01–£5.00		
£5.01–£6.00		
	Total	

(b) How many people spent more than £4?

(c) How many people spent £3 or less?

Finished Early?
➡ Go to page 348

Further Practice

(D) **1** Copy and complete this tally table of pupils' favourite subjects at school.

Subject	Tally	Frequency
Art	JHT JHT JHT JHT I	
Drama	JHT JHT JHT JHT JHT JHT JHT I	
English	JHT JHT	
French	JHT JHT II	
Maths	JHT JHT JHT JHT JHT	
Music	JHT JHT IIII	
PE	JHT JHT JHT JHT JHT JHT JHT JHT JHT I	
Science	JHT JHT JHT JHT	
Technology	JHT JHT JHT JHT JHT I	
	Total	

2 Class 8H do an essay for Mr Harris. He counts the number of words in each essay. This is what he finds.

125	162	88	104	198	150
158	135	144	106	179	175
152	166	189	113	141	108
193	96	226	164	168	121
102	85	134	128	159	172

(a) Copy and complete this tally table.

Number of words	Tally	Frequency
100 or fewer		
101–120		
181– 200		
over 200		
Total		

(b) How many essays had 120 words or fewer?

(c) How many essays were longer than 180 words?

Finished Early?
➡ Go to page 3

❷ Frequency Tables, Pictograms and Bar Charts

Remember?

Bar charts and pictograms are used to show information or **data**.

In a **bar chart**, the height of a bar shows the frequency.

You need a proper **scale** on the vertical **axis**.

The bars can be joined or separate. They have to be the same width and spaced equally.

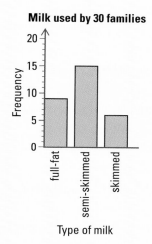

Milk used by 30 families

Word Check

axis a line used to mark the scale for a graph

In a **pictogram**, the number of pictures shows the frequency.

All the pictures have to be the same size. They have to be spaced equally.

You need a **key** to tell people what one picture means.

Milk used by 30 families

Type of milk	
Full-fat	
Semi-skimmed	
Skimmed	

Key: ▯ = 2 families

Try It Out

E **1** Ally kept a record of the weather for a month. She wrote **S** for sunny, **C** for cloudy and **R** for rainy. These are her results.

C C R R C R C C S C C S S C S S S C S S S C C S C C C R R R

(a) Draw a tally table of her data.

(b) Use your tally table to draw a bar chart. Scale on vertical axis: 1 cm = 1 day.

2 This pictogram shows the merit marks Shanaz, Mel and Ben got in one term. Use it to answer these questions.

Name	Merits
Shanaz	☺ ☺ ☺ ☺ ☺ ☺ ☺ ☺ ☺ ☺
Mel	☺ ☺ ☺ ☺ ☺ ☺
Ben	☺ ☺ ☺ ☺

Key: ☺ = 2 merit marks

(a) How many merit marks did each pupil get? Who got the most?

(b) How many marks did they get in total?

(c) Ben said to Mel, 'Together, we got more than Shanaz.' Was he right?

Learn About It

Below is a **frequency table**. It is like a tally table without the tally column. This one shows how many brothers and sisters the pupils in class 8M have.

Number of brothers and sisters per pupil	Number of pupils	Total number of brothers and sisters
0	9	0
1	12	12
2	6	12
3	2	6
4	1	4
Total	30	34

The red column is an extra one. It shows the **total** number of brothers and sisters. To get these numbers, multiply the numbers in the first two columns.

For example, 6 pupils had 2 brothers and sisters each. This makes $6 \times 2 = 12$ brothers and sisters altogether. Add the numbers in this column to find the total number of brothers and sisters in the class.

You can draw frequency tables using the data from **bar charts** or **pictograms**.

> Word Check
>
> **frequency table** a table showing the number of times something has occurred

Try It Out

F A group of Year 8 pupils were asked how many hours of TV they watched each day. The bar chart shows the results.

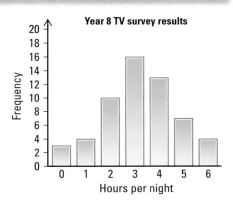

1 Copy this frequency table.

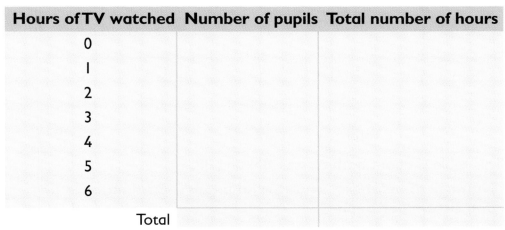

Hours of TV watched	Number of pupils	Total number of hours
0		
1		
2		
3		
4		
5		
6		
Total		

2 Use the bar chart to fill in the **Number of pupils** column.
3 Work out the numbers for the last column. Remember to multiply.
4 How many pupils took part in the survey?
5 How many pupils watch 4 or more hours of TV each day?
6 How many pupils watch less than 2 hours of TV each day?
7 Altogether, how many hours of TV do the Year 8 pupils watch in a day?
8 Where would you fit into the table?

Learn More About It

These tables show how many brothers and sisters the children in classes 8N and 8P have.

8N:

Number of brothers and sisters per pupil	Number of pupils	Total number of brothers and sisters
0	13	$0 \times 13 = 0$
1	9	$1 \times 9 = 9$
2	4	$2 \times 4 = 8$
3	0	$3 \times 0 = 0$
4	2	$4 \times 2 = 8$
Total	28	25

8P:

Number of brothers and sisters per pupil	Number of pupils	Total number of brothers and sisters
0	11	$0 \times 11 = 0$
1	11	$1 \times 11 = 11$
2	5	$2 \times 5 = 10$
3	1	$3 \times 1 = 3$
4	1	$4 \times 1 = 4$
Total	29	28

This table is about both classes. 8N and 8P:

Number of brothers and sisters per pupil	Number of pupils	Total number of brothers and sisters
0	$13 + 11 = 24$	$0 + 0 = 0$
1	$9 + 11 = 20$	$9 + 11 = 20$
2	$4 + 5 = 9$	$8 + 10 = 18$
3	$0 + 1 = 1$	$0 + 3 = 3$
4	$2 + 1 = 3$	$8 + 4 = 12$
Total	$28 + 29 = 57$	$25 + 28 = 53$

Try It Out

A4 graph paper or squared paper

Year 7 pupils were asked about
how much TV they watch.
This is a bar chart of the data.

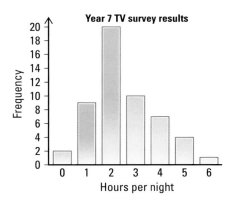

1 Copy and complete this frequency table for the data.

Hours per night	Number of pupils	Total number of hours
0		
1		
2		
3		
4		
5		
6		
Total		

2 Draw a new frequency table showing data for Year 7 and
Year 8 together, using the information from page 181.

3 Draw a bar chart from your table.
Make the scale on the vertical axis 1 cm = 2 pupils. The axis needs
to go up to 30.

4 Draw a pictogram of this data. Use 1 symbol = 2 pupils.

Practice

A4 graph paper or squared paper

H **1** Enza and Janie had a darts competition.
They had to score twenties, double twenties
or treble twenties. Any other score was a
'miss'. The bar charts shows their scores.

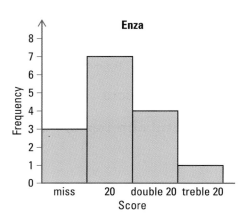

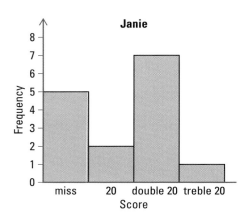

(a) Copy and complete this table for Enza's scores.

Score	Frequency	Points
miss		
20 (20 points)		
double 20 (40 points)		
treble 20 (60 points)		
Total		

(b) Draw and complete a similar table for Janie.

(c) How many darts did Enza and Janie each throw?

(d) Did they throw the same number of darts?

(e) Who won, and by how many points?

(f) Draw a new frequency table for Enza and Janie together.

(g) Draw a bar chart of the frequencies from your table.
Use a scale of 1 cm = 1 throw on the vertical axis.

2 Motormag did a survey of two streets. They asked all the families how many cars they own. These are the results.

Mosley Street

Cars per family	Frequency	Total cars
0	13	
1	40	
2	9	
3	2	
4	0	
Total		

Viscount Avenue

Cars per family	Frequency	Total cars
0	0	
1	8	
2	18	
3	4	
4	2	
Total		

(a) Copy and complete the frequency tables.

(b) Which street had more **families**?

(c) Which street had more **cars** in it?

(d) Draw a new frequency table for both streets together.

(e) Draw a pictogram showing the data from the **frequency** column of your new table. Use 1 symbol for 5 families.

(f) Draw a bar chart showing the data from the **total cars** column of your new table. Use a scale of 2 cm to 5 cars on the vertical axis.

Finished Early?
➪ Go to page 349

Further Practice

1 Norborough County Council surveyed two areas. The areas were the same size.

They recorded the different types of housing in each area.

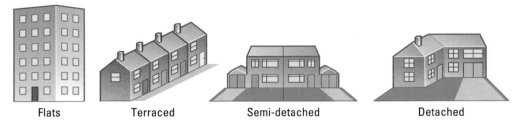

| Flats | Terraced | Semi-detached | Detached |

These frequency tables show the results.

Area X

Type of housing	Frequency
Flats	0
Terraced	12
Semi-detached	26
Detached	32
Total	

Area Y

Type of housing	Frequency
Flats	80
Terraced	140
Semi-detached	50
Detached	10
Total	

1 Copy the tables and fill in the totals.

2 How many **times** more dwellings are there in Area Y than in Area X?

3 Which area do you think is in a town or city? Why?

4 What sort of place do you think the other area is? Why?

5 Draw a new frequency table for both areas together.

> **Finished Early?**
> ➡ Go to page 349

❸ Pie Charts

Compasses, protractor

Remember?

- The angle at the centre of a whole circle is 360°.

Key Fact

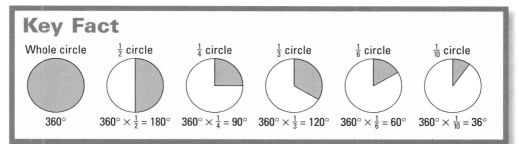

Whole circle 360°   ½ circle $360° \times \frac{1}{2} = 180°$ ¼ circle $360° \times \frac{1}{4} = 90°$ ⅓ circle $360° \times \frac{1}{3} = 120°$ ⅙ circle $360° \times \frac{1}{6} = 60°$ 1/10 circle $360° \times \frac{1}{10} = 36°$

Try It Out

1 How many degrees are there in these fractions of a circle?

(a) $\frac{1}{5}$ (b) $\frac{1}{4}$ (c) $\frac{3}{4}$ (d) $\frac{1}{6}$

(e) $\frac{5}{6}$ (f) $\frac{3}{10}$ (g) $\frac{5}{8}$

2 What fraction of a circle is ...

(a) 18°?   (b) 30°?   (c) 270°?   (d) 135°?   (e) 108°?

Learn About It

When you want to show fractions of a total, you use a **pie chart**.

A pie chart is a circle divided into **sectors**.

This pie chart shows how the pupils in class 8L travel to school. There are 30 pupils in 8L.

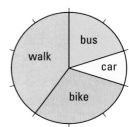

The marks around the outside divide the pie chart into 10 equal sectors. The angle at the centre of each sector is 360° ÷ 10 = 36°.

You can see that the section for going by bus takes up 2 of the 10 parts of the pie chart, so $\frac{2}{10}$ of class 8L travel to school by bus.

$\frac{2}{10}$ of 30 pupils = 2 ÷ 10 × 30 = 6. 6 pupils travel by bus.

This table shows how the pupils in 8L travel to school.

Transport	Fraction	Number of pupils
Car	$\frac{1}{10}$	$\frac{1}{10}$ of 30 = 3
Bus	$\frac{2}{10}$ (= $\frac{1}{5}$)	$\frac{1}{5}$ of 30 = 6
Bike	$\frac{3}{10}$	$\frac{3}{10}$ of 30 = 9
Walk	$\frac{4}{10}$ (= $\frac{2}{5}$)	$\frac{2}{5}$ of 30 = 12

Check the fractions: $\frac{1}{10} + \frac{2}{10} + \frac{3}{10} + \frac{4}{10} = 1$. ✓
Check the number of pupils: 3 + 6 + 9 + 12 = 30. ✓

> ### Word Check
> **pie chart** a circle divided into sectors to show fractions of the whole
> **sectors** parts into which a pie chart is divided

Try It Out

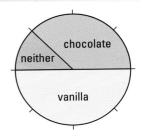

K 1 32 pupils in class 8P were asked whether they prefer vanilla or chocolate ice-cream or neither. This pie chart shows the results.

(a) Copy this table.

Type preferred	Fraction	Number of pupils
Chocolate		
Vanilla		
Neither		

(b) Work out what fraction of the class gave each answer. Complete the second column of the table.

(c) Work out how many pupils gave each answer. Complete the third column of the table.

2 In the country of Karenina, there are 36 power stations. This pie chart shows the different types.

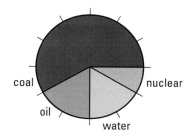

Copy and complete this table, based on the pie chart.

Type of power	Fraction	Number of power stations
Coal		
Oil		
Water		
Nuclear		

Learn More About It

To draw a pie chart, you need to work out the fraction for each sector.

- You might know the total frequency for the chart. If not, work it out.
- Divide a circle into the correct number of sectors.
- Colour and label the correct number of sections for each item.

The pupils in 8N were asked about their favourite toothpaste flavour. The table shows the results.

Follow the steps below to draw a pie chart for the data.

Flavour	Frequency
Mint	3
Spearmint	2
Fruity	2
Others	1

The total frequency is 3 + 2 + 2 + 1 = 8 pupils.

Draw a circle and divide it into 8 equal sectors. Each angle should be $360° ÷ 8 = 45°$.

Now colour and label the sections.

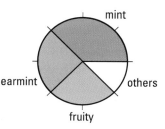

Try It Out

Type of plant	Number of beds
Flowers	5
Fruit	4
Vegetables	1

 1 In a large garden, there are 10 flower beds. The table shows what the beds are used for.

(a) How many sectors are needed on a pie chart for this data?

(b) What angle is needed for each sector?

(c) Draw a circle and divide it into sectors.

(d) Colour and label the sections of the pie chart.

2 The pupils from class 8W took part in a chip survey. The canteen staff asked them how often they have chips. These are the results:

How often	Number of pupils
Every day	9
Some days	15
Once a week	4
Never	2

(a) How many pupils took part in the survey?

(b) Work out how many degrees are needed for one pupil on a pie chart.

(c) Draw a circle and divide it up.

(d) Colour and label the pie chart.

Practice

1 Wilson's Carpets employs these people:

Job title	Number of people
Managers	2
Sales assistants	13
Warehouse workers	7
Drivers	2

(a) How many people work at Wilson's?

(b) Draw a pie chart of the data about Wilson's employees.

2 A group of 40 boys and 20 girls were asked what they usually did in the evenings.

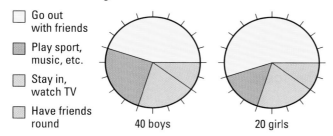

☐ Go out with friends

▨ Play sport, music, etc.

☐ Stay in, watch TV

▨ Have friends round

40 boys   20 girls

(a) Copy and complete the table.

Activity	Fraction of boys	Number of boys
Stay in, watch TV		
Have friends round		
Go out with friends		
Sport, music, etc.		

(b) Draw and complete a similar table for the girls.

(c) Write down whether what each said is RIGHT or WRONG, using the data from your tables to help you. Write down the reason for each answer.

Three pupils are shown the pie charts. This is what they say:

The same number of boys and girls stay in and watch TV.

More girls than boys go out with friends.

Twice as many boys watch TV as have friends round.

Josh   Lucy   Ben

Finished Early?
➡ Go to page 350

Further Practice

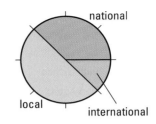

N Annabelle spent 120 minutes on the phone. Her phone bill was split into three types of call. The pie chart shows the time she used on each type of call.

(a) Copy and complete this table.

Type of call	Fraction of time	Number of minutes
Local		
National		
International		

This table shows the phone company's charges.

Type of call	Cost
Local	3p per minute
National	10p per minute
International	30p per minute

(b) Work out how much Annabelle spent on each type of call. Copy the table below and fill in the second column.

Hint: cost = pence per minute × number of minutes.

Type of call	Cost	Fraction of total cost
Local		
National		
International		

(c) How much was Annabelle's phone bill **altogether**?

Hint: add the amounts in the Cost column to find out.

(d) Work out the **fraction** of the total for each type of call. Fill in the last column.

(e) Draw a circle, divide it into 12 equal sectors and use it to draw a pie chart for the **cost** of Annabelle's calls.

Finished Early?
➡ Go to page 350

14 Two Variables

In this chapter you will learn about ...
- **1** two-way tables
- **2** scatter diagrams

▶ Two-way Tables

Learn About It

To find an entry in a table, look at the **labels** at the top or side.

labels

	A	**B**	**C**	**D**
1	A1	B1	C1	D1
2	A2	B2	C2	D2	← row 2
3	A3	B3	C3	D3
4	A4	B4	C4	D4

column B   cells

Word Check

labels letters, words or numbers at the side or top of the table which name the row, column or cell.

cell a single rectangle or 'box' in a table

column a line of cells going up and down

row a line of cells going across

Sometimes tables are split into smaller sections.

main labels   split labels

		Apples		**Bananas**	
		fresh	**mouldy**	**fresh**	**mouldy**
Cafés	**High Street**	12	3	11	2
	Back Street	6	2	5	0
Canteens	**Factory**	15	5	12	2
	Office	10	1	8	2

← main labels
← split labels

Try It Out

A Use this **distance chart** to answer the following questions.

1 How far is it...
  (a) from Leeds to Manchester?
  (b) from Bristol to Cardiff?
  (c) from London to Newcastle?
  (d) from Southampton to Exeter?
  (e) from Aberdeen to Birmingham?

Distances in kilometres To From	Aberdeen	Birmingham	Bristol	Cardiff	Exeter	Leeds	London	Manchester	Newcastle	Southampton
Aberdeen		645	805	821	910	506	795	536	371	869
Birmingham	645		141	170	258	192	189	139	334	205
Bristol	805	141		69	120	335	187	267	480	118
Cardiff	821	170	69		189	362	242	301	499	195
Exeter	910	258	120	189		446	272	382	590	170
Leeds	506	192	335	362	446		312	69	154	368
London	795	189	187	242	272	312		296	442	122
Manchester	536	139	267	301	382	69	296		218	322
Newcastle	371	334	480	499	590	154	442	218		512
Southampton	869	205	118	195	170	368	122	322	512	

2 Ralph drives a truck.
Work out how far Ralph travels ...
  (a) from London to Manchester, via Birmingham

> *Hint: this means his journey is London → Birmingham → Manchester.*

  (b) from Leeds to Aberdeen, via Newcastle
  (c) from Southampton to Exeter, via Bristol
  (d) from Cardiff to Newcastle, via Birmingham and Leeds.

Practice

B 1 This map shows where five friends live.
Copy and complete this distance chart. If there are two different routes, use the shorter one.

distance (km) To From	Alan	Jason	Minnie	Soo Lin	Suresh
Alan					
Jason					
Minnie					
Soo Lin					
Suresh					

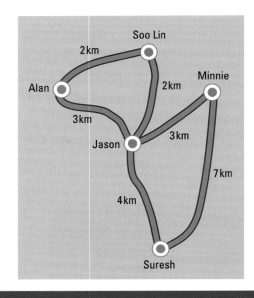

2 These tables show the hair colour and eye colour of a group of children. Use the tables to help you answer the following questions.

Boys	Hair			
Eyes	**Blond**	**Brown**	**Black**	**Ginger**
Blue	10	6	0	0
Brown	3	7	7	0
Grey	4	0	0	0
Green	0	1	1	12

Girls	Hair			
Eyes	**Blond**	**Brown**	**Black**	**Ginger**
Blue	9	2	1	0
Brown	3	11	3	2
Grey	5	0	1	0
Green	2	2	0	7

(a) How many boys had brown hair and brown eyes?
(b) How many girls had ginger hair and green eyes?
(c) How many boys had brown hair?
(d) How many girls had blue eyes?
(e) How many boys and girls had blond hair and blue eyes?
(f) How many pupils had grey eyes?
(g) How many pupils had ginger hair?

3 Each table needs $+, -, \times$ or $\div$ in the corner. Write down the correct signs.

(a)

?	2	5
10	12	15
20	22	25

(b)

?	4	3
7	28	21
5	20	15

(c)

?	10	15
8	80	120
15	150	225

(d)

?	26	40
15	11	25
20	6	20

(e)

?	20	40
4	5	10
5	4	8

(f)

?	12	8
3	36	24
25	100	200

4 This table shows how long it takes to drive from one place to another.

(a) How long does it take to drive from Mendleford to Sellis?

(b) How long does it take to drive from Hample to Stoneham?

					time in minutes to drive from one place to another
Clothley	Stoneham	Hample	Sellis	Orbury	
15	13	16	12	15	Mendleford
	25	12	10	28	Clothley
		14	26	11	Stoneham
			32	35	Hample
				8	Sellis

(c) Mr Renton lives in Sellis. He drives to his sister's house in Orbury. She isn't in, so he spends two minutes writing her a note, then drives back home. How long does this take altogether?

(d) How much longer does it take to drive from Clothley to Orbury than it does from Orbury to Stoneham?

(e) Mendleford is in the middle of all the other places. Which place is probably closest to it? Which is furthest away?

(f) The local bus service runs from Clothley to Stoneham. It takes about twice as long on the bus, as it does by car. How long is this?

Finished Early?
➡ Go to page 350

Further Practice

1 This table shows how four friends rated their favourite computer games out of 10.

	Matthew	Selina	Ashok	Rosie
Pyramid Raider	7	7	9	6
International Soccer	6	4	7	8
Speed Kings III	8	7	9	6
Platform Crazy	4	6	7	5

(a) How many points did Selina give Speed Kings III?
(b) To which game did Rosie give 8 points?
(c) Which game was Matthew's favourite?
(d) Who gave Pyramid Raider the most points?
(e) How many points did the Soccer game get altogether?
(f) How many points did Selina give altogether?
(g) Who gave the most points? How many is this?
(h) Which game got the most points? How many is this?
(i) Which game got the fewest points? How many is this?

2 Copy this table. To fill it in:
- **multiply** the two label numbers
- **add** the two label numbers
- find the **difference** between the two answers
- write it in the table.

	1	10	7	12
4			17	
15				
20				
9				

Example	7 and 4
Working	$7 \times 4 = 28$ (*Multiply the numbers.*)
	$7 + 4 = 11$ (*Add the numbers.*)
	$28 - 11 = 17$ (*Find the difference.*)
Answer	Write 17 *in the correct cell.*

Finished Early?
➡ Go to page 350

❷ Scatter Diagrams

Remember?

Using scales

- Check how many divisions (gaps) there are between the main marks.
  There may be 2, 4, 5 or 10. Make sure you know how many units each gap covers.

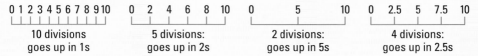

0 1 2 3 4 5 6 7 8 9 10   0   2   4   6   8   10   0   5   10   0   2.5   5   7.5   10

10 divisions   5 divisions: 2 divisions: 4 divisions:
goes up in 1s   goes up in 2s   goes up in 5s   goes up in 2.5s

Plotting and reading coordinates

- When **plotting coordinates**, the first number is on the **horizontal** or **x-axis**. The second number is on the **vertical** or **y-axis**.

y-axis: 17

x-axis: 36

(36, 17)

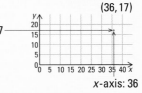

Word Check

scale a line marked with numbers at equal intervals

divisions parts of a scale, shown by marks

plot put a point onto a graph

coordinates pairs of numbers in brackets which show the position of a point on a graph, e.g. (4, 5)

axis a line on a graph on which the scale is marked

Try It Out

D **1** Write down the numbers shown by the arrows.

(a)

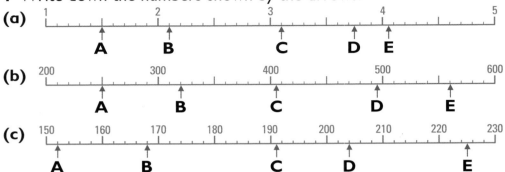

(b)

(c)

2 Write down the coordinates of each point marked on this graph.

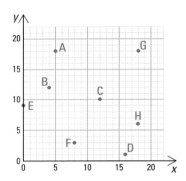

3 Draw and label a set of axes from −5 to +5.
Plot the following sets of coordinates and join the points, in order, with straight lines. Each set makes a simple shape.

(a) $(1, 1)$ $(1, 4)$ $(4, 1)$
(b) $(0, 0)$ $(3, 0)$ $(3, -4)$ $(0, -4)$
(c) $(0, 2)$ $(-3, 5)$ $(-5, -2)$ $(-2, -5)$

Learn About It

Suppose you think people who have big hands also have big feet. That would mean handspan and foot size are linked.

Draw a **scatter diagram** like this.

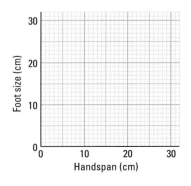

Suppose your handspan is 15 cm and your foot is 22 cm long. You plot a point as shown.

Suppose you did a survey of people's handspans and foot sizes.

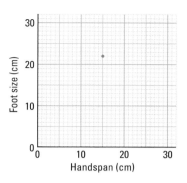

You plot one point on the scatter diagram for each person's measurements. When you had plotted all the measurements, it might look like the diagram on the right.

There is a circle around one of the points. This shows that there are **two** people with these measurements.

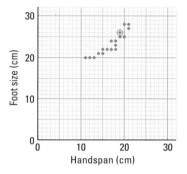

Key Fact

Sometimes it is better **not** to start the axes at 0. You can use broken axes to show this.

Do this when the points would be crammed into a small part of the graph.

Word Check

range the difference between the smallest and largest numbers on a scale or axis

Try It Out

2 mm graph paper

E 1 This table shows exam results for class 8M this year and last year.

Year 7 (%)	32	68	54	81	44	59	62	75	72	65
Year 8 (%)	45	56	50	75	60	60	54	69	72	67

Year 7 (%)	17	85	34	56	56	70	55	61	77	60
Year 8 (%)	25	88	40	58	48	75	58	57	74	70

(a) Plot the data on a scatter diagram.
Label the horizontal axis 'Year 7 Exam %' and the vertical axis 'Year 8 Exam %'. Use a scale of 1 cm to 5% and a range of 0 to 100%.

(b) What is the link between this year's marks and last year's?

2 Melanie watches the weather and records it.
She writes down how many rainy and sunny days there are in each month.

	Jan.	Feb.	Mar.	Apr.	May	Jun.	Jul.	Aug.	Sep.	Oct.	Nov.	Dec.
Rainy days	10	15	18	10	4	10	1	0	5	5	10	13
Sunny days	6	4	8	10	18	16	20	25	19	16	14	12

(a) Plot the weather data on a scatter diagram.
Label the horizontal axis 'Number of rainy days' and the vertical axis 'Number of sunny days'. Use a scale of 1 cm to 5 days and a range of 0 to 30 days.

(b) What is the link between the rainy and sunny days?

Practice

2 mm graph paper

1 This table shows class 8M's handspans and foot sizes, in centimetres.

Handspan	14	13	21	17	18	20	16	16	15	18
Foot size	21	21	29	23	24	28	22	23	22	27

Handspan	19	21	15	18	16	18	15	16	14	19
Foot size	28	30	22	26	21	28	21	24	23	27

(a) Plot the data on a scatter diagram.
Label the horizontal axis 'Handspan (cm)' and the vertical axis 'Foot size (cm)'. Use a scale of 1 cm to 5 cm.
(b) Do people with big hands usually have big feet?

2 Zac had to type 20 paragraphs. He recorded the number of words in each paragraph. He also recorded how long it took him to type. This is what he found.

Words	24	68	85	45	50	12	38	44	95	60
Time (s)	16	40	57	30	25	8	30	32	70	38

Words	15	20	6	62	44	75	23	51	32	20
Time (s)	12	15	5	51	28	55	14	31	20	18

(a) Plot the data on a scatter diagram.
Label the horizontal axis 'Number of words' and the vertical axis 'Time (seconds)'. Use a scale of 1 large square to 10 words or seconds.
(b) What is the link between number of words and time?

3 Zik is an alien from the planet Correla. Zik's class measure their heights and armspans. These are the results, in centimetres.

Height	157	145	151	149	166	139	154	150	163	132
Armspan	127	145	140	143	129	153	140	137	132	163

Height	143	163	157	140	135	159	144	133	140	152
Armspan	154	125	137	150	162	136	153	159	158	141

(a) Plot the data on a scatter diagram.
Label the horizontal axis 'Height (cm)' and the vertical axis 'Armspan (cm)'. Use a scale of 1 cm to 5 cm and a range of 120 cm to 180 cm.

(b) What is the link between height and armspan on Correla?

> **Finished Early?**
> ➡ Go to page 351

Further Practice

G Gita runs a kiosk in the park selling ice-creams and hot drinks. One year, she recorded the temperature each day. She also recorded what she sold. This table shows what Gita sold on the **warmest** day of each month.

	Jan.	Feb.	Mar.	Apr.	May	Jun.	Jul.	Aug.	Sep.	Oct.	Nov.	Dec.
Temp. (°C)	2	8	12	16	18	20	25	30	23	17	10	7
Ice-creams	0	2	4	10	22	32	50	54	28	6	3	0
Hot drinks	10	15	25	25	30	41	36	21	29	15	10	12

1 Plot a scatter diagram to show the relationship between temperature and ice-creams sold. Label the horizontal axis 'Temperature (°C)', from 0° to 30 °C, with a scale of 1 cm to 5 °C. Label the vertical axis 'Number of ice-creams sold', from 0 to 60 ice-creams, with a scale of 1 cm to 5 ice-creams.

2 Plot a similar scatter diagram to show the relationship between temperature and the number of hot drinks sold.

> **Finished Early?**
> ➡ Go to page 351

Unit 8 *Statistical Diagrams*

Summary of Chapters 13 and 14

- A **tally table** helps you to count a lot of items of bits of **data**. The **frequency** is the total for each item.

- Sometimes you need to put your data into **groups**. The groups must not overlap.

- In a pictogram, the number of pictures shows the frequency. You need a **key** to tell people what one picture means. The pictures must be of equal size. They must be spaced equally.

- A **frequency table** shows the number of times something has occurred. It is like a tally table without the tally column. Frequency tables can be combined by adding or subtracting information.

- When you want to show fractions of a total, you use a **pie chart**. A pie chart is a circle divided into **sectors**. To draw a pie chart, you need to calculate the angles for the sectors.

  1 You may already know the total frequency to be put on the chart. If not, work it out.

  2 The number of sectors is the same as the total frequency. Divide 360° by the total frequency to find out the angle size of each sector.

  3 Divide the pie chart into these sectors.

  4 Work out the number of sectors needed for each item, then colour and label them.

  Tables are made up of horizontal **rows** and vertical **columns**. A rectangle in the table is called a **cell**.

- To find an entry in a table, look at the **labels** along the top or down the side.

- A **scatter diagram** is used to investigate whether there is a link between two amounts or measurements.

Brush Up Your Number 9

 Reverse Calculations

Learn About It

Inverse operations reverse a calculation.

$12 \times 4 = 48$ and so $48 \div 4 = 12$.

Reverse calculations must be done in the opposite order to the original calculation.

An **approximate** formula for a temperature in degrees Fahrenheit (°F) in terms of degrees Celsius (°C) is
$F = 2C + 32$.

So 20 °C in °F is 20 $\boxed{\times 2}$ ▷ 40 $\boxed{+ 32}$ ▷ 72.

Starting with 72 °F the reverse of this is

20 ◁ $\boxed{\div 2}$ 40 ◁ $\boxed{- 32}$ 72

Try It Out

 Write down the inverse operations for these calculations, using number machines.

1 12 $\boxed{+ 5}$ ▷ 17

2 24 $\boxed{- 6}$ ▷ 18

3 8 $\boxed{\times 2}$ ▷ 16

4 36 $\boxed{\div 3}$ ▷ 12

5 6 $\boxed{+ 2}$ ▷ 8 $\boxed{+ 5}$ ▷ 13

6 9 $\boxed{\times 2}$ ▷ 18 $\boxed{- 6}$ ▷ 12

7 10 $\boxed{\times 3}$ ▷ 30 $\boxed{- 6}$ ▷ 24

8 14 $\boxed{+ 11}$ ▷ 25 $\boxed{\div 5}$ ▷ 5

Key Fact

Subtraction is the inverse of addition.

Division is the inverse of multiplication.

Word Check

inverse opposite

approximate nearly correct but not exact

Practice

B Use inverse operations to find the numbers fed into these number machines.

1 ? [+7] 15

2 ? [−13] 16

3 ? [×3] 27

4 ? [×12] 96

5 ? [÷8] 6

6 ? [+9]→→[×2] 30

7 ? [×4]→→[+8] 36

8 ? [×5]→→[+5] 50

9 ? [÷3]→→[+20] 25

10 ? [+17]→→[÷5] 7

C An **accurate** formula for finding the temperature in degrees Fahrenheit (°F) given the temperature in degrees Celsius (°C) is $F = \frac{9}{5}C + 32$. Find the temperature in Fahrenheit given the following Celsius temperatures. Use inverse operations to check your calculations.

Example 20 °C
Working 20 [÷5] 4 [×9] 36 [+32] 68
Check: 20 [×5] 4 [÷9] 36 [−32] 68
Answer 68 °F

1 30 °C   2 35 °C   3 45 °C
4 15 °C   5 50 °C   6 80 °C

D Use inverse operations to find the numbers fed into these number machines.

1 ? [+11] 26

2 ? [+14] 21

3 ? [−18] 4

4 ? [−9] 21

5 ? [×4] 48

6 ? [×7] 63

7 ? [÷6] 7

8 ? [+11]→→[×3] 45

9 ? [×3]→→[+9] 30

10 ? [×3]→→[+4] 40

11 ? [÷5]→→[+34] 38

12 ? [+18]→→[÷5] 8

Finished Early?
➡ Go to page 352

15 Multiples and Factors

In this chapter you will learn about ...
1. multiples
2. factors

① Multiples

> **Remember?**
> Multiplying a number by a whole number gives a **multiple**.
> So 4, 8, 12, 16, 20 ... are all multiples of 4.

Try It Out

A Write down four multiples of each of these numbers.

1 5	**2** 4	**3** 7
4 8	**5** 3	**6** 10
7 9	**8** 11	

Learn About It

Hundred grid

Every number has many multiples. 6 has the multiples 6, 12, 18, 24, etc.
All the multiples of 6 are shaded red on this *hundred grid*.

1	2	3	4	5	6	7	8	9	10
11	12	13	14	15	16	17	18	19	20
21	22	23	24	25	26	27	28	29	30
31	32	33	34	35	36	37	38	39	40
41	42	43	44	45	46	47	48	49	50
51	52	53	54	55	56	57	58	59	60
61	62	63	64	65	66	67	68	69	70
71	72	73	74	75	76	77	78	79	80
81	82	83	84	85	86	87	88	89	90
91	92	93	94	95	96	97	98	99	100

1 Cross out all the multiples of 6 on your hundred grid like this ⬚.

2 Cross out all the multiples of 4 like this ⬚. The numbers crossed out twice, like this ⬚, are multiples of 6 *and* 4.
They are called **common multiples**.

3 Common multiples are multiples of two or more numbers.
Write down the common multiples of 6 and 4 up to 100. The
lowest number in this list is called the **lowest common multiple**
(often shortened to **l.c.m.**) of 6 and 4. Write down the lowest
common multiple of 6 and 4.

4 You can work out multiples without using the *hundred grid*. Find the
first 10 multiples of 2 by multiplying 2 by 1, 2, 3, 4 and so on, up to
10. Now multiply 5 by the same numbers. Compare your two lists.
Circle the numbers that appear in both lists. These circled numbers
are common multiples of 2 and 5. The smallest of these is the
lowest common multiple of 2 and 5.

Try It Out
Hundred grid

B For each pair of numbers below, cross out the multiples of both
numbers on a *hundred grid*. Use different colours for each and stick
your grids in your book. Write down **(a)** the common multiples,
(b) the lowest common multiple for each pair of numbers.

1 4, 3	**2** 6, 9	**3** 3, 7
4 6, 8	**5** 4, 5	

> **Word Check**
> ....
> **multiple of a given number** number produced by
> multiplying the given number by another number, or itself
> **common multiple** a number which is a multiple of two or
> more numbers
> **lowest common multiple (l.c.m.)** the smallest common
> multiple of two or more numbers

Practice
C In each question below, write down …
(a) three multiples of each number
(b) any common multiples from (a)
(c) the lowest common multiple.

1 5, 6	**2** 12, 8	**3** 4, 10
4 12, 10	**5** 30, 20	**6** 8, 10

D To add or subtract fractions, make the numbers on the bottom (denominators) the same by finding a **common denominator**. You use the l.c.m. of the denominators. Write down the new denominators for these calculations.

I $\frac{}{10} + \frac{}{6}$ 2 $\frac{}{12} + \frac{}{6}$ 3 $\frac{}{15} + \frac{}{20}$

4 $\frac{}{8} - \frac{}{20}$ 5 $\frac{}{10} - \frac{}{12}$ 6 $\frac{}{6} + \frac{}{15}$

7 $\frac{}{4} + \frac{}{6}$ 8 $\frac{}{4} + \frac{}{9}$ 9 $\frac{}{9} - \frac{}{6}$

10 $\frac{}{20} - \frac{}{30}$

E Find the lowest common multiple of each group of numbers below.

Example	6, 8, 16
Working	Multiples of 6, up to 100, are 6, 12, 18, 24, 30, 36, 42, **48**, 54, 60, 66, 72, 78, 84, 90, **96**.
	Multiples of 8, up to 100, are 8, 16, 24, 32, 40, **48**, 56, 64, 72, 80, 88, **96**.
	Multiples of 16, up to 100, are 16, 32, **48**, 64, 80, **96**.
Answer	48

I 3, 4, 5   2 2, 5, 6   3 2, 5, 7

4 6, 10, 9   5 4, 9, 15   6 2, 3, 5, 7

Further Practice

> **Finished Early?**
> ➡ Go to page 352

F For each question below ...

(a) list the numbers in the outer circle that are multiples of *all* the numbers in the inner circle

(b) write down the lowest common multiple of the numbers in the inner circle.

I   2   3   4

5   6

> **Finished Early?**
> ➡ Go to page 352

❷ Factors

> ## Remember?
> A **factor** of a number is a whole number that divides exactly into it. I and the number itself are always factors.
>
> 1, 2, 4 and 8 are factors of 8.
>
> You can show factors on a **factor diagram**.
>
>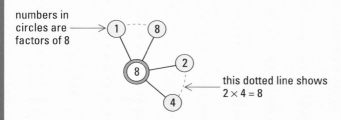

Try It Out

Ⓖ Draw factor diagrams for the following numbers.

Example   36

Working   You work out the factors in pairs.
Try to divide 36 by 1, 2, 3, 4, 5, 6.
Stop at 6 because 6 × 6 = 36 and you would only repeat factor pairs if you continued.

Answer

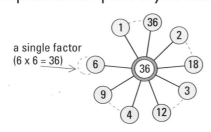

1 12	**2** 15	**3** 18
4 20	**5** 14	**6** 30
7 22	**8** 25	**9** 7
10 11		

Learn About It

These diagrams show the factors of 12 and 18.

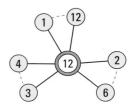
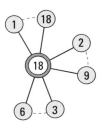

Some numbers occur in both diagrams.

The factors of 12 are 1, 2, 3, 4, 6, 12.

The factors of 18 are 1, 2, 3, 6, 9, 18.

The red numbers are factors of both 12 and 18, they are called **common factors**.

6 is the largest of the common factors. It is the **highest common factor (h.c.f.)** of 12 and 18.

The highest common factor is the largest number that will divide into both numbers.

Try It Out

H Draw factor diagrams for each number below.

List the common factors of each pair and write down their highest common factor.

1 8, 12	**2** 10, 15	**3** 16, 20
4 18, 24	**5** 12, 30	**6** 24, 32

Word Check

factor of a number a whole number that divides into it exactly

common factor a number which is a factor of two or more numbers

highest common factor (h.c.f.) the largest number that is a common factor of two or more numbers

Practice

I List the factors of each number and then write down the highest common factor of each pair.

I 15, 20	**2** 12, 30	**3** 24, 16
4 18, 24	**5** 20, 25	**6** 24, 30
7 40, 15	**8** 36, 24	**9** 36, 27
10 30, 36		

J To cancel fractions to their lowest terms, you divide the numerator and denominator by the same number. Write down the number you would divide into the numerator and denominator of each fraction to cancel it to its lowest terms.

I $\frac{8}{12}$	**2** $\frac{6}{10}$	**3** $\frac{12}{15}$
4 $\frac{12}{18}$	**5** $\frac{20}{30}$	**6** $\frac{40}{60}$
7 $\frac{36}{40}$	**8** $\frac{48}{60}$	**9** $\frac{24}{60}$
10 $\frac{75}{90}$		

> **Finished Early?**
> ➡ Go to page 352

Further Practice

K For each question below ...
 (a) list the numbers in the outer circle which are **common factors** of *all* the numbers in the inner circle
 (b) write down the highest common factor of the numbers in the inner circle.

I

2

3

4

5

6

> **Finished Early?**
> ➡ Go to page 352

16 Patterns and Sequences

In this chapter you will learn about ...
1. what's next?
2. finding the formula

1 What's Next?

Learn About It

A sequence is a list of numbers in order. The numbers are called the terms of the sequence. They grow or shrink according to a rule. You can find more terms if you work out the **rule**.

For the sequence 2, 4, 6, 8, 10 ...

| position in sequence | 1st | 2nd | 3rd | 4th | 5th |

You add 2 each time, so the sixth term is 12, the seventh term is 14, etc.

The **even numbers** make a sequence: 2, 4, 6, 8 ... You start at 2 and add 2 every time.

The **odd numbers** make a sequence: 1, 3, 5, 7 ... You start at 1 and add 2 every time.

The **square numbers** are $1^2, 2^2, 3^2, 4^2$ ... = 1, 4, 9, 16 ...

These dot patterns show the **triangle numbers**.

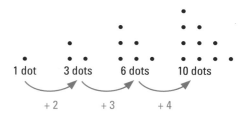

1 dot 3 dots 6 dots 10 dots
+ 2   + 3   + 4

You start at 1, then add 2, 3, 4, etc.

The sequence 1, 1, 2, 3, 5, 8, 13 … is called the **Fibonacci sequence**.
To get the next term, add the last two terms:

1 + 1 = 2

1 + 2 = 3

2 + 3 = 5

3 + 5 = 8

5 + 8 = 13 … etc.

Word Check

sequence a list of numbers that grows or shrinks according to a rule

term one number in a sequence

rule how to work out a number in a sequence

position the place of a term in a sequence

Try It Out

A Write down the next three terms of each sequence.

1 1, 3, 5, 7, 9 …

2 1, 4, 7, 10, 13, 16 …

3 2, 6, 10, 14, 18 …

4 20, 18, 16, 14, 12 …

Learn More About It

The number of objects in a pattern can make a sequence.

The number of yellow tiles in these patterns makes the sequence 8, 10, 12 …

8 yellow   10 yellow   12 yellow

Try It Out

B These dot patterns make sequences of numbers. Copy the patterns
and write the number of dots underneath each part of the pattern.
Write down the first six terms of each sequence. Draw more
patterns if this helps you.

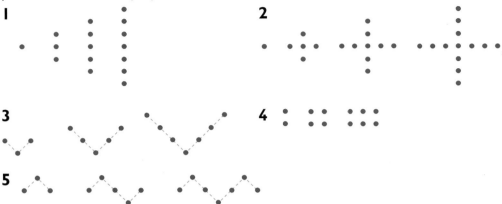

Practice

C Each pattern of matches below makes a number sequence. For each
pattern …

(a) Write down the first six terms of the sequence. Draw more
patterns if this helps you.

(b) Write down a rule for working out the terms of the sequence.

(c) Write down the tenth term of the sequence.

(d) Write down the name of the sequence, if it has a special name.

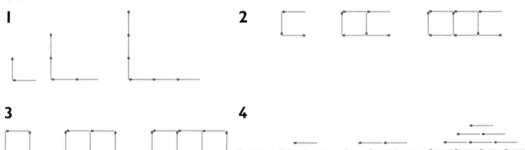

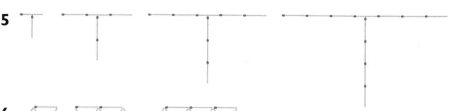

5

6

7

8

D Write down the first six terms in each of the following sequences.

1 The first term is 1. To find the next term, add 3.

2 The first term is 2. To find the next term, add 2.

3 The first term is 1. To find the next term, multiply by 3.

4 Each term is the square of its position in the sequence.

5 Each term is the cube of its position in the sequence.

6 The first term is 4 and the next term is 3 times the previous term.

7 The first two terms are 1, 1. Add the two preceding terms to find the next term.

8 The first term is 32. To find the next term, subtract 2.

> **Finished Early?**
> ➡ Go to page 353

Further Practice

E Copy these sequences and fill in the missing terms.

1 2, 4, ___, ___, 10, 12, 14, 16

2 3, 5, ___, ___, 11, 13, 15, 17

3 1, ___, 9, 16, 25, 36

4 2, 4, 8, ___, ___, 64, 128

5 3, ___, ___, 15, 19, 23, 27

6 3, 6, 9, ___, ___, ___, 21, 24

7 2, 6, ___, 54, 162, 486

8 1, 1, 2, 3, 5, 8, ___, ___, 34

F For each of the following sequences, write down ...
(a) the first eight terms
(b) the rule to find the next term.

1 2, 4, 6, 8 ...	**2** 3, 5, 7, 9 ...
3 4, 7, 10, 13 ...	**4** 1, 4, 16, 64 ...
5 2, 7, 12, 17 ...	**6** 1, 4, 9, 16, 25 ...
7 1, 3, 9, 27 ...	**8** 4, 9, 14, 19 ...
9 1, 8, 27, 64 ...	**10** 40, 36, 32, 28 ...

> **Finished Early?**
> ➡ Go to page 353

2 Finding the Formula

Learn About It

Joel is making triangles out of matchsticks.

position (*n*)   **1**   **2**   **3**   **4**

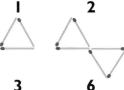 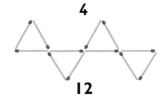

number of
matchsticks   **3**   **6**   **8**   **12**
(*T*)

He works out a **formula** to connect a term to its **position** in the
sequence.

The number of matchsticks in the pattern is *T*. Joel uses *n* for the
position. He puts his results in a table.

Position (*n*)	1 ↘ ×3	2 ↘ ×3	3 ↘ ×3	4 ↘ ×3
Number of matchsticks (*T*)	3 ↗	6 ↗	9 ↗	12 ↗

Joel sees that $n \times 3 = T$.

So the formula for the sequence is $T = 3n$.

With a formula, you can work out any term in the sequence.

The 10th term of this sequence is $10 \times 3 = 30$.

NUMBER SKILLS Add/subtract/multiply TU

Try It Out

G Write down the first six terms in a sequence with formula ...

1 $T = n + 4$ 2 $T = n + 6$

3 $T = 2n$ 4 $T = 3n - 1$

5 $T = 4n$ 6 $T = n + 3$.

> ### Key Fact
> A formula for a sequence connects a term to its position in the sequence.

Learn More About It

2, 4, 6, 8 ...

To find the formula for this sequence, draw a **difference table**.

Each time the position number goes up 1, the term goes up 2. So there must be '$n \times 2$' in the formula. The formula is $T = 2n$.

5, 7, 9, 11 ...

In this sequence, the differences are also + 2.

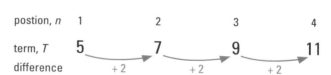

But the formula can't just be $T = 2n$. You need to add 3 to every term of the last sequence. So the formula is $T = 2n + 3$.

Word Check

difference   the number you add to get the next term

difference table   a clear way of setting out positions, terms and differences

Try It Out

H Find a formula connecting term (T) and position (n) for each of the following sequences.

1 (a) 4, 8, 12, 16 ...   (b) 5, 9, 13, 17 ...

2 (a) 5, 10, 15, 20 ...   (b) 7, 12, 17, 22 ...

3 (a) 10, 20, 30, 40 ...   (b) 9, 19, 29, 39 ...

4 (a) 6, 12, 18, 24 ...   (b) 1, 7, 13, 19 ...

Practice

I For each formula below ...
(a) write down the first six terms
(b) write down the twentieth and hundredth terms.

I $T = 2n + 1$	**2** $T = 3n + 2$
3 $T = 3n + 1$	**4** $T = 2n + 3$
5 $T = 4n + 1$	**6** $T = 5n + 1$
7 $T = 3n + 4$	**8** $T = 5n - 2$
9 $T = 3n - 1$	**10** $T = 4n - 3$

J In each of the following sequences, find a formula connecting term (T) and position (n).

I 2, 4, 6, 8 ...	**2** 3, 5, 7, 9 ...
3 5, 7, 9, 11 ...	**4** 7, 10, 13, 16 ...
5 9, 11, 13, 15 ...	**6** 6, 11, 16, 21 ...
7 5, 9, 13, 17 ...	**8** 2, 5, 8, 11 ...
9 1, 3, 5, 7 ...	**10** 1, 5, 9, 13...

Finished Early?
 Go to page 353

Further Practice

K Below are the formulae for sequences. For each ...
(a) write down the first six terms
(b) write down the thirtieth and five hundredth terms
(c) write down the difference between one term and the next.

Example	$p = 2n + 1$		
Answer	**(a)** 3, 5, 7, 9, 11, 13	**(b)** 61, 1001	**(c)** 2

I $T = n + 1$	**2** $T = 2n + 3$
3 $T = 3n + 2$	**4** $T = 5n + 1$
5 $T = 6n + 5$	**6** $T = 6n - 1$
7 $T = 3n - 2$	**8** $T = 4n - 3$

Finished Early?
 Go to page 353

Unit 9 *Number Relationships*

Summary of Chapters 15 and 16

- When you multiply a number by 1, 2, 3 … you produce **multiples**. 3, 6, 9, 12… are all multiples of 3. A **common multiple** is a multiple of two or more numbers. So 12, 24, 36 are common multiples of 4 and 3. The **lowest common multiple (l.c.m.)** is the smallest common multiple. So the l.c.m. of 4 and 3 is 12.

- A **factor** is a whole number divisor of a number. 1 and the number itself are always factors. So 1, 2, 4 and 8 are factors of 8. A **common factor** is a factor of two or more numbers. 2, 3, 6 are common factors of 12 and 18.

  The **highest common factor (h.c.f.)** is the largest common factor. 6 is the h.c.f. of 12 and 18.

- A **sequence** is a list of numbers in a specific order. The numbers are called the **terms** of the sequence.

- There are several special sequences:

  Odd numbers: 1, 3, 5, 7 …

  Even numbers: 2, 4, 6, 8 …

  Square numbers: 1, 4, 9, 16, 25 …

  Triangle numbers: 1, 3, 6, 10 …

  Fibonacci sequence: 1, 1, 2, 3, 5, 8, 13 …

- The **formula** for a sequence connects a term to its position in the sequence.

  The formula for the sequence 3, 5, 7, 9 … is $T = 2n + 1$, where T = the term and n = its position.

Brush Up Your Number 10

Place Value Calculations

Learn About It

Multiplying by 10, 100, 1000, etc. moves digits to the left.
You fill empty columns with zeros.

	× 10	× 100	× 1000	× 1 000 000
250	2500	25 000	250 000	250 000 000
2.5	25	250	2500	2 500 000
0.025	0.25	2.5	25	25 000

Dividing by 10, 100, 1000, etc. moves digits to the right.
You fill empty columns with zeros.

	÷ 10	÷ 100	÷ 1000	÷ 1 000 000
377 000	37 700	3770	377	0.377
3770	377	37.7	3.77	0.003 77
37.7	3.77	0.377	0.0377	0.000 037 7

Try It Out

A Each number machine has **4** input numbers. Work out the output
numbers.

1 6, 4100, 8.1, 0.05 ÷ 10 ?

2 55, 20 600, 0.03, 7.6 × 100 ?

3 7600, 340, 0.2, 10.66 ÷ 100 ?

4 4, 4.5, 4.55, 4.5555 × 1000 ?

5 350, 35, 27.2, 0.088 ÷ 10 ?

6 9000, 12 000, 350, 2.6 ÷ 1000 ?

7 3, 650, 1.52, 0.000 05 ÷ 1 000 000 ?

Practice

B Work out the missing numbers and operations.

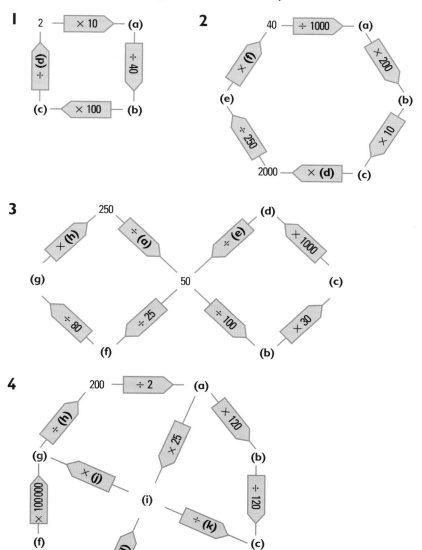

1
2 — × 10 — (a)
(d) ÷
(c) — × 100 — (b)
÷ 40

2
40 — ÷ 1000 — (a)
× (f)
(e)
÷ 250
× 200
(b)
× 10
(c)
2000 — × (d) — (c)

3
250
× (h)
÷ (a)
(g)
÷ 80
÷ 25
(f)
50
÷ (e)
(d)
× 1000
÷ 100
(c)
× 30
(b)
(b)

4
200 — ÷ 2 — (a)
÷ (h)
× 120
(g)
× 25
(b)
× (j)
(i)
÷ 120
× 10000
÷ (k)
(f)
(c)
× (l)
× 28
÷ 40
(e) — ÷ 1400 — (d)

Finished Early?
⇨ Go to page 353

17 Length and Mass

In this chapter you will learn about ...
- ① measuring and estimating length
- ② measuring and estimating mass
- ③ calculations

① Measuring and Estimating Length

Remember?

The basic unit of length is the **metre** (m).

100 **centimetres** (cm) = 1 m   10 mm = 1 cm

1000 **millimetres** (mm) = 1 m   1 **kilometre** (km) = 1000 m

---

Word Check

unit   type of measurement

centi- $\frac{1}{100}$ of a unit

milli- $\frac{1}{1000}$ of a unit

kilo-   1000 units

Try It Out

A 1 Copy and complete these sentences, using mm, cm, m or km.
   (a) A tall adult is about 2 _____ tall.
   (b) The Moon is 3460 _____ across.
   (c) A compact disc is about 200 _____ wide.
   (d) The world's tallest building is 452 _____ tall.
   (e) Martyn's handspan is 20 _____ .
   (f) A hen's egg is about 60 _____ long.

2 Measure the distance from ...

(a) A to B	**(b)** A to C	**(c)** B to D
(d) D to E	**(e)** V to W	**(f)** W to X
(g) V to Z	**(h)** A to V	**(i)** A to X
(j) V to B	**(k)** W to D	**(l)** C to Z.

Learn About It

When you use a ruler to **measure** something:
- be careful that you know what units it is measuring
- make sure you know what each small division on the ruler means
- put the zero mark of the ruler where you want to start measuring
- round off the answer if you have to
- write down the measurement straight away.

When you **estimate** a length or distance:
- make sure you estimate using a sensible unit
- compare it with something that has a length or distance you know, to give you an idea.

When you want to draw a straight line:
- draw a base line slightly longer than the one you want
- make a neat mark near one end
- measure from this mark, then make a new mark at the correct distance.

Word Check
....
estimate a good guess,
    based on what you know

When you want to draw a circle:

- make sure the compasses are tight
- make sure the pencil is sharp
- make sure the pencil is fixed and the pencil point is 'the same length' as the point of the compasses
- set the **radius** as carefully as possible
- put the point of the compasses in exactly the right place
- put more pressure on the point of the compasses than on the pencil point.

> **Word Check**
>
> **radius** the distance from the centre to the edge of a circle
>
> **diameter** the distance across the circle, through the centre; twice the radius

Try It Out

B Measure the **diameter** of each circle.

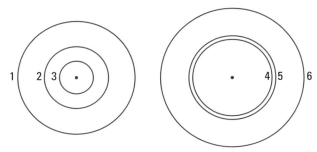

C Copy and complete the sentences.

1 A car is about _____ m long.

2 A television screen is about _____ cm wide.

3 A pigeon is about _____ cm from beak to tail.

4 A ruler is about _____ mm thick.

5 A house is about _____ m tall.

6 This book is about _____ mm thick.

7 The centre of _____ is about _____ km away.
(Fill in the first blank with your nearest big town or city.)

8 This classroom is about _____ m wide.

Plain paper, long side horizontal

D **1** Draw a straight base line at least 20 cm long.
2 Mark a point on the line within 1 cm of the left-hand end.
Label this point O.
3 Mark and label the following points.

Label	P	Q	R	S	T
Distance from O (cm)	6.8	7.5	10.8	15.3	18

Your line should look like this (bigger, of course!).

```
0              P Q   R       S   T
+----------------++---+-------+---+---
```

4 Now draw these circles with their centres at the labelled points on
the line.

Centre	P	Q	R
Radius (cm)	2.7	5	3.3

Your diagram should now look like the one below, but bigger.
Label the points U, V, W and X as shown.

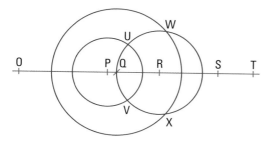

5 On your diagram, measure the distance in a straight line from ...
(a) O to U
(b) S to V
(c) T to W
(d) O to X
(e) U to V
(f) W to X.

Learn More About It

You often need to change a length from one unit into another. You need to know how many of the smaller units make the bigger unit.

If you are changing to **smaller** units, **multiply**. If you are changing to **bigger** units, **divide**.

Example	Lillian does a sponsored walk. She walks 12.3 km. How far is that in metres?
Working	There are 1000 m in 1 km. The change is to smaller units, so multiply. $12.3 \times 1000 = 12\,300$
Answer	12 300 m

Example	Steven's height is 156 cm. What is it in metres?
Working	There are 100 cm in 1 m. The change is to bigger units, so divide. $156 \div 100 = 1.56$
Answer	1.56 m

Try It Out

E Copy each line below, putting the correct operation in the number machine.

Example	? ▷ changes centimetres to millimetres
Working	10 mm = 1 cm
Answer	× 10 ▷ changes centimetres to millimetres

1 ? ▷ changes metres to centimetres
2 ? ▷ changes millimetres to centimetres
3 ? ▷ changes metres to kilometres
4 ? ▷ changes centimetres to metres
5 ? ▷ changes metres to millimetres
6 ? ▷ changes kilometres to metres
7 ? ▷ changes kilometres to centimetres

Copy and complete this table. Each row shows the same length.

Millimetres	Centimetres	Metres	Kilometres
2000	200	2	0.002
	6		
			5
8			
	48		
235			
		2.6	
			0.333
		0.81	

Practice

Write the lengths in each set in order, from shortest to longest.

1

12 cm   12 mm   2 mm   1.2 mm   1.5 cm   15 cm

Hint: change them all to millimetres first.

2

2 m   210 cm   1.2 m   12 cm   210 mm   2100 cm

Hint: change them all to centimetres first.

3

550 m   5.5 km   5000 cm   500 m   5000 m   50 km

Hint: change them all to metres first.

4

0.3 m   33 cm   3.35 cm   30 mm   0.033 m   0.3 cm

Hint: change them all to millimetres first.

Graph paper or squared paper

H **I** Draw a coordinate grid.
→ x-axis: *Scale*: 1 cm = 1 unit. *Range*: 0→10.
↑ y-axis: *Scale*: 1 cm = 1 unit. *Range*: 0→10.

2 Plot these points.
A (0, 3), **B** (5, 0), **C** (2, 8), **D** (7, 10), **E** (10, 7), **F** (9, 1).

3 Measure the following distances.

(a) AB	**(b)** BC	**(c)** CD
(d) DE	**(e)** EF	**(f)** FA
(g) AD	**(h)** CF	

> **Finished Early?**
> ⇨ Go to page 354

Further Practice

Copy and complete these sentences.

I **(a)** A baby is about 40 _____ long.
(b) The Earth is about 12 680 _____ across.
(c) A cup is about 80 _____ wide.
(d) A bus is about 1000 _____ long.

2 **(a)** A carriage on a train is about _____ m long.
(b) A piece of A4 paper is about _____ cm wide.
(c) A CD case is about _____ mm thick.
(d) The distance between my home and the nearest shopping centre is about _____ km.

3 Copy and complete this table. Each row shows the same length.

Millimetres	Centimetres	Metres	Kilometres
	120		
300			
		8	
			4.5
		21.5	
	9.3		

> **Finished Early?**
> ⇨ Go to page 354

❷ Measuring and Estimating Mass

> ## Remember?
> When you weigh something, you are finding its **mass**.
> The basic unit of mass is the **gram** (g).
> I **kilogram** (kg) = 1000 g 1000 kg = I **tonne** (t)

Try It Out

J Copy and complete these sentences using g, kg or tonnes.
1 An adult has a mass of about 70 _____.
2 A tea cup has a mass of about 160 _____.
3 The mass of a small van is about 2 _____.
4 A compact disc has a mass of about 16 _____.
5 A brick has a mass of about 2800 _____.

Learn About It

When you use **scales** to **weigh** something:
- be careful that you know what units it is measuring
- make sure you know what each small division on the scale means
- round off the answer if you have to.

When you use a **balance** to weigh something:
- be careful that you know what each weight is
- balance the weights and the thing you are weighing very carefully
- round off the answer if you have to.

When you **estimate** the mass of something
- make sure you estimate using a sensible unit
- compare it to something with a mass you know, to get an idea.

Try It Out

K Copy and complete the sentences.
1 A bike has a mass of about _____ kg.
2 A piece of A4 paper has a mass of about _____ g.
3 The mass of a cat is about _____ kg.
4 A wooden chair has a mass of about _____ g.
5 A passenger train has a mass of about _____ tonnes.

Learn More About It

You often need to change a mass from one unit to another. You need to know how many of the smaller units make the bigger unit. If you are changing to **smaller** units, **multiply**. If you are changing to **bigger** units, **divide**.

Example	May's car has a mass of 1.24 tonnes. What is that in kilograms?
Working	There are 1000 kg in 1 tonne. The change is to smaller units, so multiply. $1.24 \times 1000 = 1240$
Answer	1240 kg

Example	Kulvinder needs to weigh 600 grams of chicken for a recipe. His scales only read in kilograms. What should the reading be?
Working	There are 1000 g in 1 kg. The change is to bigger units, so divide. $600 \div 1000 = 0.6$
Answer	0.6 kg

Try It Out

L Copy each line below, putting the correct operation in the number machine.

Example	⟩ ? ⟩ changes kilograms to grams
Working	1 kg = 1000 g
Answer	⟩ × 1000 ⟩ changes kilograms to grams

1 ⟩ ? ⟩ changes kilograms to tonnes

2 ⟩ ? ⟩ changes grams to kilograms

3 ⟩ ? ⟩ changes tonnes to kilograms

4 ⟩ ? ⟩ changes tonnes to grams

Copy and complete this table. Each row shows the same mass.

Grams	Kilograms	Tonnes
	3	
	200	
		5
8		
95		
	15	
		0.43
120		
	8.6	

Match each object to the correct mass below.

1   2    3

4   5   6

7   8

A 11 kg   **B** 92 g   **C** 8.5 t   **D** 18 g
E 3.2 g   **F** 135 kg   **G** 325 g   **H** 1.75 kg

Practice

◉ Write the masses in each set in order, from lightest to heaviest.

1
900 g   1.2 kg
   0.85 kg   1 kg
1100 g   150 g

2
5t   5500 kg
   490 kg   0.5 t
550 000 g   4.8 t

Finished Early?
➡ Go to page 355

Further Practice

(P) 1 Estimate the masses of the following objects.
   (a) a frog   **(b)** a 2-litre carton of milk
   (c) a heavy book   **(d)** a television set
   (e) a skateboard   **(f)** a football

2 Write down the readings on these scales.

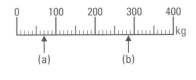

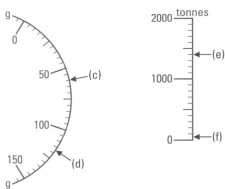

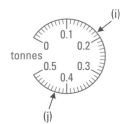

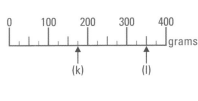

3 Put these masses in order, from lightest to heaviest.

> Hint: change them all to kilograms first.

1.5 kg, 30 g, 550 g, 250 kg, 0.25 kg,
0.3 tonnes, 2000 g, 350 kg

Finished Early?
➡ Go to page 355

3 Calculations

> ## Remember?
>
> To **round numbers**, always use the '5 and over' rule:
> - To round to the nearest **ten**, check the **units** digit. If it is 5, 6, 7, 8 or 9, round **up**. Otherwise, round **down**.
> - To round to the nearest **whole number** (unit), check the **tenths** digit (first decimal place). If it is 5, 6, 7, 8 or 9, round **up**. Otherwise, round **down**.
> - To round to the nearest **tenth** (1 d.p.), check the **hundredths** digit (second decimal place). If it is 5, 6, 7, 8 or 9, round **up**. Otherwise, round **down**.

Try It Out

1 Round these quantities to the nearest ten.
    (a) 37 kg   **(b)** 122.5 mm   **(c)** 8 tonnes   **(d)** 4.8 m

2 Round these quantities to: **(i)** 1 d.p., **(ii)** the nearest whole number.
    (a) 2.67 g   **(b)** 8.02 cm   **(c)** 130.08 m   **(d)** 15.51 kg

Learn About It

When you are doing questions on length and mass ...
- think about what operations $(+, -, \times, \div)$ to use
- make sure you use the information correctly
- ask yourself if the answer is sensible.

This question needs **two** operations:

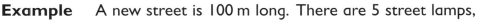

Example	A new street is 100 m long. There are 5 street lamps, spaced equally along it. How far apart are the lamps?
Working	There are 5 lamps, but that means 4 gaps. So they will be $100 \div 4 = 25$ m apart.
Answer	25 m

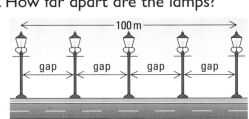

This **mass** question has several stages:

> **Example**   A goods train has an engine and 30 trucks. A truck
> carries 3.5 tonnes of rock.
> The engine has a mass of 20 tonnes. Each truck has a
> mass of 1.8 tonnes.
> What is the mass of the whole train?
>
>
>
> **Working**   1.8 + 3.5 = 5.3 t   (*Work out the mass of a full truck.*)
> 5.3 × 30 = 159 t   (*Work out the mass of 30 full trucks.*)
> 159 + 20 = 179 t   (*Add the mass of the engine.*)
> **Answer**   179 tonnes

Try It Out

1 Copy and complete this table. Write your working under the table.
Use the example in Learn About It to help you.

Length of street	Number of lamps	Distance between lamps
100 m	3	
300 m	7	
150 m	5	
1.2 km	21	
4 km	126	

2 Work out the mass of these trains. Use the example in Learn
About It to help you.

Number of trucks	Each truck holds	Mass of engine	Mass of 1 truck
10	3.5 t	20 t	1.8 t
20	3.5 t	25 t	1.8 t
25	2.7 t	31 t	1.35 t
45	4.25 t	50.5 t	2.1 t

Learn More About It

Sometimes you will get an answer that is correct but doesn't seem sensible.
If this happens, you might need to use a **different unit**.

Example	Class 8G made a line of pennies for charity. They used pennies worth £12.50. A penny is 2.05 cm wide. How long is the line of pennies?
Working	£12.50 = 1250 pence, so there are 1250 pennies. 1250 × 2.05 = 2562.5 cm This is right, but hard to imagine. You need a different unit. Divide by 100 to change it to metres. 2562.5 cm = 25.625 m
Answer	25.625 m

Sometimes you need to make your answer **simpler** to make it easier to understand. You need to **round off** your answer.

Example	Class 8G made a line of pennies 25.625 m long. This is **too accurate**. An answer to the nearest metre is better.
Working	25.635, rounded to the nearest whole number, is 26 m.
Answer	26 m, to the nearest metre

The same things can happen with mass.

Example	A penny has a mass of 3.56 g. What is the mass of 8G's line of pennies?
Working	1250 × 3.56 = 4450 g. The answer is in grams. It needs to be changed. 4450 ÷ 1000 = 4.45 kg. This is too accurate, so round it to the nearest whole kilogram: 4 kg.
Answer	4 kg, to the nearest kilogram

Try It Out

I A penny is 2.05 cm wide. To the nearest metre, what is the length of a line of pennies worth …
(a) £21?   (b) £32.50?   (c) £102.07?

2 A penny has a mass of 3.56 g. Work out the **mass** of each line of pennies in question 1.

3 5p coins are 1.75 cm wide and have a mass of 3.25 g each.
(a) How long is a line of 5p coins worth £25.30?
(b) What is the mass of the line?

Practice

I Skeletech construction sets use strips with holes in them. There is always a hole 1 cm from each end.
Here is a piece of Skeletech.

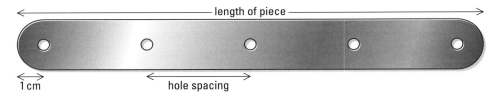

length of piece

1 cm   hole spacing

Work out the hole spacing on each of these pieces. Write your working under the table.

Piece	Length of piece	Number of holes	Hole spacing
A	6 cm	2	
B	8 cm	2	
C	10 cm	3	
D	16 cm	3	
E	20 cm	4	
F	26 cm	4	
G	30 cm	5	
H	42 cm	6	

Example	Piece **C**
Working	Piece **C** is 10 cm long. Each end is 1 cm. So the straight part is 8 cm long ($10 - 1 - 1 = 8$). There are 3 holes, so there are 2 spaces. Each space is $8 \div 2 = 4$ cm.
Answer	4 cm

2 Each piece of Skeletech is made of metal.
   1 cm of the metal has a mass of 3 g.
   A half-circle end has a mass of 2 g.
   Take off 0.5 g for each hole.
   Work out the mass of each piece.

Example	Piece **A**
Working	1 cm of the strip has a mass of 3 g. Piece **A** is 4 cm of straight strip plus 2 ends. So, before the holes are punched, it has a mass of $4 \times 3 + 2 \times 2 = 12 + 4 = 16$ g. 2 holes are punched. This takes away $2 \times 0.5 = 1$ g. $16 - 1 = 15$.
Answer	15 g

3 A boxed set of Skeletech contains the following quantities of each piece.

A	**B**	**C**	**D**	**E**	**F**	**G**	**H**
10	10	8	5	5	3	2	1

There are also **40 clips** to join the pieces together. Clips have a mass of 5 g each. The **box** has a mass of 150 g. Work out the mass of the boxed set.

4 If all the pieces in a set were laid end to end, how far would they stretch?

Finished Early?
➡ Go to page 355

Further Practice

1 A piece of A4 paper is 29.7 cm long and 21 cm wide.

Below are some other paper sizes. Work out the length and width of each.

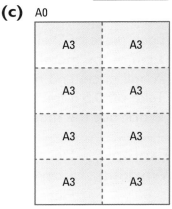

(a) A3

(b) A1

(c) A0

2 A piece of A4 paper has a mass of 6.3 g. What are the masses of each size of paper in question 1?

3 When the wheels on John's bike go round once, he travels 1.5 m. How far does he travel if his wheels go round …
(a) 100 times?
(b) 350 times?
(c) 1410 times (answer in kilometres to 1 d.p.)?
(d) 2325 times (answer in kilometres to 1 d.p.)?
(e) 6993 times (answer in kilometres to 1 d.p.)?

4 John's mum drives 18.4 km to work. When the wheels turn once, the car travels 1.2 m. How many times do the wheels turn on her way to work?

5 A ship is carrying new cars. Each car has a mass of 1200 kg. The average mass of a crew member is 75 kg. An empty ship has a mass of 1750 tonnes. It carries 225 cars. There are 36 crew members. What is the mass of the ship, crewed and loaded?

Finished Early?
➡ Go to page 355

18 Time

In this chapter you will learn about ...
1. time calculations
2. timetables

1 Time Calculations

Remember?

Units of time work in a different way to other units. This is because there are 60 seconds in a minute, 60 minutes in an hour and 24 hours in a day. They are not counted in tens, hundreds or thousands.

Times are written based on the 12-hour and 24-hour clock.

12-hour clock	9am	12 noon	2pm	11pm	12 midnight
24-hour clock	09:00	12:00	14:00	23:00	00:00

 2 minutes and 45 seconds is not the same as 2.45 minutes!

Try It Out

A
1. Change the following times to seconds.
   (a) 2 minutes (b) 5 minutes (c) $1\frac{1}{2}$ minutes (d) 1 hour
2. Change the following times to minutes.
   (a) 240 seconds (b) 150 seconds (c) 2 hours (d) 8 hours
3. Change the following times to hours.
   (a) 300 minutes (b) 90 minutes (c) 3 days (d) $1\frac{1}{2}$ days
4. Change these times to the 12-hour clock.
   (a) 13:00 (b) 17:30 (c) 09:10 (d) 23:55
5. Change these times to the 24-hour clock.
   (a) 2.45pm (b) 5.15am (c) 12 midnight (d) 8.40pm

Learn About It

To add and subtract times, you can work in separate units.

Example	Add 3 hours, 46 minutes and 32 seconds to 11 hours, 27 minutes and 51 seconds.
Working	Set out the calculation:

$$
\begin{array}{ccc}
h & m & s \\
3 & 46 & 32 \\
11 & 27 & 51 \\
\hline
14 & 73 & 83 \\
\end{array}
$$

Change 83 seconds into 1 minute and 23 seconds.

$$
\begin{array}{ccc}
h & m & s \\
14 & 74 & 23 \\
\end{array}
$$

Change 74 minutes into 1 hour and 14 minutes.

Answer	15 hours, 14 minutes and 23 seconds

Or you can change all the times to the same unit, the smallest in the question.

Example	The winning time in a race was 56 minutes and 40 seconds. Josie's time was 1 hour, 10 minutes and 24 seconds. How much later than the winner did she finish?
Working	1 hour = 60 × 60 seconds = 3600 seconds

10 minutes = 60 seconds × 10 = 600 seconds

So Josie took = 3600 + 600 + 24 seconds
            = 4224 seconds.

The winner took 56 × 60 + 40 = 3360 + 40 = 3400 seconds.

The difference = 4224 − 3400 = 824 seconds.

824 ÷ 60 = 13 remainder 44

Answer	13 minutes and 44 seconds

Try It Out

B This table shows world records for the marathon. They have changed a lot in the last century.

Year	Time (h:m:s)	Year	Time (h:m:s)
1896	3:03:05	1958	2:15:17
1908	2:55:19	1969	2:08:34
1920	2:32:35	1981	2:08:18
1935	2:26:42	1988	2:06:50
1947	2:25:39	1998	2:06:05

1 Between which years was the smallest change?
2 Between which years was the biggest change?
3 How much faster has the marathon become since 1896?
4 Copy the table, rounding all the times to the nearest minute.
5 Frank ran the London marathon last year. He ran the first half of the race in 2 hours, 30 minutes, 18 seconds and the second half in 2 hours, 57 minutes, 36 seconds. What was his total time?

Learn More About It

You can use the same methods to multiply or divide times.

Multiplying time can be done in separate units.

Example	A machine takes 2 minutes and 35 seconds to make a toy boat. How long does it take to make 2 dozen boats?
Working	2 dozen = 2 × 12 = 24 boats 2 minutes × 24 = 48 minutes 35 seconds × 24 = 840 seconds = 14 minutes 48 minutes + 14 minutes = 62 minutes = 1 hour, 2 minutes
Answer	1 hour, 2 minutes

To divide times, you must change them to the **same** unit.

Example	Reg Morris of Walsall is the world kipper eating champion. He prepared and ate 27 kippers in 17 minutes and 6 seconds! How long did each kipper take?
Working	Divide 17 minutes 6 seconds by 27. 17 minutes 6 seconds = $17 \times 60 + 6 = 1026$ seconds $1026 \div 27 = 38$
Answer	38 seconds

Try It Out

C 1 Javed's CD collection is very strange. All the tracks on each CD last exactly the same time.
Work out how long each of these CDs last.

CD Title	Track length (m:s)	Number of tracks
(It's) All the Same to Me	9:15	8
Spin Sector	13:31	5
Nice and Even Does It	5:58	12
Time and Time Again	5:44	10
Divided We Fall	9:54	7

2 The prize in a snail race went to the owner of the fastest snail.
Work out how long each snail took to cover 1 metre.
Write the names of the snails in order, from fastest to slowest.

Name of snail	Distance covered (m)	Time (h:m:s)
Lightning	2	0:15:12
The Flash	5	0:38:15
Linford	12	1:24:00
Bluebird	7	0:51:06
Turbo	6	0:38:30

Practice

D **1** These are the times taken by athletes in a triathlon race.

Name	Swim 1 km (m:s)	Cycle 35 km (h:m:s)	Run 10 km (h:m:s)	Total (h:m:s)	Position in race
Jessica Fraser	12:11	1:20:05	43:15		
Kate O'Connor	14:03	1:18:04	46:16		
Ruth Coates	15:34	1:06:17	48:57		
Jane Harrison	16:22	1:13:37	51:05		
Jenn Powell	16:49	1:25:26	55:51		
Roxanne MacLaurin	16:56	1:12:19	1:00:15		
Jude d'Entremont	17:38	1:04:09	52:49		
Melanie Wallace	21:33	1:38:29	1:00:41		

(a) Copy the table.
(b) Work out the times for the **total** column. Write your working underneath. Fill in the column.
(c) Work out the positions in the race (first, second, etc.). Fill in the last column.

2 One week, Wei Ling wrote down the times it started and finished raining each day. This is what she wrote.

	Mon	Tue	Wed	Thu	Fri	Sat	Sun
Started raining							The Sun shone
Finished raining							all day!

(a) For how long did it rain each day?
(b) For how long did it rain over the whole week?

3 Yana travelled a long way to visit her family. She recorded how long it took. This is what she recorded: 2 hours 12 minutes, 2 hours 15 minutes, 1 hour 48 minutes, 2 hours 25 minutes, 4 hours 4 minutes, 2 hours 10 minutes. Work out ...
(a) the total time taken for her journey
(b) the mean time for a stage of her journey.

> Remember: to find the average or **mean** of a group of times, you add up all the times, then divide by the number of times.

4 Five music students are going to play pieces at a concert. These are the lengths of the pieces:
7 minutes 15 seconds, 4 minutes 35 seconds, 5 minutes 21 seconds, 4 minutes, 8 minutes 44 seconds.

Work out the mean length of the pieces.

> **Finished Early?**
> ➡ Go to page 356

Further Practice

E Here is a section from a TV guide.

Channel 3		Channel 4	
6:00	Local News	6:00	Wildlife
6:25	News & Weather		documentary
7:00	Emmerdale	7:00	Channel 4 News
7:30	Coronation Street	7:55	Video Snapshot
8:00	The Big Match	8:00	Brookside
9:45	Drama: *Police Story*	8:30	The Film Show
11:05	Late News	9:00	Drama: *Paramedic!*
11:20	Local News &	10:00	Life in the City
	Weather	10:30	Film: *Romeo and Juliet*
11:25–1:15	Athletics highlights	12:05–12:15	Weather Watch

1 Write down how long each programme lasts.

2 Cynthia has to go out. She wants to record *Emmerdale*, *Coronation Street* and *Brookside*.
(a) How long do these programmes last altogether?

(b) Cynthia has a 180-minute video. It already has a film on it that lasts 1 hour and 40 minutes. Can she fit the soaps onto it?

(c) If your answer to (b) was yes, how much spare tape is there? If your answer was no, how much of *Brookside* will she miss?

3 Jake wants to record The Big Match and *Romeo and Juliet*. Will they fit on a blank 180-minute tape? If so, how much tape is left? If not, how much of *Romeo and Juliet* will Jake miss?

> **Finished Early?**
> ➡ Go to page 356

❷ Timetables

Learn About It

A **timetable** is used when a lot of time information has to be shown. This is a bus timetable.

LINCOLN-SWANPOOL-BIRCHWOOD							Service 99
Monday to Saturday only							
	S	NS					S
Lincoln City Bus Station	0715	0745		:45		1945	2015
The Junction	—	0755	then	:55		1955	—
Swanpool Almond Avenue	0730	0800	at	:00		2000	2030
Birchwood The Wildlife Inn	0732	0802	these	:02		2002	2032
Birchwood The Neighbourhood Centre	0740	0810	minutes	:10	until	2010	2040
Birchwood The Wildlife Inn	0742	0812	past	:12		2012	2042
Swanpool Almond Avenue	0745	0815	each	:15		2015	2045
The Junction	0750	0820	hour	:20		2020	2050
LINCOLN City Bus Station	0800	0830		:30		2030	2100
NOTES							
S – Saturday only NS – Not Saturday							

Notice that:

- The **S** means a bus **only** runs on Saturdays. **NS** means a bus **doesn't** run on Saturdays. The **NOTES** at the bottom of the timetable tell you this.
- Some buses don't stop everywhere. There is a — to show where a bus does not stop.
- There isn't a column for every bus. The buses run every hour. If you want to reach a certain place, look at the minutes past each hour. For example, a bus arrives at Lincoln at 0930, 1030, 1130, etc.

Try It Out

F Answer the following questions using the bus timetable below.

LINCOLN-SWANPOOL-BIRCHWOOD								*Service 99*
Monday to Saturday only								
	S	NS						S
Lincoln City Bus Station	0715	0745		:45		1945		2015
The Junction	—	0755	then	:55		1955		—
Swanpool Almond Avenue	0730	0800	at	:00		2000		2030
Birchwood The Wildlife Inn	0732	0802	these	:02		2002		2032
Birchwood The Neighbourhood Centre	0740	0810	minutes	:10	until	2010		2040
Birchwood The Wildlife Inn	0742	0812	past	:12		2012		2042
Swanpool Almond Avenue	0745	0815	each	:15		2015		2045
The Junction	0750	0820	hour	:20		2020		2050
LINCOLN City Bus Station	0800	0830		:30		2030		2100
NOTES								
S – Saturday only NS – Not Saturday								

1 Write down the times of all the buses leaving Lincoln Bus Station on a Saturday.

Hint: there are 14 altogether.

2 What time does the first bus on a Monday stop at the Wildlife Inn?

3 How long does it take from Birchwood Centre to the Junction?

4 Jessica is shopping in Lincoln on Saturday. She wants to be back at Birchwood Centre by six o'clock. Which bus should she catch from the Bus Station?

5 Pete arrives at Almond Avenue bus stop at 8.55am. How long does he have to wait for the Lincoln bus?

6 Ryan is meeting someone at the Wildlife Inn at 6.15pm on Saturday. He gets to the Bus Station at 5.50. How late will he be?

Practice

G Use the train timetables on the next page to answer the following questions.

1 What time does the 0900 from Newcastle arrive in London?

2 Adam is travelling from Newcastle. He wants to be in Peterborough by 11.30 am. He wants to have his breakfast on the train. Which train should he catch?

North East England and Scotland to London

Mondays to Fridays

	✗		✗	✗	✗		✗	✗	✗
Aberdeen				0508e		0650e	0755		
Dundee		0616e	0639e	0720e	0805e	0906			
Edinburgh	0700	0800	0900	0930	1000	1031	1100	1130
Berwick-on-Tweed	0739		0945	1010	1039		1141	
Newcastle	0828	0900	0928	1032	1056	1126	1157	1231	1255
Darlington	0902	0930	0955	1103	1123	1157		1305	
York	0932	1001	1026	1131	1151	1229	1248	1333	1346
Doncaster	0958	1026	1053	1158		1254		1400	
Peterborough	1050	1112	1230o		1256	1344	1401	1446	1456
London King's Cross	1145	1211	1235	1336	1350	1443	1458	1543	1554

NOTES: e change at Edinburgh   ✗ restaurant service
o change at Doncaster

London to North East England and Scotland

Mondays to Fridays

	✗	✗	✗	✗ FX	✗ FO	✗	✗		
London King's Cross	1700	1730	1800	1820	1820	1830	1900	2000	2200
Peterborough		1814		1906	1906	1919	1944	2044	2259
Doncaster			1930			2017	2032	2132	2355
York	1847	1926	1956	2017	2017	2042	2057	2157	0020
Darlington	1914	1954	2024	2049	2049	2110	2125	2230	0048
Newcastle	1946	2029	2055	2126	2126	2147	2200	2310	0139
Berwick-on-Tweed		2124	2140		2212		2251		
Edinburgh	2114	2214	2223		2300		2337		
Dundee	2254e	0004e			0038e				
Aberdeen	0018e								

NOTES: e change at Edinburgh   ✗ restaurant service   FX not Fridays
FO Fridays only

3 How long does the 1800 from King's Cross take to reach Darlington?

4 Scott lives in Dundee. He needs to be in London by 2pm. Which train should he catch?

5 How many stations does the 1100 from Edinburgh stop at?

6 Duncan needs to get home to Aberdeen from London. What is the latest train he can catch?

7 Look at the 1820 train from King's Cross. What is different about it on Fridays?

8 Siobhan needs to get home to Dundee from York on a Tuesday. What is the latest train she can catch?

> **Finished Early?**
> ➡ Go to page 357

Further Practice

H This is part of a train timetable.

North-West England to The Midlands and East Anglia									
Saturdays									
	✗	✗		✗	✗	✗			
Liverpool Lime Street	1352	1452	1552	1652	1752	1852	1952	2052	
Warrington Central	1418	1518	1618	1718	1818	1918	2018	2118	
Manchester Piccadilly	1443	1543	1643	1743	1843	1943	2043	2145	2228
Stockport	1453	1553	1653	1753	1853	1953	2053	2155	2238
Sheffield	1540	1638	1747	1840	1940	2038	2140	2238	2340
Chesterfield	1554	1654	1801	1854	1954	2053	2154	2302	0002
Nottingham	1625	1733	1840	1926	2041	2130	2229	2344	0042
Grantham	—	1813	—	—	2112	—	—	—	—
Peterborough	—	1852	2001	—	2143	—	—	—	—
Ely	—	1925	2033	—	2231	—	—	—	—
Thetford	—	1952	2100	—	2251	—	—	—	—
Norwich	—	2026	2129	—	2326	—	—	—	—

NOTES: ✗ food trolley service

Use the timetable to answer the following questions.

1 **(a)** What time does the 1352 from Liverpool arrive at Chesterfield?
(b) How long is that journey?

2 Vandra is in Stockport. She wants to be home in Ely before 10pm. What is the latest train she can catch?

3 Mel is in Grantham. She needs to arrive in Norwich before 10pm. Which train should she catch?

4 John just misses the 2145 at Manchester. How long does he have to wait for the next train?

5 Sanjay gets on the 1840 train at Sheffield. He is travelling to Peterborough.
(a) What mistake has he made?
(b) How long must he wait for the next train?
(c) How long does his journey take altogether?

6 Alyssa travels on the 1418 from Warrington to Nottingham. While in Nottingham she loses her timetable. She remembers that the train home leaves at 2035. It takes the same time as her first journey. What time will she get back to Warrington?

7 The train company alters the last train so that it starts at Liverpool instead of Manchester.
Work out the times that will go in the two blank spaces on the timetable.

Finished Early?
➡ Go to page 357

Unit 10 *Measures*

Summary of Chapters 17 and 18

- To **estimate** a length or distance, compare it with something with a length or distance you know, to give you an idea. Make sure you estimate using a sensible **unit**.

- When you **weigh** something you are finding its **mass**. Make sure you know what each small division on the scale means.

- To **estimate** the mass of something, compare it with something that has a mass you know, to give you an idea. Make sure you estimate using a sensible **unit**.

- 100 **centimetres** (cm) = 1 m   1000 mm = 1 m
  10 **millimetres** (mm)= 1 cm   1 **kilometre** (km) = 1000 m
  1 **kilogram** (kg) = 1000 grams (g) 1000 kg = 1 **tonne** (t)

- To change from one unit to another:
  1 Work out how many of the smaller units make the bigger unit.
  2 If you are changing to **smaller** units, **multiply**.
    If you are changing to **bigger** units, **divide**.

- Units of time work in a different way to other units. This is because there are 60 seconds in a minute, 60 minutes in an hour and 24 hours in a day. They are not grouped in tens, hundreds or thousands.
  Times are written using either the 12-hour or the 24-hour clock.

12-hour	2am	8.30am	12 noon	4pm	7.30pm	10pm	12 midnight
24-hour	02:00	08:30	12:00	16:00	19:30	22:00	00:00

  To add and subtract times, work in separate units or change all measurements to the same unit.

- You can organise information about time in a **timetable**.

Brush Up Your Number 11

 ## Calculation Shortcuts

Learn About It

Here are some calculation shortcuts.

Calculation	Shortcut	Example	Working
Add 9	Add 10	$46 + 9$	$46 + 10 = 56$
	Subtract 1		$56 - 1 = 55$
Add 99	Add 100	$73 + 99$	$73 + 100 = 173$
	Subtract 1		$173 - 1 = 172$
Subtract 99	Subtract 100	$248 - 99$	$248 - 100 = 148$
	Add 1		$148 + 1 = 149$

Try It Out

 Calculate the following using shortcuts. Explain how you worked out each answer.

1. (a) $26 + 9$ (b) $45 + 9$ (c) $94 + 9$ (d) $138 + 9$
2. (a) $37 - 9$ (b) $72 - 9$ (c) $166 - 9$ (d) $331 - 9$
3. (a) $27 + 99$ (b) $135 + 99$ (c) $252 + 99$ (d) $585 + 99$
4. (a) $136 - 99$ (b) $290 - 99$ (c) $462 - 99$ (d) $948 - 99$

Learn More About It

Here are some more shortcuts.

Calculation	Shortcut	Example	Working
Multiply by 9	Multiply number by 10	23×9	$23 \times 10 = 230$
	Subtract number		$230 - 23 = 207$
Multiply by 99	Multiply number by 100	7×99	$7 \times 100 = 700$
	Subtract number		$700 - 7 = 693$

NUMBER SKILLS **Four operations with HTU**

Calculation	Shortcut	Example	Working
Multiply by 5	Multiply by 10 Divide by 2	28×5	$28 \times 10 = 280$ $280 \div 2 = 140$
Multiply by 50	Multiply by 100 Divide by 2	14×50	$14 \times 100 = 1400$ $1400 \div 2 = 700$
Divide by 5	Divide by 10 Multiply by 2	$90 \div 5$	$90 \div 10 = 9$ $9 \times 2 = 18$
Divide by 50	Divide by 100 Multiply by 2	$600 \div 50$	$600 \div 100 = 6$ $6 \times 2 = 12$

Try It Out

B Calculate the following using shortcuts. Show your working.

1 (a) 13×9 **(b)** 25×9 **(c)** 78×9 **(d)** 560×9
2 (a) 7×99 **(b)** 35×99 **(c)** 14×99 **(d)** 89×99
3 (a) 12×5 **(b)** 23×5 **(c)** 52×5 **(d)** 140×5
4 (a) 6×50 **(b)** 16×50 **(c)** 88×50 **(d)** 240×50
5 (a) $80 \div 5$ **(b)** $120 \div 5$ **(c)** $230 \div 5$ **(d)** $480 \div 5$
6 (a) $300 \div 50$ **(b)** $700 \div 50$ **(c)** $1000 \div 50$ **(d)** $2400 \div 50$

Practice

C Calculate the following using shortcuts. Show your working.

1 24×50 **2** $70 \div 5$ **3** 23×9 **4** $76 + 99$
5 $332 - 99$ **6** $800 \div 50$ **7** 6×99 **8** $420 \div 5$
9 82×50 **10** 99×68 **11** $256 + 9$ **12** 5×860
13 $843 - 99$ **14** $4800 \div 50$ **15** 9×46 **16** $334 + 99$

D Answer these questions using a shortcut.
1 Brad is 47. Carmen is 9 years older. How old is she?
2 Exercise books cost 68p each. How much do 5 cost?
3 Simon has used 99 minutes of his 360-minute video tape.
How much recording time is left?
4 A coach has 50 seats. How many coaches
are needed for 1200 football supporters?

> **Finished Early?**
> Go to page 358

19 Perimeter and Area

In this chapter you will learn about ...
1. perimeters
2. calculating areas of rectangles
3. calculating areas of parallelograms and triangles

P 1 Perimeters

Remember?

The **perimeter** of a shape is the distance all the way round the outside.

Perimeter = $a + b + c + d + e$

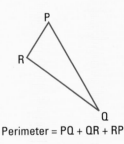

Perimeter = PQ + QR + RP

Sometimes you can measure the perimeter; sometimes you have to calculate it.

If you want to show that lines are the same length, use special marks.

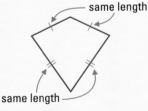

same length

same length

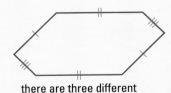

there are three different lengths of line in this shape

Learn About It

You work out perimeters by adding lengths.

The perimeter of this shape is
$4 + 6 + 8 + 5 + 7 = 30$ cm.

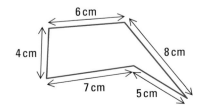

6 cm

4 cm

8 cm

7 cm

5 cm

If the sides are of equal lengths, you can calculate the perimeter by multiplying.

The perimeter of this triangle is
3×10 cm = 30 cm.

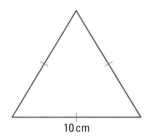

Sometimes you need to subtract lengths to work out the missing sides first.

The red line is $7 - 4 = 3$ cm.
The blue line is $8 - 3 = 5$ cm.
So the perimeter is:
$7 + 8 + 4 + 5 + 3 + 3 = 30$ cm.

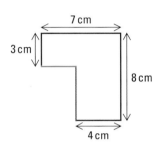

Try It Out

Ⓐ **1** Find the lengths shown by letters in these shapes.

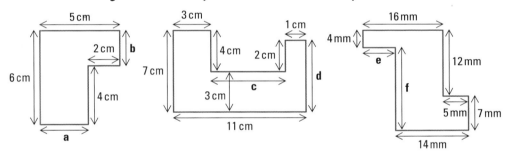

2 Work out the perimeter of each shape.

(a)

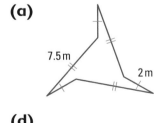

(b)

(c)

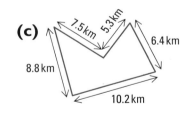

(d)

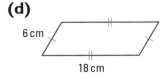

(e)

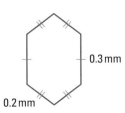

(f)

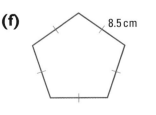

Learn More About It

If you know the perimeter, you can work out the missing length of a side.

Example	The perimeter of this garden is 26 m. How long is it?
Working	The hedge is 4 m long. The other end of the garden is also 4 m. That makes 4 + 4 = 8 m altogether. That leaves 26 − 8 = 18 m for the long sides. Both long sides are the same, so they are each 18 ÷ 2 = 9 m.
Answer	9 m

Try It Out

B Work out the missing lengths.

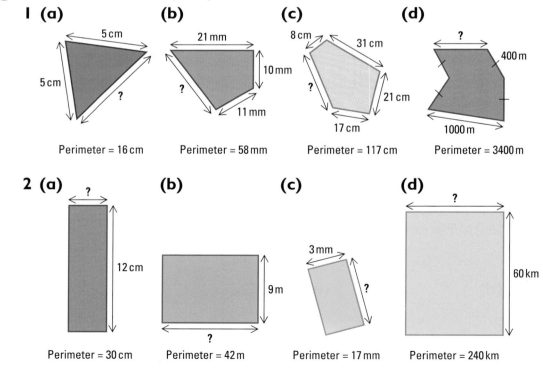

1 (a) 5 cm 5 cm ?
Perimeter = 16 cm

(b) 21 mm 10 mm 11 mm ?
Perimeter = 58 mm

(c) 8 cm 31 cm 21 cm 17 cm ?
Perimeter = 117 cm

(d) ? 400 m 1000 m
Perimeter = 3400 m

2 (a) ? 12 cm
Perimeter = 30 cm

(b) 9 m ?
Perimeter = 42 m

(c) 3 mm ?
Perimeter = 17 mm

(d) ? 60 km
Perimeter = 240 km

Practice

1 This is a plan of a country estate.
What is the perimeter of …
(a) the South Meadow?
(b) the East Meadow?
(c) the West Meadow?
(d) the whole estate?

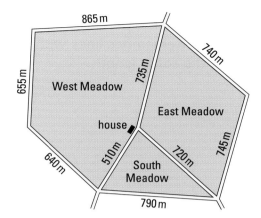

2 This is a plan of a country house and garden.

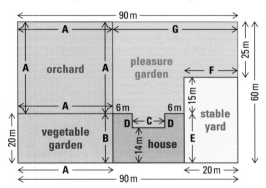

(a) Copy the diagram. Calculate the missing measurements.
They are lettered in the order you should work them out.
Sides with the same letter are the same length.
(b) What is the perimeter of the vegetable garden?
(c) What is the perimeter of the house?
(d) What is the perimeter of the pleasure garden?

Finished Early?
➡ Go to page 358

Further Practice

D **1** Work out the perimeter of each shape within the mosaic pattern below. Remember, lines with the same marks (/ or // or ///) are the same length.

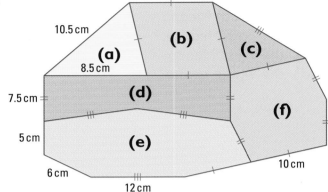

2 Work out the missing lengths.

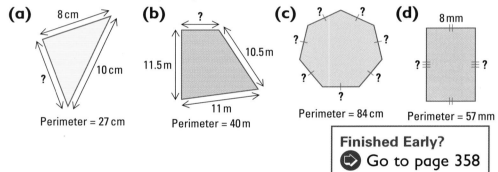

(a) 8 cm / 10 cm / ?
Perimeter = 27 cm

(b) ? / 11.5 m / 10.5 m / 11 m
Perimeter = 40 m

(c) ? / ? / ? / ? / ? / ?
Perimeter = 84 cm

(d) 8 mm / ? / ?
Perimeter = 57 mm

Finished Early?
➡ Go to page 358

T **2** **Calculating Areas of Rectangles**

Remember?

- **Area** is the amount of surface something occupies.
- Area is measured in **square** units such as square centimetres (cm^2).
  There are $10 \times 10 = 100 \ mm^2$ in $1 \ cm^2$.
  There are $100 \times 100 = 10\,000 \ cm^2$ in $1 \ m^2$.

1 cm
1 cm

- Area of a rectangle = length × width.
- In a square, the length and width are the same. Multiply the side of a square by itself – **square** it – to find the area.

Try It Out

1 Find the area of each of the following rectangles.
   (a) 2 cm × 5 cm   **(b)** 7 m × 4 m   **(c)** 20 mm × 10 mm

2 Find the area of each of the following squares.
   (a) 4 cm sides   **(b)** 10 km sides   **(c)** 2 m sides

Learn About It

Sometimes, the length and width of a rectangle are given in different units. You can't multiply them straight away to find the area. You have to change the unit of one so they match.

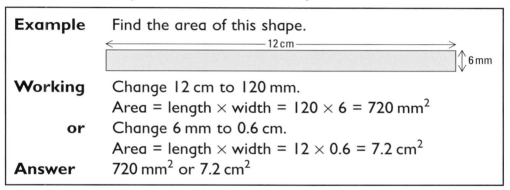

Example	Find the area of this shape.
Working	Change 12 cm to 120 mm. Area = length × width = 120 × 6 = 720 mm²
or	Change 6 mm to 0.6 cm. Area = length × width = 12 × 0.6 = 7.2 cm²
Answer	720 mm² or 7.2 cm²

Compound shapes are made by joining simple shapes.

You can also make them by taking a shape out of another shape.

Work out the area of a compound shape by adding or subtracting the areas of the shapes it's made of.

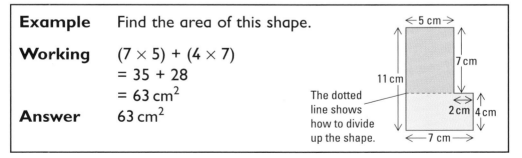

Example	Find the area of this shape.
Working	(7 × 5) + (4 × 7) = 35 + 28 = 63 cm²
Answer	63 cm²

The dotted line shows how to divide up the shape.

Word Check

compound shape a shape made by joining two or more shapes or taking shapes out of others

---

Try It Out

F Draw a sketch diagram of each shape below. Work out and label any missing lengths.

Work out the area of each shape. Show your working.

I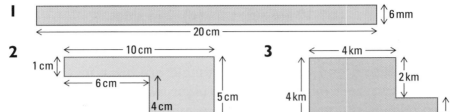

2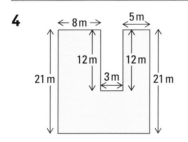

3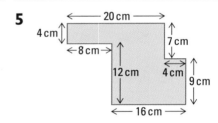

| *Hint: add two rectangles together.* | *Hint: add two rectangles together.* |

4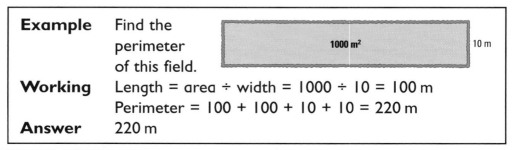

5

| *Hint: take a small rectangle from a big rectangle.* | *Hint: take two small rectangles from a big rectangle.* |

Learn More About It

If you know the area of a rectangle and the length of one side, you can work out the length of the other side. Divide the area by the length of the known side.

Once you know the length and width, you can work out the perimeter.

Example	Find the perimeter of this field.
Working	Length = area ÷ width = 1000 ÷ 10 = 100 m
	Perimeter = 100 + 100 + 10 + 10 = 220 m
Answer	220 m

1000 m²   10 m

Sometimes the area and sides of a rectangle are given in different units. You can't divide them straight away. You have to change one so they match.

Squares are slightly different. To find the side of a square, work out the **square root** of the area.

Example	A square tarpaulin covers 9 m². How long is each side?
Working	$\sqrt{9} = 3$ (because $3 \times 3 = 9$)
Answer	3 m

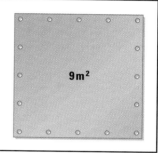

9 m²

Try It Out

For each rectangle, find **(a)** the missing length **(b)** the perimeter.

1

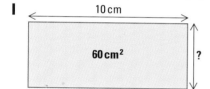

10 cm

60 cm²

?

2

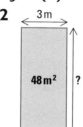

3 m

48 m² ?

3

50 mm

75 mm² ↕ ?

4

144 m² ?

5

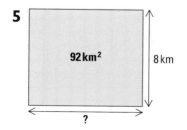

92 km²

8 km

?

6

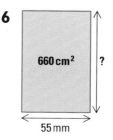

660 cm² ?

55 mm

Practice

 This plan shows some houses and their gardens on a small estate. The paths are all 2 m wide.

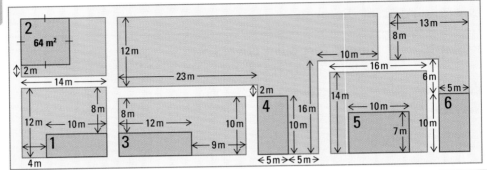

> **key**
> ▇ house
> ▨ garden
> ☐ path

A **plot** is the total area taken up by a house **and** its garden.

1 Copy and complete this table. Write your working underneath.

House number	Area of house (m²)	Area of plot (m²)	Area of garden (m²)
1			
2	64		
3			
4			
5			
6			

2 Work out the total area of the estate.

I All sorts of things come on rolls. If you unroll them, you get long, thin rectangles! If you know the width of the roll and the area of the rectangle, you can calculate the length.

Work out how long the following rolls are. Write your working underneath. Use sensible units for the answers.

	Type of roll	Width	Area	Length
1	Sticky tape	2.5 cm	8250 cm^2	
2	Kitchen towels	0.25 m	3.6 m^2	
3	Bin liners	20 cm	45 000 cm^2	
4	Toilet roll	11 cm	33 000 cm^2	
5	Carpet	3.5 m	84 m^2	
6	Wallpaper	0.56 m	22.4 m^2	
7	Parcel tape	5 cm	25 000 cm^2	
8	Party streamer	0.5 cm	125 cm^2	

Finished Early?
➡ Go to page 359

Further Practice

J Work out the area of each numbered part of this diagram. Draw a sketch diagram first.

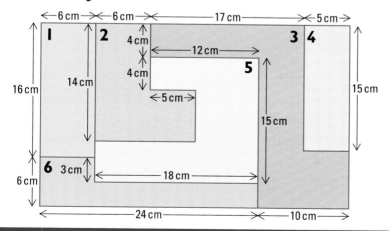

K Work out the missing lengths in the following rectangles. Draw and label a sketch diagram of each one.

1 Area = 40 cm², length = 8 cm
2 Area = 100 m², width = 8 m
3 Area = 2 m², length = 8 m
4 Area = 4 cm², length = 20 cm
5 Area = 1 km², width = 50 m
6 Area = 10 m², width = 25 mm

Finished Early?
➡ Go to page 359

T ❸ Calculating Areas of Parallelograms and Triangles

Learn About It

On the diagram, the red line has a special name – the **height** of the parallelogram. The height is always **perpendicular** (at right angles) to the base. The line at the bottom of the parallelogram has a special name – the **base**

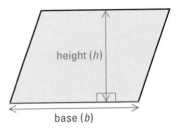

height (h)

base (b)

> ### Key Fact
> Area of a parallelogram = base × height

Example Find the area of this parallelogram.

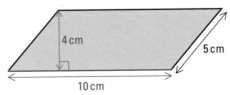

4 cm

5 cm

10 cm

Working The base is 10 cm. The height is 4 cm.
Area = base × height
= 10 × 4
= 40 cm²

Answer 40 cm²

You can measure the height at different places. It's always the same, even *outside* the parallelogram. You always measure it straight up from the base, at right angles.

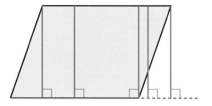

> ### Word Check
> **parallelogram** a four-sided shape with two pairs of parallel sides
> **base** the 'bottom' of a shape; called its length
> **(perpendicular) height** the distance going up at 90° from the base of a parallelogram to the opposite side

Try It Out

Find the areas of these parallelograms.

1
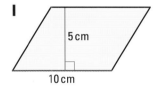
5 cm
10 cm

2
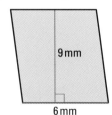
9 mm
6 mm

3
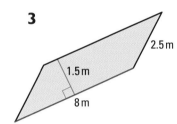
2.5 m
1.5 m
8 m

4
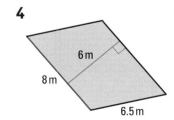
6 m
8 m
6.5 m

5
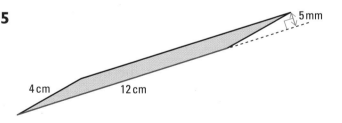
5 mm
4 cm
12 cm

Learn More About It

Triangles have bases and heights too. On these pictures, the base is shown in blue. The height is shown in red.

All these triangles have the same area because they all have the same length of base and are of equal height.

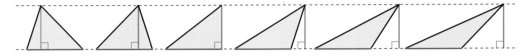

> # Key Fact
> Area of a triangle = base × height ÷ 2

Example Find the area of this triangle.

Working The base is 8 cm.
The height is 6 cm.
A = base × height ÷ 2
  = 8 × 6 ÷ 2
  = 48 ÷ 2
  = 24 cm²

Answer 24 cm²

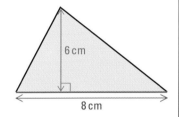

Word Check

(perpendicular) height the distance from the top corner or **apex** of a triangle to the base, meeting it at 90°

Try It Out

A Find the areas of these triangles.

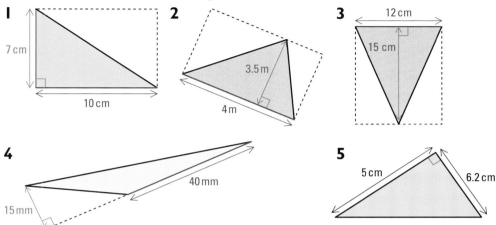

1 7 cm, 10 cm

2 3.5 m, 4 m

3 12 cm, 15 cm

4 40 mm, 15 mm

5 5 cm, 6.2 cm

Practice

A4 squared paper or dotted paper, long side horizontal

Draw coordinate axes on your paper.

→ x-axis: *Scale*: 1 cm = 1 unit. *Range*: 0→15.

↑ y-axis: *Scale*: 1 cm = 1 unit. *Range*: 0→15.

For each question below:

(a) plot the coordinates

(b) join the points in order, with straight lines, to make the shape

(c) measure and label the base and height

(d) work out the area of the shape.

1 $(0, 0) \rightarrow (6, 0) \rightarrow (8, 4) \rightarrow (2, 4) \rightarrow (0, 0)$

2 $(9, 0) \rightarrow (15, 0) \rightarrow (14, 3) \rightarrow (8, 3) \rightarrow (9, 0)$

3 $(6, 5) \rightarrow (15, 5) \rightarrow (9, 7) \rightarrow (0, 7) \rightarrow (6, 5)$

4 $(1, 8) \rightarrow (3, 8) \rightarrow (3, 15) \rightarrow (1, 8)$

5 $(4, 13) \rightarrow (14, 13) \rightarrow (4, 15) \rightarrow (4, 13)$

6 $(4, 8) \rightarrow (11, 8) \rightarrow (5, 12) \rightarrow (4, 8)$

7 $(12, 7) \rightarrow (15, 7) \rightarrow (14, 12) \rightarrow (12, 7)$

8 $(10, 10) \rightarrow (12, 10) \rightarrow (11, 12) \rightarrow (10, 10)$

I This is a map of a farm.
The fields are labelled
(a) to **(e)**.
Work out the area of
each field.

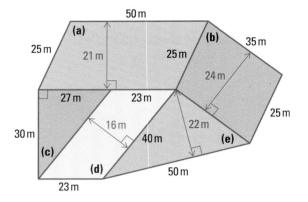

*Hint: use your fingers or
a piece of paper to cover
up parts of the diagram
you're not using.*

2 What is the area of the whole farm?

*Hint: add up all your
answers from question 1.*

Further Practice

Protractor

P For each question below:
(a) draw the triangle using the
information given
(b) draw the perpendicular height
and measure it to the nearest
0.1 cm
(c) work out the area of the triangle.

height
(draw
this last)

angle P
(draw this
second)

base
(draw this first)

angle Q
(draw this
third)

	Base (cm)	Angle P	Angle Q
1	10	40°	40°
2	6	30°	80°
3	12	60°	20°
4	8	70°	70°
5	5	30°	120°

Finished Early?
➡ Go to page 359

20 Volume and Capacity

In this chapter you will learn about ...
1 volumes of cuboids
2 capacity

1 Volumes of Cuboids

Learn About It

Volume is the amount of space taken up by a 3D object. Volume is measured in **cubic** units such as cubic metres (m^3).

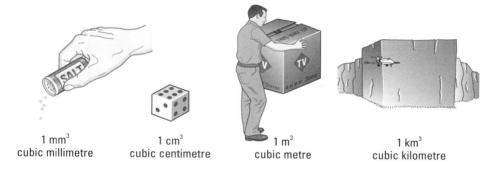

1 mm^3	1 cm^3	1 m^3	1 km^3
cubic millimetre	cubic centimetre	cubic metre	cubic kilometre

This cuboid is made from 1 cm cubes.
It is 5 cm long, 4 cm wide and 3 cm high.

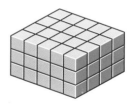

There are 3 layers of cubes.

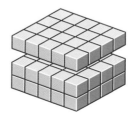

Each layer is made of 4 rows of 5 cubes each. That's $4 \times 5 = 20$ cubes.

So the whole cuboid uses $3 \times 20 = 60$ cubes.

The volume is **60 cm³**.

You don't need to count the layers of cubes. You just use the measurements of the cuboid.

The length is 5 cm.

The width is 4 cm.

The height is 3 cm.

$5 \times 4 \times 3 = 60$ cm³

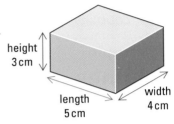

Key Fact

Volume of a cuboid
= length × width × height

Word Check

cuboid a solid box shape – all its faces are squares or rectangles

volume the amount of space a 3D object takes up

Try It Out

A Work out the volume of each cuboid.

1

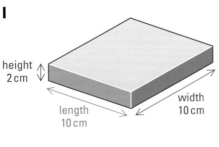

2

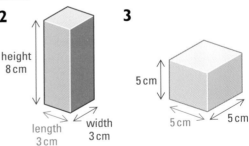

3

4

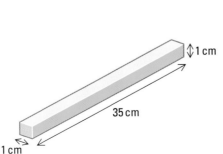

5

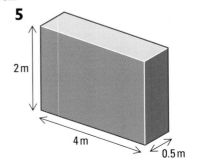

Learn More About It

Sometimes, the measurements of a
cuboid are given in different units.

When finding volume, you must
have all the measurements in the
same unit.

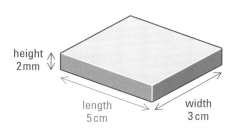

Example

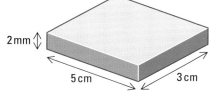

Working   Change 2 mm to 0.2 cm.

Volume = length × width × height
= 5 × 3 × 0.2 = 3 cm³.

or   Change 5 cm to 50 mm.

Change 3 cm to 30 mm.

Volume = length × width × height
= 50 × 30 × 2 = 3000 mm³.

Answer   3 cm³ or 3000 mm³

3000 mm³ is the same as 3 cm³.
1000 mm³ = 1 cm³

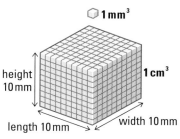

There are 100 cm in 1 m.
So there are 100 × 100 × 100 cm³ in 1 m³.
That's 1 000 000 cm³!

volume = length × width × height
= 10 × 10 × 10
= **1000 mm³**

Key Fact

1000 mm³ = 1 cm³
1 000 000 cm³ = 1 m³

Try It Out

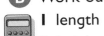

B Work out the volume of each cuboid.

1 length 1.5 cm, width 4.8 mm, height 8.5 mm
2 height 24 cm, width 13 cm, length 2.6 m
3 12 m by 14 m by 2.5 cm
4 2 mm by 3 mm by 20 cm
5 length 4.2 m, width 2.5 m, height 1.3 cm

Practice

C Here are some objects. Work out the volume of each one.

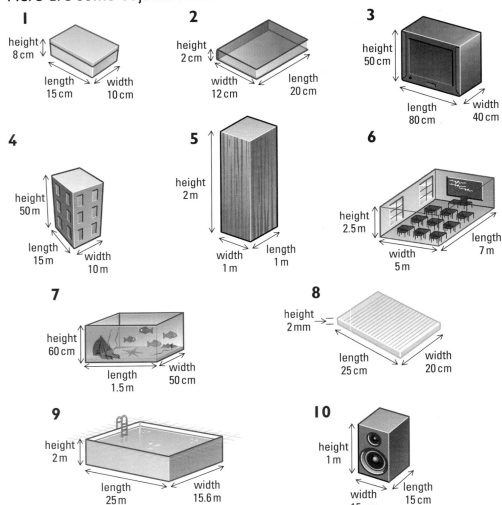

1
height 8 cm
length 15 cm
width 10 cm

2
height 2 cm
width 12 cm
length 20 cm

3
height 50 cm
length 80 cm
width 40 cm

4
height 50 m
length 15 m
width 10 m

5
height 2 m
width 1 m
length 1 m

6
height 2.5 m
width 5 m
length 7 m

7
height 60 cm
length 1.5 m
width 50 cm

8
height 2 mm
length 25 cm
width 20 cm

9
height 2 m
length 25 m
width 15.6 m

10
height 1 m
width 15 cm
length 15 cm

D **1** This is a picture of a shelf unit.
There are 3 shelves, 6 battens
and 2 end cheeks. All the wood
used was 2 cm thick.
(a) Work out the volume of wood
used for each of the parts.
(b) Work out the volume of wood
in the whole shelf unit.

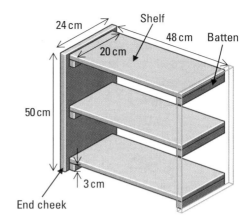

Shelf
24 cm
48 cm   Batten
20 cm
50 cm
3 cm
End cheek

2 Tins of Dino Beans come in 3 sizes.

Small
6.5 cm
5 cm
DINO BEANS   Volume = 166 cm³

Regular
7.5 cm
10 cm
DINO BEANS   Volume = 442 cm³

Jumbo   12 cm
12 cm
DINO BEANS   Volume = 1357 cm³

The tins are packed into boxes, like this.

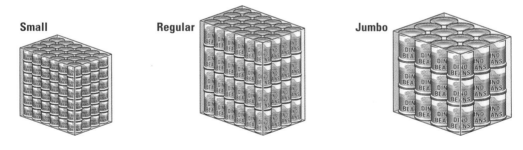

Small   Regular   Jumbo

(a) **(i)** How many **small** size tins fit into a box?
(ii) Work out the length, width and height of the box.
(iii) Work out the volume of the box.
(iv) What volume inside the box is taken up by the tins?
(v) What volume of air is inside the box?
(b) Repeat part (a) for the Regular size tins.
(c) Repeat part (a) for the Jumbo size tins.

Finished Early?
➡ Go to page 360

Further Practice

E Work out the volume of each cuboid.
Show your working.

	Length	Width	Height	Volume
1	5 cm	3 cm	8 cm	
2	10 m	2 m	2 m	
3	6 cm	4 cm	14 cm	
4	5 mm	5 mm	30 mm	
5	3 m	50 cm	1 m	
6	12 cm	12 cm	2 mm	
7	8 m	2.5 m	2.5 m	
8	4.4 km	3 km	2.1 km	

Finished Early?
➡ Go to page 360

❷ Capacity

Remember?

Volume of liquids is called **capacity**.
Capacity is measured in special units: **litres** (l), **centilitres** (cl) and **millilitres** (ml).

Key Fact

100 cl = 1 l
1000 ml = 1 l
10 ml = 1 cl

Word Check
....
capacity the volume of
  a liquid, or a container
  for liquid

Try It Out

F Copy and complete the table. The three quantities in each row should be equal.

	Millilitres	Centilitres	Litres
1	3000		
2			2
3		45	
4			12.55
5	25		
6			80

Learn About It

It's important to be able to estimate:
- an amount of liquid
- the capacity of a container.

You can use a few everyday things to compare.

teaspoon	coffee mug	cola bottle	motor oil bottle	bucket	bath
5 ml	250 ml	1 litre	5 litres	15 litres	300 litres

When you do capacity calculations, use a sensible size of unit for the answer.

Round the answer if you have to.

Example Jackie wants to share equally among herself and
6 friends a 1-litre bottle of cola.
How much will they each get to drink?

Working There are 7 people who want a drink.
1 l ÷ 7 = 0.142 857 14 ... l each.
= 142.857 14 ... ml each *(Change to a more
useful unit.)*

Answer 143 ml, to the nearest millilitre
(Round your answer sensibly.)

Try It Out

G 1 A can contains 330 ml of cola.
Samantha buys a 12-pack of cans at the supermarket.
How much cola is there altogether, in litres?

2 This ice-cube tray needs 300 ml of
water to fill it. About how much
water is there in each ice-cube?

3 Tim is making punch for a party.
He uses two 70-cl bottles of grape juice, 1.5 litres
of lemonade and 400 ml of fruit cordial.
(a) How much punch does this make?
(b) The glasses he uses to serve the punch hold 200 ml each.
How many glasses can he serve? Is there any left over?

Tim empties into his punch $2\frac{1}{2}$ trays of ice-cubes like those in
question 2.
(c) How much extra volume do they add?
(d) What is the total volume of the punch now?

Practice

H Calculate these amounts.
1 300 ml + 60 cl   **2** 1 l – 15 ml   **3** 3 l + 600 ml
4 80 cl – 150 ml   **5** 100 ml + 50 cl   **6** 10 l – 375 cl

I 1 Henry ran the tea stall at the school fête. He charged 30p per cup.
(a) He took £37.50 in cash. How many cups did he sell?
(b) A teacup holds 200 ml. How much water did he use?
(c) The kettle held 1.7 l. How many times did he have to fill it?

2 A carton of tropical fruit juice holds 220 ml.
(a) A bottle of tropical fruit juice holds the same as 7 cartons.
What is the capacity of the bottle?
(b) 4% of tropical fruit juice is mango juice. How much mango
juice is there in ...
(i) a carton?
(ii) a bottle?

3 Kajal's shampoo comes in 200-ml bottles. Kajal washes her hair 4 times a week. She has to buy a new bottle of shampoo every 4 weeks.

(a) How many times can she wash her hair with one bottle?

(b) How much shampoo does she use each time she washes her hair?

(c) One day, Kajal bought an extra large bottle. This lasted her 10 weeks. How much was in the bottle?

(d) If Kajal grew her hair longer she would have to use more shampoo. If she used 25 ml each time, how many washes would she get from a large bottle?

(e) How often would she have to buy shampoo if she grew her hair?

> **Finished Early?**
> ➡ Go to page 360

Further Practice

1 Calculate these amounts.

(a) 200 ml + 50 cl

(b) 1 l − 25 ml

(c) 2 l + 500 ml

(d) 70 cl − 125 ml

(e) 4 l − 250 cl

(f) 100 ml + 200 cl

(g) 2 l − 375 ml

2 Work out the amount of liquid in each multi-pack.

	Liquid	Amount in 1 bottle or carton	Number per pack	Total amount (litres)
(a)	Orange juice	200 ml	12	
(b)	Milk	500 ml	8	
(c)	Wine	70 cl	12	
(d)	Fizzy drink	330 ml	6	
(e)	Cider	440 ml	4	
(f)	Lemonade	1.5 l	6	

> **Finished Early?**
> ➡ Go to page 360

Unit 11 *Mensuration*

Summary of Chapters 19 and 20

Perimeter

- The **perimeter** of a shape is the distance all the way round the outside. The perimeter of a shape is the length of all its sides added together.
- Special marks show that the sides of a shape are the same length.

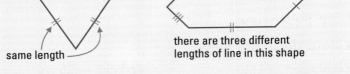

same length

same length

there are three different
lengths of line in this shape

  If all the sides are the same length, the perimeter is the length of a side multiplied by the number of sides.
- Sometimes you need to **subtract** lengths to work out the length of unknown sides first.
- You can use perimeters to work out unknown lengths.

Area

- **Area** is the amount of **surface** a shape has.
  Area is measured in square units such as square centimetres (cm^2).
  There are $10 \times 10 = 100$ mm^2 in 1 cm^2.
  There are $100 \times 100 = 10\,000$ cm^2 in 1 m^2.

  Rectangles
  - Area of a rectangle = length $\times$ width
  - Sometimes the length and width of a rectangle are given in different units. You can't multiply them straight away to find the area. You have to convert one so the units match.
  - If you know the area of a rectangle and the length of one side, you can work out the length of the other side.
    Divide the area by the length of the side you know.

Parallelograms

- Area of a parallelogram
  = base × height
- You can find unknown lengths in
  a parallelogram by dividing area
  by base or height, just like in a
  rectangle.

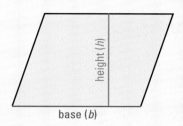

Triangles

- In a triangle, the area is base × height ÷ 2.
  The other sides of the triangle are **not** part of the working.
- **Compound shapes** are made by putting simple shapes
  together or taking one shape out of another.

Volume

- **Volume** is the amount of space a 3D object takes up.
  You measure volume in **cubic** units such as mm^3, cm^3, m^3 or
  km^3.
  $$1000\ mm^3 = 1\ cm^3 \qquad 1\ 000\ 000\ cm^3 = 1\ m^3$$
  $$1\ 000\ 000\ 000\ mm^3 = 1\ m^3$$
- Volume of a cuboid = length × width × height

Capacity

- The volume of liquids is called **capacity**.
- Capacity is measured in special units such as litres (l),
  centilitres (cl) and millilitres (ml).
  $$100\ cl = 1\ l \qquad 1000\ ml = 1\ l \qquad 10\ ml = 1\ cl$$

Brush Up Your Number 12

T ● Money

Learn About It

Money can be in pounds (£) or pence (p), £1 = 100p.

To change pounds to pence, multiply by 100, so £3.50 = 350p.

To change pence to pounds, divide by 100, so 235p = £2.35.

To add or subtract money, all amounts must be in either pounds or pence.

A customer pays for items worth £2.35, 70p and £1.20 with £5.

Joe does these calculations to work out the change.

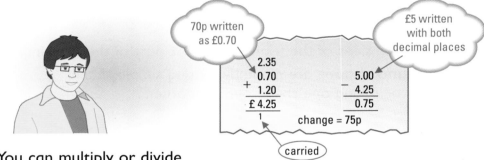

70p written as £0.70

£5 written with both decimal places

$$\begin{array}{r} 2.35 \\ 0.70 \\ + \; 1.20 \\ \hline £\,4.25 \\ {}_{1} \end{array}$$

$$\begin{array}{r} 5.00 \\ - \; 4.25 \\ \hline 0.75 \end{array}$$

change = 75p

carried

You can multiply or divide.

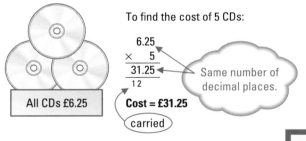

All CDs £6.25

To find the cost of 5 CDs:

$$\begin{array}{r} 6.25 \\ \times \quad 5 \\ \hline 31.25 \\ {}_{1\,2} \end{array}$$

Same number of decimal places.

Cost = £31.25

carried

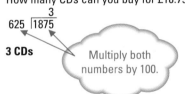

How many CDs can you buy for £18.75?

$$625\,\overline{)1875}\;^{3}$$

3 CDs

Multiply both numbers by 100.

Always put the units in your answer.

Try It Out

A Calculate the following.

1 £1.25 + £2.50   2 £5.00 − £3.75
3 £6.50 × 4   4 180p ÷ 6
5 70p + £3.20   6 £8.50 − 95p
7 £7.20 ÷ 12   8 35p × 9

> ## Key Fact
> To change pounds to pence, multiply by 100.
> To change pence to pounds, divide by 100.
> To add or subtract money, all amounts must be in the same unit.

Practice

B For each question below, work out ...

(a) the total cost of the purchases

(b) the change the customer receives.

Daily Best
newspaper 70p

Jazz Sounds
magazine £1.50

Daily Informer
newspaper 40p

New Music
magazine £2.00

Daily Knowledge
newspaper 45p

Computers Now
magazine £1.75

1 the *Daily Best* and *New Music*, paid for with £5

2 *New Music* and *Computers Now*, paid for with £4

3 *New Music* and *Jazz Sounds*, paid for with £5

4 the *Daily Best* and the *Daily Knowledge*, paid for with £2

5 *New Music*, *Jazz Sounds* and *Computers Now*, paid for with £10

6 the *Daily Informer* and *Computers Now*, paid for with £20

7 the *Daily Best* and *Computers Now*, paid for with £2.50

8 *New Music* and the *Daily Knowledge*, paid for with £2.60

9 the *Daily Best*, the *Daily Knowledge* and the *Daily Informer*, paid for with £5

10 all six newspapers and magazines, paid for with £10.

C 1 One packet of sweets costs 70p.

    (a) How much do 12 cost?

    (b) How many can you buy for £3.50?

2 One computer game costs £12.50.

    (a) How much do 10 cost?

    (b) How many can you buy for £50?

3 One roll of tape costs 60p.

    (a) How much would 5 cost?

    (b) How many can you buy for £7.20?

Finished Early?
➡ Go to page 361

21 Averages

In this chapter you will learn about ...
1 mode and median
2 mean and range
3 comparing sets of data

P 1 Mode and Median

Remember?

Sets of data have different kinds of average. **Mode** and **median** are two of them.

The Mode

Seven friends looked in their pockets to see how many £1 coins they had. This is what they found.

Angharad	Ben	Chloë	Davinder	Eve	Frank	Gary
£4	£3	£2	£2	£4	£2	£3

This table shows how the data looks when it is better organised.

The amount that appears most often is **£2**. More people had £2 than any other amount. This is the **mode** of the data.

Amount	Frequency
£2	3
£3	2
£4	2

The Median

Write the amounts of money in order.

£2, £2, £2, £3, £3, £4, £4

The amount in the middle of the list is the **median**.

Word Check

data information or facts
frequency how many times something occurs
mode the data item that appears most often
median the value in the middle data item, when written in order

Try It Out

A **I** Write down the mode of each set of numbers.
 (a) 4, 6, 5, 4, 8, 6, 4
 (b) 200, 100, 200
 (c) 26, 22, 23, 27, 27
 (d) 8.5, 8.7, 9, 8.6, 8.7, 9.1, 9, 8.7, 8.5
 (e) 1, 100, 1, 1, 1, 100, 100, 1, 100, 1, 1, 1, 100, 100, 100

2 Write each set of numbers from question 1 in order, from smallest to largest. Circle the median.

Learn About It

This is a table of the number of pets owned by the pupils in class 8P.

There is a 'tie' for the mode.
1 and 2 have the same frequency. They are *both* modes.
It is possible to have more than one mode.

Number of pets	Frequency
0	5
1	8
2	8
3	4
4	3

Look at this set of numbers:
100, 400, 300, 500, 200.

There is just one of each number. So they all have the same frequency. There *isn't* a mode.

The pupils in 8P weighed themselves.
These are their masses in kilograms.

45	49	33	36	44	52	35	57	39
49	38	44	55	32	48	42	39	51
49	49	46	32	39	50	45	44	34

It's hard to see a pattern. The data needs to be better organised by being put into groups. These groups are sometimes called **classes** or **class intervals**. This doesn't have anything to do with the class you're in at school.

The classes must not overlap.

> **Word Check**
> **class** grouped data items
> **modal class** the class with the highest frequency

1 Copy and complete this **tally** table.

Mass (kg)	Tally	Frequency
31–35		
36–40		
41–45		
46–50		
51–55		
56–60		

2 The class with the highest frequency is called the **modal class**.
It's the **mode** of data that has been put into groups.
Copy and complete this statement about the masses of the pupils in 8P. 'The modal class is ___–___ kg.'

Try It Out

B Find the mode of each set of numbers below. You don't need to put the numbers into groups.

1

| 5 | 7 | 5 | 4 | 4 | 6 | 5 | 4 |

2

| 13 | 16 | 14 | 14 | 10 | 12 | 13 | 10 | 15 | 16 |

3	10	6	10	8	6	6	10

4	27	29	22	26	28
	26	25	28	29	20
	27	24	21	26	23

5	28	23	22	25	21	24	30	29

1 When the pupils in 8P were still in Year 7, they measured themselves. These were their heights, in centimetres.

170	144	162	139	150	161	136
149	161	136	162	163	154	148
164	154	150	163	167	166	159
166	164	158	171	144	160	140

(a) Copy and complete the tally table, putting the data into groups.

(b) What is the modal class?

Height (cm)	Tally	Frequency
136–140		
141–145		
146–150		
151–155		
156–160		
161–165		
166–170		
171–175		

2 The pupils in 8P measured themselves again this year. Everybody has grown 3 cm.

(a) Write down the new height list.

(b) Draw a new tally table.

(c) Has the modal class changed?

Learn More About It

Sometimes you need to do a simple calculation to find the median. Look at these numbers. They are already written in order.

   5   7   8   9

There isn't a middle number.

The middle position is in between 7 and 8 so you have to use the number **halfway** between.

   5   7   8   9
             ↑
            7.5

The median is 7.5.

Sometimes, the two middle numbers are the same. This makes it even easier.

   6   10   13   13   15   19

The median is 13!

Here is 8P's pet data again.

Number of pets	Frequency
0	5
1	8
2	8
3	4
4	3

To find the median, write out a list in order.

0 0 0 0 0 1 1 1 1 1 1 1 1 ②② 2 2 2 2 2 2 3 3 3 3 4 4 4

14 numbers on the left   median   14 numbers on the right

The median is 2 pets.

Word Check

median the value of the middle item when data is written in order

Try It Out

D Find the median of each set of numbers.

1 | 38 | 33 | 32 | 35 | 31 | 34 | 40 | 29 |

2 | 11 | 14 | 12 | 12 | 18 | 10 | 11 | 8 | 13 | 14 |

3 | 6 | 8 | 6 | 5 | 5 | 7 | 6 | 5 |

4

84	94	88	99	88
96	98	98	92	99
90	99	85	89	83
88	98	84	84	92

E **1** Charlie works at a chocolate factory. His job is to check that the boxes contain the right number of sweets. Today he is checking boxes of Mint Stix. He counts the Mint Stix in 50 boxes.

Number per box	37	38	39	40	41
Frequency	2	10	18	12	8

(a) Which position in the list is the median?

(b) Find the median number per box.

(c) There are supposed to be 40 in a box. Should Charlie say there are the right number in each box, too many or too few?

2 The pupils in 8R all wrote their names 10 times, as quickly as possible. They recorded how long it took. These are the results, in seconds.

Time (seconds)	40	45	50	55	60
Frequency	2	4	8	8	6

(a) Write out the list of times in full.

(b) Find the median time for the class.

Practice

(F) **1** Bimla and Toby compared their maths tests through the year. This is what they scored.

Test	1	2	3	4	5	6	7	8	9
Bimla	10	19	20	11	10	17	10	18	15
Toby	9	11	12	8	13	10	12	12	11

(a) Calculate the mode for each person.

(b) Calculate the median for each person.

(c) Both Bimla and Toby said, 'I did better than you.' Who was right, and why?

2 Shelley works for the traffic police. She recorded the speeds of 40 vehicles that passed her. These are the results, in miles per hour (mph).

60	62	73	72	95	35	75	68	80	77
71	78	53	68	72	72	62	73	82	57
75	76	70	29	73	44	71	63	38	72
75	46	80	65	58	70	54	47	68	80

(a) Copy and complete this table using the data above.

(b) What is the modal class?

(c) What kind of road do you think this was?

(d) Do you think the drivers of the cars could see Shelley?

Speed (mph)	Tally	Frequency
0–20		
21–30		
31–40		
41–50		
51–60		
61–70		
71–80		
81–100		

3 Stella has 10 hens. One month, she wrote down how many eggs they laid each day. These are her results.

5	9	10	10	3	9	7	5	8	8
6	9	8	2	8	8	3	5	4	10
9	3	9	10	8	10	2	10	8	8

(a) Draw a tally table of the number of eggs laid.
(b) What was the modal number of eggs?
(c) How many days were in this month?
(d) Write out the list in order.
(e) Find the median number of eggs.

Finished Early?
➡ Go to page 362

Further Practice

1 Find the mode and median of each set of numbers.

(a)

| 5 | 8 | 7 | 5 | 4 |
| 5 | 3 | 7 | 2 | 7 |

(b)

| 0 | 2 | 2 | 0 |
| 1 | 3 | 3 | 1 |

(c)

| 24 | 32 | 25 | 24 | 27 | 15 |
| 20 | 30 | 36 | 50 | 12 | 50 |

(d)

54	53	55	45	60	21
32	50	54	60	35	68
44	68	66	33	32	54
35	60	20	45	71	40

2 The pupils in 8S did a survey to find out how many hours of TV they watched each night. The pictogram shows the results.

TV survey by 8S	
1 hour	▢
2 hours	▢ ▢ ▢
3 hours	▢ ▢ ▢ ▢ ▢ ▢
4 hours	▢ ▢ ▢ ▢ ▢
5 hours	▢

KEY: ▢ stands for 2 pupils

(a) Draw a frequency table for this data.

(b) What is the modal number of hours?

(c) Write the list of hours in order.

(d) What is the median number of hours?

3 The pupils in 8P were asked to take off their watches and to stand up. They had to sit down when they thought a minute had passed. These are the numbers of seconds they waited before sitting down.

54	35	58	43	55	71	51
41	48	50	56	53	36	56
63	40	46	59	26	44	49
54	50	60	38	43	48	71

(a) Copy and complete the tally table.

Time (seconds)	Tally	Frequency
21–30		
31–40		
41–50		
51–60		
61–70		
71–80		

(b) What is the modal class?

Finished Early?
➯ Go to page 362

NUMBER SKILLS Add HTU

❷ Mean and Range

Remember?

The Mean

- When people say 'average', they are usually talking about the **mean**.
- To calculate the mean of a set of data:
  - work out the total of all the data values
  - divide this by the number of data items.

Example Find the mean of these numbers.

5	6	4	2	4	5	3	8	2	3

Working The total is 42. There are 10 numbers.
$42 \div 10 = 4.2$

Answer 4.2

- The mean doesn't have to be one of the numbers in the list.

The Range

- The range of a set of numbers tells you how 'spread out' they are.
It is the difference between the largest and smallest numbers.

Example Find the range of these numbers.

5	6	4	2	4	5	3	8	2	3

Working Largest = 8, smallest = 2.
$8 - 2 = 6$

Answer 6

Try It Out

H Find the mean and range of each set of numbers.

1

5	5	3	2	4	4	5	4

2

13	16	14	14	10	12	13	10	15	16

3

28	23	22	25	21	24	32	29

4

27	29	22	26	28
26	25	28	29	20
27	24	21	26	23

5

103	113	107	113	107
115	117	117	111	118
109	118	104	108	102
107	117	103	103	111

6

10	6	10	5	5	6	10

Learn About It

When you have data in a frequency table, you need to do some extra calculations to work out the **mean**.

This table shows the number of paper clips in 10 boxes.

Number of paper clips in a box	Number of boxes	Number of paper clips
18	1	18 × 1 = 18
19	5	19 × 5 = 95
20	3	20 × 3 = 60
22	1	22 × 1 = 22
Total	10	195

The mean number of paper clips in a box is:

total number of paper clips ÷ number of boxes = 195 ÷ 10 = 19.5.

Word Check

mean the average data value

range the 'spread' of the data; the difference between the smallest and largest data values

Try It Out

1 At Weston Farm they keep ducks. Some of the ducks lay an egg every day, but most don't. One week, the farmer kept a record. Here are the results.

Eggs laid	Number of ducks	Number of eggs
0	1	
1	0	
2	1	
3	4	
4	7	
5	8	
6	7	
7	8	
Total		

(a) How many ducks are there altogether?

(b) Copy the table. Fill in the **Number of eggs** column.

(c) How many eggs did the ducks lay altogether?

(d) What is the mean number of eggs a duck lays in a week?

2 The pupils in 8M did a survey. They wanted to find out how many brothers and sisters everyone had.

(a) Copy and complete the table.

(b) What is the mean number of brothers and sisters in 8M?

Number of brothers and sisters	Number of pupils	Total number of brothers and sisters
0	7	
1	13	
2	6	
3	0	
4	1	
5	0	
6	1	
Total		

3 Luxibrite test a sample of their light bulbs. They record how long each one lasts, to the nearest 50 hours.

Lifetime of bulb (hours)	Number of bulbs	Number of hours
0	2	
50	9	
100	15	
150	24	
200	89	
250	49	
300	12	
Total		

(a) Copy and complete the table.

(b) What is the mean lifetime of a bulb?

Practice

J **1** Safebury's food store carried out a survey of their customers. They asked people whether they shopped for food every week or every month.

(a) The weekly shoppers were asked how much they spent on food each week, to the nearest £10. These are the results.

Amount per week (£)	10	20	30	40	50	60	70	80	90	100
Number of customers	2	5	12	35	20	8	3	2	0	0

Draw a frequency table. Calculate the mean amount spent per week.

(b) The monthly shoppers were asked how much they spent on food each month, to the nearest £20. These are the results.

Amount per month (£)	20	40	60	80	100	120	140	160	180	200
Number of customers	0	1	2	5	5	10	27	29	14	5

Draw a frequency table. Calculate the mean amount spent per month.

(c) Safebury's want to know who spends more on average, weekly or monthly shoppers.

Work out the mean spending in a year for each group. Who spends the most?

> *Hint: multiply weekly amounts by 52. Multiply monthly amounts by 12.*

2 Mike ran a game at his village fête. People threw darts at this special dartboard.

This bar chart shows what people won.

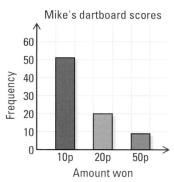

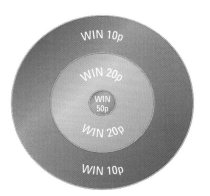

(a) Draw and complete a frequency table for the data.

(b) Calculate the mean amount won.

3 A sample of names from the telephone directory were checked. This table records how long the surnames were.

Letters in surname	3	4	5	6	7	8	9	10	11
Frequency	5	30	101	131	108	64	34	22	5

(a) What is the mean length of the surnames?

(b) What is the modal length?

(c) What is the median length?

> **Finished Early?**
> ➡ Go to page 363

Further Practice

K **1** This table shows the ages of the members of a youth club.

(a) Copy and complete the table.

(b) What is the mean age of the members?

Age	Number of members	Number of years
11	20	
12	14	
13	14	
14	12	
15	9	
16	1	
Total		

2 This table shows the results of a survey of the arrival times of a number of trains on the PasTran network.

Minutes late	Number of trains	Number of minutes
0	14	
1	13	
2	8	
3	4	
4	6	
5	10	
10	5	
Total		

(a) Copy and complete the table.

(b) What is the mean number of minutes by which PasTran trains are late?

> **Finished Early?**
> ➡ Go to page 363

❸ Comparing Sets of Data

Learn About It

These are the last 20 throws made by a shot putter, in metres.

A. Putter				
14	15	15	14	13
17	13	15	17	12
12	17	18	14	14
11	15	15	13	16

These are the last 20 throws made by another athlete.

B. Chucker									
17	20	15	15	18	13	15	12	22	11
14	20	20	15	16	9	19	20	13	16

The table below is called a **comparison table**. It lets you **compare** the results for the two athletes.

	Mean (m)	Best (m)	Worst (m)	Range (m)
A. Putter	14.5	18	11	7
B. Chucker	16	22	9	13

You can see that Chucker's mean is better than Putter's. However, Chucker is not as **consistent** as Putter. That means that the length of his throws varies a lot more. The **range** is bigger. Chucker's best throw is longer than Putter's, but Chucker's worst throw is shorter.

If you were choosing one of the shot putters to be in a team, you'd probably choose Putter, who is more consistent. Just having the best throw doesn't make you the best choice.

Word Check

comparison table a table comparing two sets of data

consistent staying about the same, reliable

Try It Out

 L These are the last 20 times by a 400-metre runner, in seconds.

C. Runner	53.6	58.2	56.2	53.8	56.9	56.3	55.8	55.1	53.1	53.1
	54.9	53.5	54.2	54.5	54.6	56.3	54.1	55.1	55.7	55.0

These are the last 20 times by another runner.

D. Asher	55.8	55.6	57.2	56.8	56.2	56.6	57.2	56.0	56.6	56.8
	57.0	56.2	56.4	55.6	55.6	56.4	55.2	56.4	57.2	57.2

1 Copy and complete this comparison table. Write your working underneath.

	Mean	Fastest	Slowest	Range
C. Runner				
D. Asher				

2 (a) Who has the fastest time?

(b) Whose mean time is the fastest?

(c) Who has the slowest time?

(d) Who is the more consistent runner?

Practice

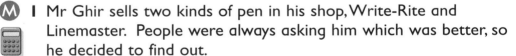 **M 1** Mr Ghir sells two kinds of pen in his shop, Write-Rite and Linemaster. People were always asking him which was better, so he decided to find out.

He tested 10 of each type of pen. He drew a long line with each pen until it ran out. This table shows the lengths of the lines in metres.

Write-Rite (m)	1220	1170	1200	1180	1230
	1180	1230	1150	1230	1210
Linemaster (m)	1200	1220	1190	1220	1140
	1300	1290	1370	1430	1140

(a) Copy and complete this comparison table. Write your working underneath.

	Mean	Longest	Shortest	Range
Write-Rite (m)				
Linemaster (m)				

(b) Which type of pen lasted longer, on average?

(c) Which type of pen was more consistent?

(d) Should Mr Ghir recommend Write-Rite or Linemaster pens to his customers? Give your reasons.

2 Briggs Batteries tested two of their brands of batteries, Powerplus and Xtralife, to see which type lasted longer. These pictograms show the results.

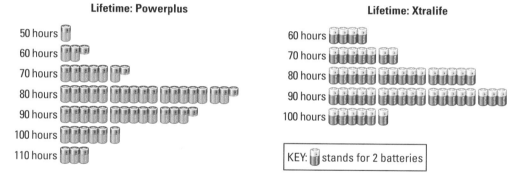

Lifetime: Powerplus

Lifetime: Xtralife

KEY: stands for 2 batteries

(a) Draw a frequency table for Powerplus batteries. Remember to include a column for multiplying.

(b) Calculate the mean lifetime of a Powerplus battery.

(c) Draw a frequency table for Xtralife batteries.

(d) Calculate the mean lifetime of an Xtralife battery.

(e) Draw a comparison table for the two types of battery.

(f) Which do you think are the best batteries, and why?

3 David uses two taxi firms
regularly, Luxicabs and
Zoom Taxis.

He decides to try to find out which is the best firm. He records
how many minutes it takes the taxi to come when he rings.

Zoom Taxis	5	16	18	16	22	5	4	10	16	8
Luxicabs	14	17	12	12	16	16	15	13	15	13
	13	17	17	16	18	16				

(a) Work out the mean waiting time for Zoom Taxis.

(b) Work out the mean waiting time for Luxicabs.

(c) Draw a comparison table.

(d) For each of the following situations, write down which taxi
firm David should use. Give reasons for your answers.
If there is no reason to choose one or the other, say so.
 (i) David is late and needs to get to the station quickly.
 (ii) He is going out for the evening and has plenty of time.
 (iii) He is booking a taxi in advance to take him to
  an interview.

> **Finished Early?**
> ➡ Go to page 364

Further Practice

1 SADA supermarkets check their fruit.
Mrs Checkers is in charge.
One month, Mrs Checkers thinks that
the yellow grapefruit are too small. They
are supposed to be the same weight as
the pink grapefruit.
She picks one of each off the shelves and
weighs them. They are both 269 g.
She is still not happy, so she weighs 20
of each.

These are the weights in grams.

Pink		269	298	268	273	280	278	263	280	299	294
grapefruit		279	283	261	263	281	296	268	275	264	282
Yellow		269	199	289	240	194	203	239	193	224	210
grapefruit		279	276	217	288	234	266	220	240	239	273

(a) Work out the mean weight of the pink grapefruit.

(b) Work out the mean weight of the yellow grapefruit.

(c) Copy and complete this comparison table.

	Mean	Heaviest	Lightest	Range
Pink				
Yellow				

(d) Is Mrs Checkers right in thinking that the yellow grapefruit
are too small?
What should she write in her report about the grapefruit?

2 Three friends are comparing their exam results.

	Javed	Wendy	Simone
Maths	79%	69%	81%
English	77%	36%	74%
Science	72%	61%	71%
French	77%	42%	94%
German	75%	34%	81%
Technology	72%	61%	62%
Art	73%	40%	79%
Music	88%	48%	55%
Drama	67%	35%	80%
Lifeskills	70%	58%	73%

(a) Calculate the mean mark for each person.

(b) Copy and complete this comparison table.

	Mean	Highest mark	Lowest mark	Range
Javed				
Wendy				
Simone				

(c) Who got the lowest marks?

(d) Who was the most consistent?

(e) Who got better marks, Javed or Simone? How do you know?

> **Finished Early?**
> ➡ Go to page 364

Unit 12 *Processing Data*

Summary of Chapter 21

- **Data** is facts or **information. Data items** are single pieces of data, like someone's shoe size or the population of a country.

  The **frequency** of a data item is the number of times it occurs in a list.

  Sometimes you need to put the data into groups called **classes** or **class intervals**. The classes must not overlap.

The mode

- The **mode** is the data item that occurs most often. It has the highest frequency.

  The **modal class** is the class with the highest frequency, for data that has been put into groups.

- You can have more than one mode or modal class.

The median

- Write the data items in order. The value of the data item in the middle of the ordered list is the **median**.

  If you have an even number of data items, there isn't a middle one. The median is **halfway** between the two middle data items.

The mean

- To calculate the **mean** of a set of data:

  1 work out the total value of all the data items

  2 divide this by the number of data items.

The range

- The **range** of a set of data tells you how 'spread out' the data items are. It is the difference between the largest and smallest data item values.

Comparing sets of data

- Draw a **comparison table**.

  Compare the means to see which is bigger.

  Compare the ranges to see which is more **consistent**.

Brush Up Your Number 13

Fraction Calculations

Learn About It

To work out $\frac{1}{2}$ of an amount, divide it by 2.

To work out $\frac{1}{5}$ of an amount, divide it by 5.

To work out a fraction of something when the fraction doesn't have 1 on the top:

- divide by the number on the bottom (denominator)
- multiply the answer by the number on the top (numerator).

For example, $\frac{2}{3}$ of 48 kg = 48 ÷ 3 × 2

$$= 16 \times 2$$
$$= 32 \text{ kg.}$$

Try It Out

A In each of the following questions, two of the calculations have the same answer. Write down which is the odd one out.

1 **(a)** $\frac{1}{2}$ of 24p   **(b)** $\frac{1}{5}$ of 60p   **(c)** $\frac{1}{4}$ of 64p

2 **(a)** $\frac{1}{4}$ of 40 cm   **(b)** $\frac{1}{2}$ of 80 cm   **(c)** $\frac{1}{5}$ of 50 cm

3 **(a)** $\frac{3}{4}$ of £12   **(b)** $\frac{1}{8}$ of £24   **(c)** $\frac{1}{2}$ of £18

4 **(a)** $\frac{2}{3}$ of 42 kg   **(b)** $\frac{1}{4}$ of 120 kg   **(c)** $\frac{1}{3}$ of 90 kg

5 **(a)** $\frac{5}{8}$ of 24 cars   **(b)** $\frac{3}{4}$ of 20 cars   **(c)** $\frac{3}{8}$ of 32 cars

6 **(a)** $\frac{3}{10}$ of 150 books **(b)** $\frac{2}{5}$ of 125 books **(c)** $\frac{1}{2}$ of 100 books

7 **(a)** $\frac{4}{9}$ of 54 hours **(b)** $\frac{2}{5}$ of 50 hours **(c)** $\frac{1}{3}$ of 72 hours

8 **(a)** $\frac{9}{20}$ of 240 km   **(b)** $\frac{1}{4}$ of 420 km   **(c)** $\frac{7}{10}$ of 150 km

Learn More About It

When you add or subtract fractions, they must have the same **denominator**.

Sometimes you need to change one of the fractions to match the other.

Sometimes you need to change **both** fractions.

> **Example** $\frac{5}{12} + \frac{3}{8}$
>
> **Working** Change the denominator to 24.
>
> $\frac{5}{12} = \frac{10}{24}$
>
> $\frac{3}{8} = \frac{9}{24}$
>
> $\frac{10}{24} + \frac{9}{24} = \frac{19}{24}$
>
> **Answer** $\frac{19}{24}$

Try It Out

B Calculate the following. Cancel your answers to their lowest terms if necessary.

1 (a) $\frac{3}{10} + \frac{4}{10}$ (b) $\frac{6}{7} - \frac{2}{7}$ (c) $\frac{11}{24} + \frac{5}{24}$ (d) $\frac{13}{18} - \frac{5}{18}$

2 (a) $\frac{1}{2} + \frac{3}{8}$ (b) $\frac{3}{5} + \frac{3}{10}$ (c) $\frac{1}{6} - \frac{1}{24}$ (d) $\frac{1}{3} + \frac{5}{18}$

3 (a) $\frac{11}{12} - \frac{3}{5}$ (b) $\frac{9}{10} - \frac{6}{7}$ (c) $\frac{1}{4} + \frac{1}{6}$ (d) $\frac{3}{5} + \frac{1}{6}$

4 (a) $1 - \frac{1}{4}$ (b) $1 - \frac{7}{8}$ (c) $1 - \frac{2}{11}$ (d) $1 - \frac{11}{15}$

Practice

C Use these fraction strips for the following calculations.

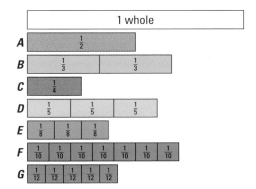

1 Write down the fraction each set shows.

2 Calculate the following.

   (a) $C + D$ (b) $D + E$

   (c) $D - A$ (d) $E + G$

   (e) $G - E$ (f) $B - D$

3 The **whole** strip is 12 cm long. Work out the length of each fraction strip.

> **Finished Early?**
> ➡ Go to page 365

22 Chance

In this chapter you will learn about ...
1. theoretical probability
2. predicting results
3. experimental probability

1 Theoretical Probability

Remember?

Anything that happens by chance has a **probability**.
Probability describes how likely something is to happen.

A probability is a **number** between 0 and 1.

That means you can write it as a **fraction,** a **decimal** or a **percentage**.

You can put any probability onto the **probability scale**.

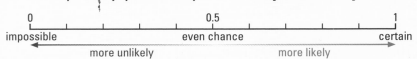

When you flip a coin there is an even chance of getting a head.

The probability is $\frac{1}{2}$ or 0.5. In mathematics, it is *not* correct to say things like '5 to 1', '1 chance in 6', etc.

In mathematics, probabilities can only be expressed as fractions, decimals or percentages.

Try It Out

A **1** Match each statement below with one of these words:
IMPOSSIBLE, UNLIKELY, EVEN, LIKELY, CERTAIN.

(a) Somewhere in the world today, a baby will be born.
(b) 1 + 2 = 4
(c) Someone in your family will win £1 000 000 on the lottery.

(d) You will have some homework to do tonight.
(e) The Sun will rise tomorrow morning.
(f) Your teacher will walk into the room wearing a funny hat.
(g) You will say the word 'the' today.
(h) You will eat chips today.
(i) The school fire alarm will sound this week.
(j) You will oversleep tomorrow morning.

2 Copy the following. Add ✓ or ✗ to each to show whether it can be a probability or not. If you put ✗, give a reason.

(a) $\frac{1}{3}$ **(b)** 1 chance in 2 **(c)** $\frac{5}{8}$
(d) 3 to 1 **(e)** $\frac{1}{12}$ **(f)** 1
(g) 0.25 **(h)** 50–50 **(i)** $\frac{10}{15}$
(j) 61% **(k)** 6 to 1 **(l)** 6.1

Learn About It

In mathematics, anything that is controlled by chance is called an **event**. The results of an event are called **outcomes**.

Outcomes have **probabilities**. Instead of writing a probability as a sentence, such as 'The probability of getting a head is $\frac{1}{2}$', you can write $P(\text{head}) = \frac{1}{2}$ for short.

For example:

Event	Outcomes	Probabilities
Flip a coin	head	$P(\text{head}) = \frac{1}{2}$
	tail	$P(\text{tail}) = \frac{1}{2}$

Key Fact

If all the outcomes of an event are equally likely, work out the probabilities like this:
• count how many different outcomes there are
• the probability is $\frac{1}{\text{number of outcomes}}$.

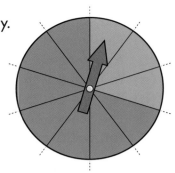

Sometimes outcomes **are not** all equally likely.

$\frac{3}{10}$ of the spinner is blue.

$\frac{7}{10}$ of the spinner is green.

$P(\text{blue}) = \frac{3}{10}$ or 0.3

$P(\text{green}) = \frac{7}{10}$ or 0.7

$P(\text{blue}) + P(\text{green}) = \frac{3}{10} + \frac{7}{10}$

$\qquad\qquad\qquad\qquad = \frac{10}{10}$

$\qquad\qquad\qquad\qquad = 1$

> ### Key Fact
> The sum of the probabilities of all the outcomes **always** equals 1.

Word Check

event something that is controlled by chance

outcomes the possible results of an event

probability the likelihood of getting a given outcome

equally likely having the same probability

P(outcome) the probability that a particular outcome will happen

Try It Out

B Work out $P(\text{red})$ and $P(\text{yellow})$ for each spinner.

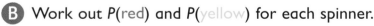

1
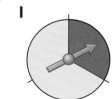

2
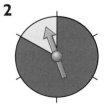

3
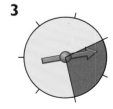

4
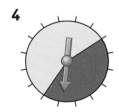

Practice

 1 Imagine rolling an ordinary die. What is the probability you will roll …

(a) a 4?
(b) an even number?
(c) a number higher than 3?
(d) not a 6?
(e) a prime number?
(f) a 7?

2 Robin has a bag of letter tiles. There are 4 B tiles, 3 A tiles and 5 G tiles. If he picks a tile at random, what is …

(a) P(B)?
(b) P(A)?
(c) P(G)?

3 Miriam drives to work.

(a) The probability she will be held up at the railway crossing is 0.2. What is the probability she will not be held up?

(b) The probability she will get a space in the **free** car park is 0.55. What is the probability she will have to use the **other** car park?

4 There is a 2% probability that a new Luxibrite light bulb won't work. What is the probability that it **does** work?

5 Four friends pass round a bag of mixed sweets. They each take **one** sweet in turn.

(a) Philip chooses first. There are 6 fruit sweets, 4 mints and 2 chocolates in the bag. Calculate the probabilities of his getting each type of sweet.

(b) Philip takes a sweet. It is a mint. He passes the bag to Stephanie. Calculate the probabilities of her getting each type of sweet.

 There are fewer sweets in the bag after each friend takes one.

(c) Stephanie takes a fruit sweet. She passes the bag to Lai Chu. Calculate the probabilities of her getting each type of sweet now.

(d) Lai Chu takes a sweet. It is a chocolate. She passes the bag to Eddie. Calculate the probabilities of his getting each type of sweet now.

(e) Eddie takes a sweet. It is a chocolate. He passes the bag back to Philip. Calculate the probabilities of his getting each type of sweet now.

> **Finished Early?**
> ➡ Go to page 366

Further Practice

D **I** Work out *P*(green) and *P*(blue) for each spinner.

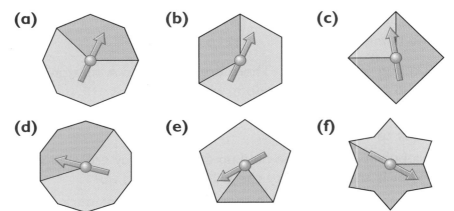

(a)   **(b)**   **(c)**

(d)   **(e)**   **(f)**

2 There are 52 playing cards in a normal pack.
There are four **suits** – hearts (♥), spades (♠), diamonds (♦) and clubs (♣).
The **number** cards are 1 (ace)–10 of each suit.
The **court** cards are the jack (11), queen (12) and king (13).

When a pack has been shuffled, if you chose one card at random what is the probability of taking ...

(a) the ace (1) of spades?

(b) a king?

(c) a number card?

(d) an even-numbered club (the queen counts as even)?

(e) a red card?

(f) a black 3?

(g) a court card (king, queen or jack)?

(h) an odd-numbered card (the jacks and kings count as odd)?

(i) a higher card than a 7 (the court cards are higher)?

(j) a red card that is 4 or less?

Finished Early?
➡ Go to page 366

❷ Predicting Results

Learn About It

You can use probability to **estimate** how many times something will happen.

On this spinner, the probability of landing on black is $\frac{1}{3}$.

Suppose you spin the pointer 60 times. How many times do you expect it to land on black?

P(black) = $\frac{1}{3}$. You'd expect it to come up $\frac{1}{3}$ of the time.

$\frac{1}{3}$ of 60 = 60 ÷ 3 = 20 times.

This is called the **expected number** of times, or **expected frequency**.

The expected number of times the spinner will land on orange is

$\frac{2}{3}$ of 60 = 60 ÷ 3 × 2 = 40 times.

When you are testing probability, each 'go' is called a **trial**.

Imagine you do 100 trials with this spinner.

Copy and complete the following statements.

P(grey) = _____
Expected number of grey = _____ of 100 = _____ times.

P(blue) = _____
Expected number of blue = _____ of 100 = _____ times.

P(mauve) = _____
Expected number of mauve = _____ of 100 = _____ times.

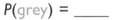

Key Fact	**Word Check**
expected number = probability × number of trials	**expected number** an estimate of how many times an outcome will happen
	expected frequency expected number
	trial an event made to happen

Try It Out

E 1 When you press a robot's nose, it does one of the things written on its body. The probability it will do each thing is written there too.

(a) Imagine you press each robot's nose 100 times. Write down the expected number for each outcome.

> **Example**
> **Working**
> $P(\text{beep}) = 0.4$
> $0.4 \times 100 = 40$
> $P(\text{hoot}) = 0.6$
> $0.6 \times 100 = 60$
> **Answer** beeps = 40
> hoots = 60
>
> $P(\text{beep}) = 0.4$
> $P(\text{hoot}) = 0.6$

(b) Some of the robots sometimes do nothing. You can tell this if the probabilities do not add up to 1. If this is true, write down $P(\text{do nothing})$ as well, and calculate the expected frequency.

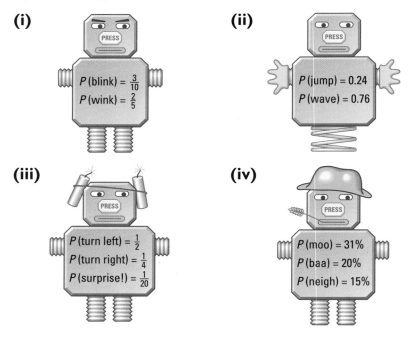

(i)
$P(\text{blink}) = \frac{3}{10}$
$P(\text{wink}) = \frac{2}{5}$

(ii)
$P(\text{jump}) = 0.24$
$P(\text{wave}) = 0.76$

(iii)
$P(\text{turn left}) = \frac{1}{2}$
$P(\text{turn right}) = \frac{1}{4}$
$P(\text{surprise!}) = \frac{1}{20}$

(iv)
$P(\text{moo}) = 31\%$
$P(\text{baa}) = 20\%$
$P(\text{neigh}) = 15\%$

2 When Jim goes out in the evening, there is a $\frac{1}{3}$ probability he will see his friend Farukh. One month, he goes out 18 times. How many times do you expect he saw Farukh?

3 When a book is printed and bound, there is a probability of 0.003 that it will have a loose page. In a batch of 10 000 books, how many would you expect to have loose pages?

Practice

F **1** At Dairy Dream they make yogurt. A machine fills the pots with yogurt. Most of the time, the amount of yogurt in a pot is just right. Sometimes there is too much (an **overweight** pot) or too little (an **underweight** pot). The probabilities vary depending on the type of the pot.

Mass of pot (g)	P(overweight)	P(correct)	P(underweight)
125	2%		3%
250	1%		3%
500	1%		2%

(a) Copy and complete the table.
(b) The Dairy Dream manager wanted to know how many pots would be overweight, underweight or just right each day. Copy and complete this table for a day's work.

Mass of pot (g)	Number of pots filled	Number of pots expected to be ...		
		overweight	correct	underweight
125	1000			
250	600			
500	500			

G Zorah is running a game at a charity fair. People pay 20p to throw a dart at this board. There's an equal chance of landing on each square.

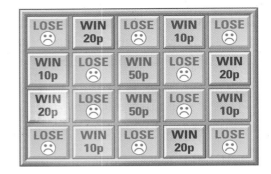

1 What is the probability that the square you land on will say …

(a) LOSE?   (b) WIN 10p?   (c) WIN 20p?   (d) WIN 50p?

2 In 100 trials, what are the expected frequencies for each kind of square?

3 Imagine you are running Zorah's game. 100 people have a go. Suppose that the numbers come up as expected.

(a) How much money would you take?

(b) How much would you have to pay out to winners who landed on the 10p squares?

> *Hint: expected number × 10p.*

(c) How much would you have to pay out to winners who landed on the 20p squares?

(d) How much would you have to pay out to winners who landed on the 50p squares?

(e) How much would you pay out altogether?

(f) How much profit would you make for charity?

4 Do you think this game is fair?

> **Finished Early?**
> ➡ Go to page 367

Further Practice

(H) **1** Work out *P*(grey) and *P*(pink) for each spinner.

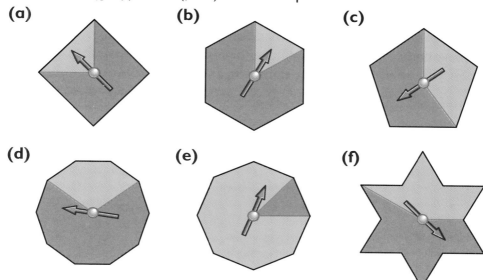

(a)   **(b)**   **(c)**

(d)   **(e)**   **(f)**

2 Each spinner from question 1 is given 120 spins.
Copy and complete the table.

Spinner	Expected number of ...	
	grey	pink
(a)		
(b)		
(c)		
(d)		
(e)		
(f)		

Finished Early?
➡ Go to page 367

ⓣ❸ Experimental Probability

Learn About It

Experimental probability is about using an experiment to **estimate** probability. It is different to **theoretical probability**, when you just **think** about an event and predict what will happen.

Suppose you flipped a coin 100 times and these were the results.

Outcome	Tally	Frequency
Heads	JHT JHT JHT JHT JHT III	28
Tails	JHT JHT JHT JHT JHT JHT JHT JHT JHT JHT JHT JHT JHT JHT II	72

You would probably think something was wrong with the coin.

You would expect to have got about the same number of heads and tails.

This coin is more likely to land on tails than heads. The coin is **unfair** or **biased**.

Out of 100 trials, 28 were heads.

So the **experimental** probability is $P(\text{head}) = \frac{28}{100}$

$$= 0.28.$$

Tails came up 72 times out of 100, so $P(\text{tail}) = \frac{72}{100}$

$$= 0.72.$$

If the coin is fair, these probabilities are 0.5.

You can show this clearly on a probability scale.

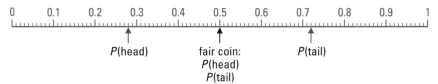

Key Fact

experimental probability = frequency ÷ number of trials

Word Check
....

experimental probability an estimate of
probability, made by doing trials or experiments

theoretical probability probability calculated
by working out the mathematics affecting
an event

biased unfair – when the outcomes seem equally
likely, but aren't

Try It Out

1 (a) Copy and complete the table of probabilities for throwing
a dice.

Outcome	Frequency	Probability
1	15	P(1) =
2	18	P(2) =
3	35	P(3) =
4	0	P(4) =
5	15	P(5) =
6	17	P(6) =
Total		1

(b) There is something unusual about this dice. What do you
think it is?

2 Dominic has an old car. He uses it every day. Every day during June, he wrote down whether the car started on the first try or not. He put a ✓ on his calendar if it did, and a ✗ if it didn't.

June			
6 MON ✗	13 MON ✗	20 MON ✓	27 MON ✗
7 TUE ✗	14 TUE ✓	21 TUE ✗	28 TUE ✗
1 WED ✓	8 WED ✗	15 WED ✗	22 WED ✗	29 WED ✗
2 THU ✗	9 THU ✗	16 THU ✓	23 THU ✗	30 THU ✓
3 FRI ✗	10 FRI ✓	17 FRI ✗	24 FRI ✗
4 SAT ✓	11 SAT ✗	18 SAT ✓	25 SAT ✗
5 SUN ✗	12 SUN ✗	19 SUN ✗	26 SUN ✓

Copy and complete this table.

Outcome	Frequency	Probability
Started first try		P(✓) =
Didn't start first try		P(✗) =
Total		1

Practice

J For each of the following experiments:

    (a) draw a tally table

    (b) carry out 100 trials and tally the results (except question 4, which only has 50 trials)

    (c) count your tally marks to get the frequency

    (d) work out the probabilities.

1 Point Up?

Drawing pin

Drop a drawing pin on to your desk from a height of about 30 cm. Record whether it lands point up 📌 or point down 🔩.

Outcome	Tally	Frequency	Probability
Point up			P(up) =
Point down			P(down) =
Total		100	1

2 Biased Dice

Squared paper, scissors, glue or sticky tape, scrap paper

On squared paper, copy the net of the dice on the right. Make each square 4 cm wide.

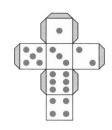

Before you fold up the net and stick the flaps, tape or glue a small wad of paper to the inside of one of the faces. This weights the dice so it will be biased in favour of one number.

Outcome	Tally	Frequency	Probability
1			P(1) =
2			P(2) =
3			P(3) =
4			P(4) =
5			P(5) =
6			P(6) =
Total		100	1

3 Shove It!

A4 squared paper, coin, tape or blue-tack

Draw this board using lines 4 cm apart. Put it on the edge of your desk. Make sure it can't move by using tape or blue-tack.

Put a coin on the Start line.
Knock the coin along the board with one shove, aiming for line 4.
Copy and complete this table of results.

Outcome	Tally	Frequency	Probability
1			P(1) =
2			P(2) =
6			P(6) =
7			P(7) =
Total		100	1

4 Quadruple Flip

Coin, counter or other small object

On the game board below, one 'trial' means working from **Start** to one of the letters by flipping a coin four times. Use something small, such as a counter, to mark your place on the board.

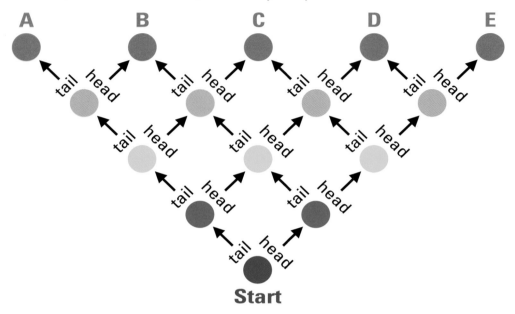

Do 50 trials, then copy and complete this table.

Outcome	Tally	Frequency	Probability
A			P(A) =
B			P(B) =
C			P(C) =
D			P(D) =
E			P(E) =
Total		50	1

> **Finished Early?**
> ⮕ Go to page 368

Further Practice

1 Michael did an experiment. He repeatedly flipped three coins. Each time, he wrote down whether the coins showed a mixture of heads and tails, or all showed the same. Copy and complete this table of his results.

Outcome	Frequency	Probability
Mixed	27	P(mixed) =
Same	73	P(same) =
Total		1

2 Kirsty's watch isn't very accurate. She always sets it in the morning. She checks it at night. In April, she decided to write down what her watch did. Every day, she wrote 'F' for fast, 'S' for slow and 'R' for right. This is what her calendar looked like at the end of the month.

	4 MON S	11 MON F	18 MON F	25 MON F
	5 TUE F	12 TUE F	19 TUE F	26 TUE S
	6 WED S	13 WED F	20 WED F	27 WED F
April	7 THU F	14 THU F	21 THU R	28 THU R
1 FRI S	8 FRI F	15 FRI S	22 FRI F	29 FRI F
2 SAT F	9 SAT S	16 SAT R	23 SAT S	30 SAT S
3 SUN F	10 SUN F	17 SUN S	24 SUN F	

Copy and complete this table.

Outcome	Frequency	Probability
Fast		P(F) =
Slow		P(S) =
Right		P(R) =
Total	30	1

3 A spinner was spun 60 times. The pointer stopped in the green sector 15 times. It stopped in the yellow sector 45 times. Draw what you would expect the spinner to look like.

Finished Early?
➡ Go to page 368

Unit 13 *Probability*

Summary of Chapter 22

- A probability is a **number** from 0 to 1 that describes how likely something is to happen. You can write it as a **fraction**, **decimal** or **percentage**. You can put any probability on a **probability scale**.

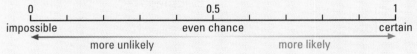

'The probability of getting a head is $\frac{1}{2}$' can be written as $P(\text{head}) = \frac{1}{2}$.

- In mathematics, anything that is controlled by chance is called an **event**. The results of an event are called **outcomes**. Outcomes have **probabilities**.

Event	Outcomes	Probability
Flip a coin	head	$\frac{1}{2}$
	tail	$\frac{1}{2}$

Outcomes that have the same probability are called **equally likely**. The probability is $\frac{1}{\text{number of outcomes}}$.

Fair dice and coins have equally likely outcomes. In a **biased** or **unfair** event, the outcomes seem equally likely, but are not.

If you add together the probabilities of **all** the possible outcomes for one event, you always get 1.

- You can use probability to **estimate** how many times something will happen. This is called the **expected number** of times, or **expected frequency**.

expected frequency = probability × number of trials

- **Experimental** probability is about using an experiment to **estimate** probability.

experimental probability = frequency ÷ number of trials

Finished Early?

Brush Up Your Number 1

Place Value and Ordering with Whole Numbers

1 **(a)** Write down six three-digit numbers using these digits: 4, 7, 2. You can repeat digits. Here's a start: 247, 777, 242 ...
  (b) Order the numbers from smallest to largest.
2 **(a)** Write down ten four-digit numbers using these digits: 5, 2, 7.
  (b) Order the numbers from smallest to largest.
3 **(a)** Write down three digits of your own. Make ten 5-digit numbers using your digits.
  (b) Order the numbers from smallest to largest.
4 Make ten bigger numbers, e.g. of 7 digits, using your three digits from question 3. Order them from smallest to largest.

Chapter 1 *Negative Numbers*

Working with Negative Numbers

1 **(a)** Work out $(-2) + 3$.
  (b) If you change all the signs, the calculation becomes $(+2) - 3$. Does this give the same answer?
2 **(a)** Calculate $(-2) + 3 - 4$.
  (b) Changing all the signs gives $(+2) - 3 + 4$. How does the answer change?
3 **(a)** What happens to the answer when you change all the signs?
  (b) Test the rule with some longer calculations.

4 Work out 3 − 5 + 2.

5 (a) Write down five calculations that give the answer 0.
Each calculation must be longer than the one before.

(b) If you change all the signs in your calculations from part (a),
what would the answers be? Try it and see.

❷ Adding and Subtracting Negative Numbers

1 Russell calculates −3 + 2 − 4 + 7 − 1 + 5 like this:
first he adds the numbers that come after a plus sign:
2 + 7 + 5 = 14
then he adds the numbers that come after a minus sign:
3 + 4 + 1 = 8.
To get the answer, he subtracts the second total from the first:
14 − 8 = 6, so −3 + 2 − 4 + 7 − 1 + 5 = 6.
Check his answer, working from left to right.

2 Use Russell's method to work out the following calculations.
Check your answers using another method.
(a) −4 + 2 − 3 + 5 − 1
(b) 4 − 2 − 3 − 4 + 5 + 6
(c) −2 + 5 + 3 − 4 − 6 − 2 + 1
(d) − 1 + 2 − 3 + 4 − 5 + 6 − 7 + 8 − 9 + 10

3 (a) Work out −3 + 2 − 5 + 4.
(b) Imagine that each sign is stuck to the number that follows it,
like this:
−3 +2 −5 +4.
Rearrange the numbers: −5 +2 −3 +4 (keep the signs with
the same numbers).
Work out the new calculation: −5 + 2 − 3 + 4. Do you get the
same answer?
(c) Rearrange the numbers different ways, keeping the signs with
them. Do you always get the same answer?
(d) Investigate using other calculations, e.g. 3 − 5 − 1 + 2 − 8.

Brush Up Your Number 2

Addition and Subtraction of Whole Numbers

On a bank statement the **balance** is the money that is in the account. The **credit** column shows amounts added to the balance. The **debit** column shows amounts subtracted from the balance.

Copy this table and complete the balance column.

Debit (£)	Credit (£)	Balance (£)
		2 500 000
650 000		
	125 000	
	1 225 500	
565 400		
624 430		
	345 725	
1 112 345		
	3 435 000	
1 125 250		
	120 050	
133 465		
540 385		

How can you check that the final balance is correct?
Check your answer this way.

Chapter 2 *Coordinates and Graphs*

 Squared paper

❶ Coordinates

1 **(a)** Draw *x*- and *y*-axes and label them from −10 to 10.

   (b) Draw a quadrilateral (a 4-sided figure) on your axes and find the coordinates of the corners.

   (c) Write the coordinates of the corners on a separate piece of paper and swap with another pupil. Draw each other's shapes on your graphs and check that they are correct.

2 Repeat question 1 using a pentagon (5 sides).

3 Repeat question 1 using a hexagon (6 sides).

4 Repeat question 1 using a shape with a larger number of sides.

❷ Reading Graphs

A shop sells records, cassettes and CDs. Their yearly sales from 1985 to 1998 are shown on the graph.

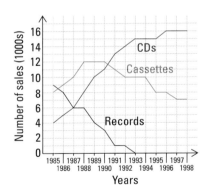

1 Which product's sales dropped the most?

2 Which product's sales increased the most?

3 What was the difference between record and cassette sales in 1990?

4 What was the difference between cassette and CD sales in 1988?

5 When did CD sales first become larger than cassette sales?

6 Describe each line in words and explain what happened to the sales of that product.

❸ Drawing Graphs

£1 = 12 Norwegian kroner

£1 = 2.5 Australian dollars

Draw two conversion graphs to convert up to £20 to kroner and to Australian dollars. Use them to answer the following questions.

(a) What is £14 in kroner?
(b) What is £18 in Australian dollars?
(c) What is 100 kroner in pounds?
(d) What is 100 kroner in Australian dollars?
(e) What is 40 Australian dollars in pounds?
(f) What is 40 Australian dollars in kroner?
(g) What is 23 Australian dollars in kroner?

Brush Up Your Number 3

Multiplication Tables

Work out the 11 and 12 times tables.
Practise them, then get a friend to test you.

Chapter 3 *Angles*

❶ Estimating, Measuring and Drawing Angles

Protractor

This is how to draw an equilateral triangle like the one on the right.

(a) Draw a line 5 cm long.
(b) Draw a second 5 cm line at 60° to the first.
(c) Draw a third 5 cm line at 60° to the second. This line should meet the other end of the first line.

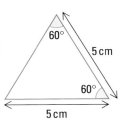

By following the same method but using different angles, you can draw other regular shape.
For each question, draw the shape made when each side is 5cm and each angle is the one given.

1 90°   **2** 108°   **3** 120°   **4** 135°   **5** 144°.

❷ Angle Facts

Protractor

1 Draw a pair of straight lines crossing each other.

2 Measure the four angles between the lines. Write the sizes of the angles on your diagram. The fact that angles on a straight line add up to 180° should help you to measure accurately.

3 Draw eight more pairs of crossed lines. Measure the angles and write their sizes on your diagrams.

4 Write down any connection you can see between the angles where two lines cross.

❸ Triangles

Protractor

Extending one of the sides of a triangle forms an **exterior** angle.

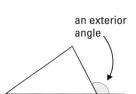

an exterior angle

1 Draw ten triangles, making them different sizes and shapes.

2 Extend one of the sides of each triangle to make an exterior angle.

3 Measure all the angles and all the exterior angles of your triangles. Mark the angles on your diagrams.

4 Make a table listing the exterior angles in your triangles and the two angles farthest away from the exterior angle.

5 Look at the numbers in your table and write down a connection between the exterior angle and the two angles, furthest away from it.

6 Draw three more triangles and, without measuring the exterior angle, predict what it will be by measuring the two interior angles furthest away from it. Test your prediction by measuring the exterior angle.

④ Quadrilaterals

Protractor

1 (a) Draw five parallelograms of different sizes. Mark in the diagonals (the lines joining the corners) and measure the angles at the centre and the lengths of the diagonals to where they cross.

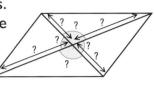

(b) Describe how the diagonals of a parallelogram cross.

2 (a) Draw five rectangles and measure the lengths and angles.

(b) What can you say about how the diagonals of a rectangle cross?

3 Repeat the same activity with squares.

Chapter 4 *Symmetry*

---

① Line Symmetry

Squared paper

Using the lines on these axes, you can make a shape with line symmetry of order 8. Start with a shape in one section.

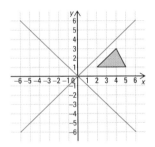

The diagram on the right shows the result if you keep reflecting the drawing in the lines.

Draw a simple shape of your own and keep reflecting your shape until you have completed the pattern.

Repeat this with other shapes.

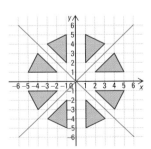

② Rotational Symmetry

Protractor

- To draw a shape with rotational symmetry of order 3, start with three lines meeting at angles of 120°.
- Draw a shape in one angle.
- Now rotate the shape through 120° twice to complete the diagram.

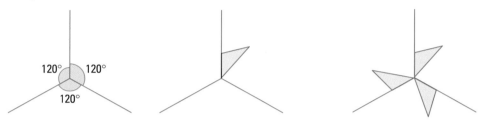

Draw shapes of your own with rotational symmetry of order:

1 4   **2** 6   **3** 8   **4** 9   **5** 10.

Chapter 5 *Three Dimensions*

① Solids

1 Copy and complete this table.

Name	Faces	Corners	Edges
Cube	6	8	12
Triangular prism			
Square-based pyramid			

2 Write down a rule to find the number of edges from the numbers of corners and faces.

3 See if your rule works for a tetrahedron and a hexagonal pyramid.

② Drawing Solids

Triangular dotted paper, cubes

Make a shape from cubes and draw it viewed from three different positions. Shade the same side on each drawing.

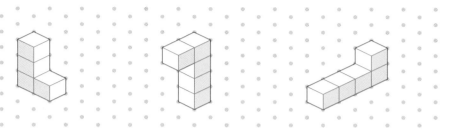

Make five more shapes. Draw each one in three different ways.

③ Nets

Cubes, card, scissors

Use about six cubes to make a solid shape. Draw the net of your solid.

Swap your net with another pupil and make each other's solids. Compare the solids made from each net with the original shape.

Repeat this with other shapes made from different numbers of cubes.

> # Brush Up Your Number 4

● Rounding Whole Numbers

Numbers are usually rounded to 10, 100, 1000, etc. but they can be rounded to other numbers.

Round each number below to the nearest:

(a) 25	(b) 50	(c) 250	(d) 500	(e) 2500.
1 3224	**2** 5176	**3** 12 480	**4** 13 204	
5 18 775	**6** 4312	**7** 7894	**8** 6213	
9 9562	**10** 39 422	**11** 321 183	**12** 21 325	

Chapter 6 *Decimals*

❶ Decimals

Add together the numbers and fractions in each circle below.
Write your answer as decimals.

Example

$\frac{3}{10}$ 2

$\frac{7}{1000}$ 400

$\frac{5}{100}$

Working $400 + 2 + \frac{3}{10} + \frac{5}{100} + \frac{7}{1000}$

$= 400 + 2 + 0.3 + 0.05 + 0.007$

$= 402.357$

Answer   402.357

I

50   7
200
$\frac{3}{100}$

2

$\frac{5}{1000}$ 4
2000   50
$\frac{3}{10}$

3

4   $\frac{3}{10}$
$\frac{5}{1000}$ 70
$\frac{3}{10000}$

4

8   10
$\frac{4}{10000}$ $\frac{3}{10}$
$\frac{3}{100}$

5 Make a number circle like the ones above by splitting five decimals into four or five parts. Swap with another pupil and work out each other's decimal totals.

❷ Rounding Decimals

Here are six statements and six comments. Match each statement with the correct comment.

Statements

A After adding the interest I should have £125.3472 in my account at the end of the year.

B The winner of the 200 m race took 23.62 seconds and the runner up took 23.64 seconds.

C The length of a car is 5.333 333 m.

D The recipe calls for 12.4951 g of flour.

E Jane timed her journey to school at 25 minutes 48.25 seconds.

F A bee can collect 0.002 g of nectar from a flower.

Comments

U
There are too many decimal places, round it to the nearest whole number or 1 d.p.

V
This should probably be rounded to the nearest minute.

W
You need all three decimal places. If you rounded it, the statement would be nonsense.

X
You need to use both decimal places.

Z
You cannot measure that amount. Round it to 1 d.p.

Y
This should be rounded to 2 decimal places.

❸ Adding and Subtracting Decimals

For each of these calculations …
(a) work out the answer and round it to the nearest whole number
(b) round each number to the nearest whole number, then work out the answer using the rounded numbers
(c) find the difference between the answers to (a) and (b).

1 12.5 + 32.6

2 34.55 + 13.65

3 33.45 + 26.3

4 66.32 + 43.7

5 123.44 + 45.6 + 14.7

6 16.6 + 12.5 + 34.75

7 38.4 − 12.8

8 42.6 − 18.3

9 45.5 − 27.4

10 26.55 − 13.75

11 226.4 − 148.9

12 106.9 − 32.5

❹ Place Value Calculations

Copy and complete this table.

	Item	Cost of 1	Cost of 10	Cost of 100
1	Book	£4.55		
2	Magazine	£0.85		
3	Video game		£235.50	
4	Calculator			£695
5	Motor bike		£15 650	
6	Computer	£499.99		
7	Printer			£16 449
8	Mobile phone		£234.50	

❺ Multiplying and Dividing Decimals

For each of these calculations …
(a) work out the answer and round it to the nearest whole number
(b) round each number to the nearest whole number, then work out the answer using the rounded numbers
(c) find the difference between the answers to (a) and (b).

1 2.3×3.5		**2** 5.4×2.1	
3 8.4×1.5		**4** 7.6×3.2	
5 12.5×2.1		**6** 7.8×0.5	
7 3.2×4.2		**8** $4.8 \div 0.6$	
9 $15.6 \div 1.2$		**10** $1.28 \div 1.6$	
11 $1.65 \div 1.5$		**12** $7.2 \div 1.8$	

Brush Up Your Number 5

Multiplying Whole Numbers

1 **(a)** Think of a two-digit number, for example, 26.

(b) Square it. | *Remember: squaring means multiplying by itself.*

(c) Now multiply one less than the number by one more than the number. If you started with 26, you would work out 25×27.

(d) Write down anything you notice about the two answers.

2 Repeat question 1 three more times with different starting numbers. Write down what you notice. Is there a pattern?

Chapter 7 *Formulae and Expressions*

Substitution

Here are some formulae for finding the areas of shapes.

1 Area = bh (with h and b labelled)

2 Area = a^2 (with a labelled)

3 Area = $ab - c^2$ (with b, c, a labelled)

4 Area = $b^2 - a^2$ (with b, a labelled)

5 Area = $\frac{1}{2} bh$ (with h, b labelled)

Find the area of each shape when a = 3 cm, b = 4 cm, c = 2 cm, h = 5 cm.

❷ Making Formulae

1 (a) Make as many formulae as you can, starting with $a =$.
Use the letters b and c, the operation $+$ and the number 2.
For example, $a = b + 2$, $a = b + c + 2$, $a = b^2$

(b) Find the value of a by substituting $b = 2$ and $c = 5$ in each formula.

2 (a) Make as many formulae as you can, starting with $p =$.
Use the letters q and r, the operation $\times$ and the number 3.
For example, $p = 3 \times q$, which you can write as $p = 3q$.

(b) Find the value of p by substituting $q = 4$ and $r = 2$ in each formula.

3 (a) Make as many formulae as you can, starting with $g =$.
Use the letters d and e, the operations $\times$ and $+$ and the numbers 2 and 5. For example, $g = 2 \times d + e$, which you write as $g = 2d + e$.

(b) Find the value of g by substituting $d = 3$ and $e = 4$ in each formula.

❸ Simplifying Expressions

1 Make up three expressions that simplify to $2a$.
For example, $5a - 3a = 2a$.

2 Make up three expressions that simplify to $3c + 2d$.
For example, $5c - 2c + d + d$.

3 Make up three expressions that simplify to:
(a) $4mn$ **(b)** $10k + 4$ **(c)** $a + b + c$.

Chapter 8 *Equations*

❶ Making Equations

I How many marbles in a full bag?

Marvin bought
2 bags of marbles.

He took six out
of a bag.

There were 14 marbles
left altogether.

Write down the problem as an equation. Use *b* for the number of
marbles in a bag.

2 Make up your own marbles problem like the one above.

(a) Decide:

- how many bags to buy, e.g. 3
- how many marbles you will take out of the bags, e.g. 6
- how many marbles will be left, e.g. 18.

(b) Write an equation, using *b* for the number of marbles in a bag,
e.g. $3b - 6 = 18$.

3 How many marbles in a full bag?

Ann emptied 3 bags
of marbles into a box.

She added 6
more marbles.

Now there are 21
marbles in the box.

Write down the problem as an equation.

4 (a) Make up your own marbles problem like the one above.

(b) Write an equation.

5 (a) Make up four more marbles problems.

(b) Write an equation for each one.

❷ Solving Equations

I This is an equation generator: n ▢ ● = ●

Using the equation generator, choose from the following numbers and operation signs to make five equations.

▢ $+, -, \div, \times$ ● $1, 2, 4, 5, 8$

Example	Choose $\times, 4, 5$
Working	n ▢× ●4 = ●5
	$n \times 4 \qquad = 5$
	$4n \qquad = 5$ (*Write 4n instead of n4.*)
Answer	$4n = 5$

2 Solve your equations by working backwards. The answers may be negative, fractions or decimals. Use a calculator if you need to.

❸ Equations with Two Operations

I Solve these equations by working backwards.

Example	$\dfrac{n}{3} - 2 = 4$
Working	Start with the answer: 4
	Add 2: $\qquad\qquad\qquad$ $4 + 2 = 6$
	Multiply by 3: $\qquad\quad$ $6 \times 3 = 18$
Answer	$n = 18$

(a) $\dfrac{m}{3} + 4 = 9$ $\qquad$ **(b)** $\dfrac{g}{2} + 3 = 7$ $\qquad$ **(c)** $\dfrac{a}{5} - 1 = 3$

(d) $\dfrac{d}{3} - 4 = 6$ $\qquad$ **(e)** $\dfrac{k}{10} + 5 = 12$ $\qquad$ **(f)** $\dfrac{s}{2} - 20 = 30$

2 (a) Write the two equations below, filling in the boxes with your own numbers. The red box must have the smallest number in each equation.

$$\dfrac{n}{\square} + ▢ = \square \qquad\qquad \dfrac{n}{\square} - ▢ = \square$$

(b) Solve your equations.

Brush Up Your Number 6

● Dividing Whole Numbers

I Look at this pattern.

1000 $\boxed{\div 2}$> 500 $\boxed{\div 2}$> 250 $\boxed{\div 2}$> 125 $\boxed{\div 2}$> 62 $\boxed{\div 2}$> 31 $\boxed{\div 2}$> 15 $\boxed{\div 2}$> 7 $\boxed{\div 2}$> 3 $\boxed{\div 2}$> I $\boxed{\div 2}$> 0

The remainders have been ignored (e.g. 125 ÷ 2 is really 62 remainder I).
After 1000, **ten** numbers were written down altogether.

2 Work out what will happen if you continue the pattern below, ignoring the remainders. Stop when you reach 0.

1000 $\boxed{\div 3}$> ? $\boxed{\div 3}$> ? $\boxed{\div 3}$> ? ...

How many numbers did you write down after 1000?

3 Repeat this for

1000 $\boxed{\div 4}$>
1000 $\boxed{\div 5}$>
1000 $\boxed{\div 6}$>, up to **1000** $\boxed{\div 10}$>.

4 Use your results to copy and complete the table.

5 If you have time, draw a graph like the one below to illustrate your results.

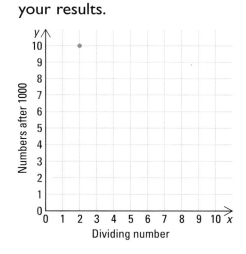

Dividing number	How many numbers after 1000?
2	10
3	
4	
5	
6	
7	
8	
9	
10	

Chapter 9 *Computation*

❶ Mixed Operations and Brackets

1 **(a)** Work out $10 - 2 \times 3 - 1$.

(b) Put in some brackets, e.g. $(10 - 2) \times 3 - 1$. Work out the answer. Remember to work out the brackets first.

(c) Put the brackets in a different place, e.g. $10 - (2 \times 3 - 1)$. Work out the answer.

(d) Put the brackets in a different place and work out the answer.

(e) What do you notice?

2 Can you make three different answers for each calculation by putting brackets in different places?

(a) $4 \times 7 + 3 \times 2$

(b) $12 \div 6 - 3 - 1$

(c) $2 \times 8 - 3 \times 2$

(d) $4 \times 6 - 4 \div 2$

3 Some calculations have brackets inside other brackets, for example: $3 \times (7 - (5 - 3))$.

Work out the calculations below, as follows:

- work out the inside (blue) brackets first
- then work out the outside (red) brackets
- finish the calculation
- use a calculator to check your answer.

(a) $2 \times (4 \times (3 + 5))$

(b) $(20 - (7 - 3)) \times 4$

(c) $10 + (7 - (2 + 3))$

(d) $(12 - (2 \times 5)) - 1$

(e) $15 - (4 \times (5 - 2))$

❷ Powers

1 **(a)** Calculate $3^2 \times 4^2$.

   (b) Calculate $(3 \times 4)^2$.

   Remember: brackets first.

   (c) What do you notice about the answers?

2 **(a)** Calculate $2^2 \times 5^2$.

   (b) Calculate $(2 \times 5)^2$.

   (c) What do you notice about the answers?

3 **(a)** Choose any two numbers, e.g. 3 and 7.

   (b) Square each number, *then* multiply the answers, e.g. $3^2 \times 7^2 = ?$

   (c) This time, multiply your two chosen numbers first, *then* square the answer, e.g. $(3 \times 7)^2$.

   (d) What do you notice about the answers?

   (e) Write down a rule, if you can find one.

4 Try different numbers of your own. Does your rule always work?

❸ Square Roots

1 Calculate $\sqrt{4} \times \sqrt{9}$.

2 Calculate $\sqrt{(4 \times 9)}$. Remember to calculate brackets first.

3 What do you notice about the answers to questions 1 and 2?

4 **(a)** Calculate $\sqrt{16} \times \sqrt{25}$.

   (b) Calculate $\sqrt{(16 \times 25)}$.

   (c) What do you notice about the answers?

5 **(a)** Choose any two square numbers, e.g. 9 and 100.

   (b) Find the square root of each number first, then multiply the answers together, e.g. $\sqrt{9} \times \sqrt{100}$.

   (c) This time, multiply the numbers first, then find the square root of the answer, e.g. $\sqrt{(9 \times 100)}$.

   (d) What do you notice about the answers?

   (e) Write down a rule, if you can find one.

6 Try different square numbers of your own. Does your rule always work?

Brush Up Your Number 7

Fraction Diagrams

Squared paper

1 Copy this rectangle onto squared paper.

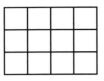

2 Shade the rectangle like this.
Write down the fraction.

3 Shade the rectangle different ways to show the same fraction.

4 Shade and label different fractions.

5 Copy these shapes.
Shade as many fractions as you can.
Write down each fraction you shade.

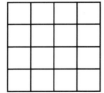 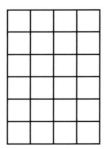 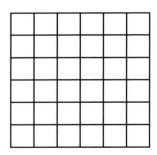

Chapter 10 *Fractions*

➊ Equivalent Fractions

You can compare fractions that have the same denominator.
For example, $\frac{7}{20}$ is bigger than $\frac{3}{20}$ because 7 is bigger than 3.

1 Write the following fractions from smallest to largest.

$\frac{25}{36}, \frac{12}{36}, \frac{31}{36}, \frac{29}{36}, \frac{7}{36}$

The fractions $\frac{3}{4}$ and $\frac{2}{3}$ do not have the same denominator.

To make their denominators the same:

- multiply the denominators together:
  $4 \times 3 = 12$

- make equivalent fractions that have this new denominator:
  $\frac{3}{4} = \frac{9}{12}$ and $\frac{2}{3} = \frac{8}{12}$.

Now you can compare the fractions.
$\frac{9}{12}$ is larger than $\frac{8}{12}$, so $\frac{3}{4}$ is bigger than $\frac{2}{3}$.

2 Compare the fractions in each pair and write down which is larger.

(a) $\frac{2}{5}, \frac{1}{2}$

(b) $\frac{5}{6}, \frac{3}{4}$

(c) $\frac{3}{8}, \frac{1}{3}$

(d) $\frac{5}{9}, \frac{4}{7}$

(e) $\frac{7}{10}, \frac{2}{3}$

3 Make up two fractions, using the numbers 1 to 10, then compare your fractions. Do this five times.

❷ Mixed Numbers

1 Megan changes improper fractions to mixed numbers like this.

Example	$\frac{24}{10}$
Working	$24 \div 10 = 2$ remainder 4 *(She leaves cancelling*
	$\frac{24}{10} = 2\frac{4}{10}_5 = 2\frac{2}{5}$ *until the end.)*
Answer	$\frac{24}{10} = 2\frac{2}{5}$

Convert these fractions to mixed numbers, then cancel to their lowest terms.

(a) $\frac{9}{6}$ **(b)** $\frac{14}{4}$ **(c)** $\frac{21}{9}$ **(d)** $\frac{45}{10}$

(e) $\frac{16}{12}$ **(f)** $\frac{90}{40}$ **(g)** $\frac{24}{18}$ **(h)** $\frac{75}{30}$

2 Repeat question 1. This time, cancel first, then change to mixed numbers.

3 Which method do you prefer? Explain your answer.

4 Megan wrote down the mixed number $2\frac{7}{5}$. This is wrong because $\frac{7}{5}$ is improper. Write the following mixed numbers correctly.

Example	$2\frac{7}{5}$
Working	Convert $2\frac{7}{5}$ to an improper fraction: $5 \times 2 + 7 = 17$.
	$2\frac{7}{5} = \frac{17}{5}$
	Convert $\frac{17}{5}$ back to a mixed number:
	$17 \div 5 = 3$ remainder 2, so $\frac{17}{5} = 3\frac{2}{5}$.
Answer	$3\frac{2}{5}$

(a) $1\frac{9}{5}$ **(b)** $2\frac{5}{3}$ **(c)** $1\frac{7}{4}$ **(d)** $3\frac{5}{2}$

(e) $4\frac{13}{10}$ **(f)** $5\frac{7}{6}$ **(g)** $3\frac{21}{5}$ **(h)** $6\frac{33}{10}$

(i) $2\frac{10}{8}$ | *Remember to cancel.* | **(j)** $5\frac{20}{6}$

③ Decimals and Fractions

1 Convert $\frac{1}{3}$ to a decimal using your calculator.
What do you notice about the answer?

2 Convert $\frac{1}{99}$ to a decimal using your calculator.
What do you notice about the answer?

0.3434343434 … is called a **recurring decimal**. The digits 34
recur (repeat themselves) for **ever** and make a pattern. You can
write this decimal like this: $0.\dot{3}\dot{4}$.

3 Convert these fractions to decimals. Which give recurring
decimals?

   (a) $\frac{20}{99}$ **(b)** $\frac{7}{8}$ **(c)** $\frac{8}{333}$ **(d)** $\frac{7}{11}$ **(e)** $\frac{15}{32}$

4 (a) Make up your own recurring decimal using two digits,
e.g. 0.3636363636.

  (b) Make a fraction out of 99 using your two digits, e.g. $\frac{36}{99}$.

  (c) Convert your fraction to a decimal using your calculator.
What do you notice?

5 Make five fractions which give recurring decimals.

Chapter 11 *Calculating with Fractions*

---

① Adding and Subtracting Fractions

Naomi adds these fractions together.

$$\frac{1}{6} + \frac{2}{9} = \frac{9}{54} + \frac{12}{54} = \frac{9+12}{54} = \frac{\overset{7}{\cancel{21}}}{\underset{18}{\cancel{54}}} = \frac{7}{18}$$

She has to cancel her answer. This could mean that her common
denominator, 54, was too big.

Look at the denominators of $\frac{5}{6}$ and $\frac{2}{9}$.

Both 6 and 9 can be divided by 3, so you can divide the common
denominator, 54, by 3 to make it smaller: $54 \div 3 = 18$.

18 is the **lowest common denominator (l.c.d.)**. It's easier to use
than 54 because the answer won't need to be cancelled.

Here is the same calculation, this time using the l.c.d.

$$\frac{1}{6} + \frac{2}{9} = \frac{3}{18} + \frac{4}{18} = \frac{3+4}{18} = \frac{7}{18}$$

I Calculate the following by finding the lowest common denominator.

(a) $\frac{9}{10} - \frac{3}{8}$ (b) $\frac{4}{9} + \frac{1}{4}$ (c) $\frac{6}{7} - \frac{1}{2}$ (d) $\frac{7}{12} + \frac{3}{8}$

(e) $\frac{1}{6} + \frac{3}{8}$ (f) $\frac{3}{10} + \frac{4}{15}$ (g) $\frac{5}{6} - \frac{1}{4}$ (h) $\frac{7}{10} + \frac{1}{6}$

(i) $\frac{5}{9} - \frac{5}{12}$ (j) $\frac{7}{8} - \frac{9}{20}$ (k) $\frac{5}{6} - \frac{8}{15}$ (l) $\frac{3}{4} - \frac{7}{10}$

2 Work these out the best way. Sometimes you need to use the lowest common denominator.

(a) $\frac{2}{5} + \frac{3}{10}$ (b) $\frac{1}{4} + \frac{1}{6}$ (c) $\frac{3}{5} - \frac{1}{3}$ (d) $\frac{7}{8} - \frac{3}{4}$

(e) $\frac{5}{6} - \frac{3}{10}$ (f) $\frac{4}{9} + \frac{5}{12}$ (g) $\frac{2}{3} + \frac{5}{6}$ (h) $\frac{6}{7} - \frac{2}{3}$

(i) $\frac{7}{8} - \frac{7}{10}$ (j) $\frac{9}{10} - \frac{3}{20}$ (k) $\frac{1}{3} + \frac{4}{15}$ (l) $\frac{2}{9} + \frac{5}{6}$

❷ Multiplying and Dividing Fractions

I (a) Choose any three fractions from the list below and multiply them together.

$$\frac{1}{2} \qquad \frac{2}{3} \qquad \frac{3}{4} \qquad \frac{5}{6} \qquad \frac{5}{8} \qquad \frac{6}{7} \qquad \frac{7}{9} \qquad \frac{9}{10}$$

(b) Repeat with two more sets of three fractions.

2 Repeat question I with groups of **(a)** four, **(b)** five, **(c)** six fractions.

3 Multiply together all eight fractions from question I.

> *Remember: cancel any numerator with any denominator; when you have cancelled, multiply the numerators and multiply the denominators.*

❸ Fractions of an Amount

I Make three fractions that add up to I. Do it like this:

- choose three numbers that add up to 20, e.g. 5, 6, 9
- make the numbers into three fractions with denominator 20, e.g. $\frac{5}{20}, \frac{6}{20}, \frac{9}{20}$
- these fractions add up to I:

$$\frac{5}{20} + \frac{6}{20} + \frac{9}{20} = \frac{5+6+9}{20} = \frac{20}{20} = 1$$

- cancel your fractions to their lowest terms, e.g. $\frac{5}{20} = \frac{1}{4}$, $\frac{6}{20} = \frac{3}{10}$, $\frac{9}{20}$ doesn't cancel.

2 Make your own fruit cocktail. Do it like this:
- choose three fruits, e.g. apple, pear, grape
- give each fruit one of your fractions, e.g. $\frac{1}{4}$ apple juice, $\frac{3}{10}$ pear juice, $\frac{9}{20}$ grape juice.

3 Copy and complete the table below to show how much of each type of fruit juice you need to mix each quantity of cocktail. Use your own fruits and fractions

Amount of cocktail (cl)	Fruit juice (cl)		
	Apple ($\frac{1}{4}$)	Pear ($\frac{3}{10}$)	Grape ($\frac{9}{20}$)
80			
30			
1500			

4 (a) Draw a new table. Add an extra column for a fourth type of fruit juice.

(b) Make up a new cocktail using four fruits and complete the table. Choose your own fruits and fractions.

5 Make up a new cocktail with five fruits.

Chapter 12 *Percentages*

❶ Percentages

You can use percentages to add and subtract fractions.

Example	$\frac{1}{4} - \frac{1}{10}$
Working	Change $\frac{1}{4}$ to 25% and $\frac{1}{10}$ to 10%.
	$\frac{1}{4} - \frac{1}{10} = 25\% - 10\% = 15\%$
	$= \frac{15}{100} = \frac{3}{20}$ (Cancel to lowest terms.)
Answer	$\frac{1}{4} - \frac{1}{10} = \frac{3}{20}$

1 Work out the following using percentages.

(a) $\frac{1}{2} - \frac{2}{10}$ (b) $\frac{7}{10} - \frac{1}{4}$ (c) $\frac{1}{4} + \frac{7}{10}$

(d) $\frac{1}{10} + \frac{1}{2}$ (e) $\frac{3}{4} + \frac{4}{10}$ (f) $1\frac{3}{4} - \frac{7}{10}$

2 Choose one red and one blue fraction from below to make up five addition sums of your own. Work them out using percentages.

$\frac{1}{10}, \frac{2}{10}, \frac{3}{10}, \frac{4}{10}, \frac{5}{10}, \frac{6}{10}, \frac{7}{10}, \frac{8}{10}, \frac{9}{10}$ $\frac{1}{4}, \frac{1}{2}, \frac{3}{4}, 1\frac{1}{2}, 2\frac{3}{4}, 3\frac{1}{4}$

3 Make up five subtractions. Work them out using percentages.

❷ Percentages of an Amount

1 A carton of fruit juice contains orange, apple and pear juice. You have to decide how much of each juice it contains.

2 Choose a percentage for each fruit. They must add up to 100%. For example: 40% orange, 25% apple and 35% pear.

3 Choose how much juice there will be altogether: 50 cl, 80 cl, 120 cl, 150 cl, 200 cl, 300 cl.

4 Calculate the amount of each juice in the carton.

5 Now invent your own four-fruits drink.

❸ Percentage Increase and Decrease

1 You can increase £60 by 23% using the following quick method.
Start with 100%.
Add 23% to get 123%.
123% of £60
= 123 ÷ 100 × 60
= 1.23 × 60
= £73.80

2 Use the quick method to calculate the following. Write your answers to the nearest penny.

(a) increase £34 by 10%   (b) increase £9 by 98%

(c) increase 45p by 3%   (d) increase £7.34 by 39%

You can decrease £60 by 23% using the following quick method.
Start with 100%.
Take away 23% to get 77%.
77% of £60
= 77 ÷ 100 × 60
= 0.77 × 60
= £46.20

3 Use the quick method to calculate the following. Write your
answers to the nearest penny.
(a) decrease £80 by 10%   **(b)** decrease £12 by 2%
(c) decrease 55p by 32%   **(d)** decrease £19.71 by 11%

Brush Up Your Number 8

● Calculating with Large Numbers

Astronomers measure the distances to stars using **light years** (LY).
A light year is 9 460 920 000 000 km.

Work out how far away these stars are in kilometres.

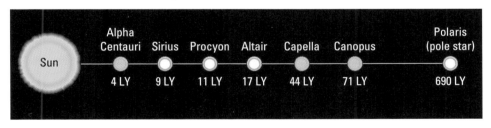

Hint: for Polaris, multiply by 69, then multiply by 10.

Chapter 13 *Using Tables and Charts*

➊ Tallying and Grouping

Alicia does a survey. She asks 50 people the number of their house or flat. If the house only has a name, she writes 0. This is what she writes.

25	0	3	142	10	105	9	4	19	186
22	131	28	0	40	12	45	0	50	4
9	15	62	38	2	12	0	148	2	165
66	33	88	10	0	6	146	13	42	27
61	137	8	17	55	25	3	25	0	20

I Use Alicia's survey to copy and complete this tally table.

This is a big table. You will need a full page.

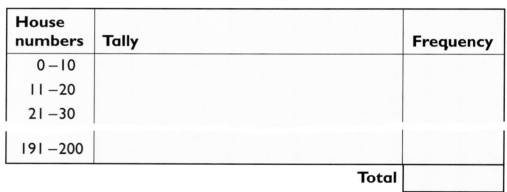

House numbers	Tally	Frequency
0 – 10		
11 – 20		
21 – 30		
191 – 200		
Total		

2 Now use Alicia's survey to copy and complete this tally table.

House numbers	Tally	Frequency
0 – 20		
21 – 40		
41 – 60		
181 – 200		
Total		

3 What do you notice about the frequencies in this table? How are they connected to the last table?

4 Use what you found out to copy and complete this table. Do **not** count!

House numbers	Tally	Frequency
0 –40		
41 –80		
161 –200		
	Total	

② Frequency Tables, Pictograms and Bar Charts

This table shows the results of a sports competition. Four schools took part. They could win gold, silver or bronze medals for each event.

School	Medals		
	Gold	Silver	Bronze
Kirkley School	4	4	6
John Adams College	5	10	6
Mount School	8	2	6
Queen Anne High School	3	4	2

1 Work out the medal total for each school.

2 (a) Work out the total number of winners of each type of medal.
  (b) What do you notice?
  (c) How many events were there in the competition?

3 Draw a bar chart showing the medals won by each school.

❸ Pie Charts

1 This section is about investigating how we use letters in English.
   What fraction of a piece of text is vowels (a, e, i, o, u)?
   What fraction is consonants (the other letters)?
   Have a guess at the answer now. Write it down and draw a rough
   pie chart to show your answer.

2 Find a book or magazine that has lots of text. A maths book isn't a
   good choice! Draw a blank tally table with two rows, one for
   vowels and one for consonants.

3 Pick a part of your book or magazine. Tally the vowels and
   consonants until you have a total of 360 letters.
   Draw a pie chart of the results. How does it compare with your
   guess?

Chapter 14 *Two Variables*

---

❶ Two-way Tables

1 Tables where the labels are used in calculations are called
   function tables.

   Here are three ways to combine the numbers. Copy and complete
   each table.

   (a) Add the two numbers together.

   > **Example**   3 and 5 → 3 + 5 → 8
   >
   > | | 1 | 2 | 5 | 10 |
   > |----|---|---|---|----|
   > | 1 | | | | |
   > | 3 | | | 8 | |
   > | 6 | | | | |
   > | 12 | | | | |

   (b) Subtract the number in the left column from the number in the
   top row.

   > **Example**   5 and 3 → 5 − 3 → 2
   >
   > | | 1 | 2 | 5 | 10 |
   > |----|---|---|---|----|
   > | 1 | | | | |
   > | 3 | | | 2 | |
   > | 6 | | | | |
   > | 12 | | | | |

(c) Use the number in the left column as the tens digit and the number in the top row as the units digit.

Example	3 and 5 → 35				

	1	2	5	10
1				
3			35	
6				
12				

2 (a) Make up a rule of your own for a function table.

(b) Copy the table above and fill it in using your rule.

(c) Copy the table again and fill in **half** the answers. Challenge a friend to work out the rule and complete the table.

❷ Scatter Diagrams

A coin

The results of this coin-flipping experiment should make a good scatter diagram.

1 Draw a table like this to record the results.

Number of flips	10	12	14	16		28	30
Number of heads							

On the first 'go', flip the coin 10 times. Record the number of heads.

Next time, flip it 12 times, then 14, etc. Carry on until you reach 30 flips.

Draw a scatter diagram of your results. The axes should be labelled 'Number of flips' and 'Number of heads'. Does it tell you anything about the numbers of flips and heads?

2 Think of another coin experiment and carry it out. Draw a scatter diagram of the results.

Brush Up Your Number 9

● Reverse Calculations

The formula for finding a temperature in degrees Fahrenheit (°F), given the temperature in degrees Celsius (°C) is $F = \frac{9}{5}C + 32$.

Find the temperature in Celsius when the temperature is:

1 122 °F   **2** 97 °F   **3** 75 °F   **4** 145 °F   **5** 63 °F

6 144° F   **7** 32 °F   **8** 212 °F   **9** 318 °F   **10** 23 °F

Chapter 15 *Multiples and Factors*

❶ Multiples

The lowest common multiple of 1 and 2 is 2.
The lowest common multiple of 1, 2 and 3 is 6.
The lowest common multiple of 1, 2, 3 and 4 is 12.

Continue this pattern to find the lowest common multiple of 1, 2, 3, 4, 5, 6, 7, 8, 9 and 10.

❷ Factors

Complete this table to list the factors of the numbers 1 to 20.

Number	Factors	Number of factors
1	1	1
2	1, 2	2
3	1, 3	2
4	1, 2, 4	3

1 Write down a list of all the numbers with only **two** factors. What is special about these numbers? What are they called?

2 Write down a list of numbers with an **odd** number of factors. What is special about these numbers? What are they called?

Chapter 16 *Patterns and Sequences*

❶ What's Next?

Make up five different sequences of numbers. Remember, they must follow a rule. Write down the first six terms of each sequence.

Write down the rule that describes how each sequence is made.

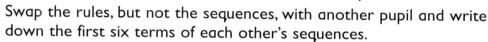 Swap the rules, but not the sequences, with another pupil and write down the first six terms of each other's sequences.

❷ Finding the Formula

The sequences below are made using the sequence of squares $(1, 4, 9, 16, 25 \ldots)$ or cubes $(1, 8, 27, 64 \ldots)$. Find a formula for each. The formula should involve n^2 or n^3 (n = number).

1 2, 8, 18, 32, 50 ...   **2** 0, 3, 8, 15, 24 ...

3 4, 7, 13, 19, 28 ...   **4** 1, 7, 17, 31, 49 ...

5 0, 6, 16, 30, 48 ...   **6** 1, 8, 27, 64 ...

7 2, 9, 28, 65 ...   **8** 2, 16, 54, 128 ...

Brush Up Your Number 10

● Place Value Calculations

1 Work out 60×60.

Lots of other pairs of numbers multiply to give this answer. Find as many as you can.

2 Work out $1000 \div 20$.

Lots of other pairs of numbers divide to give this answer. Find as many as you can.

Chapter 17 *Length and Mass*

❶ Measuring and Estimating Length

Compasses

1 Draw the following triangle.

10 cm, 8 cm, 6 cm

- Draw a base line. Make two marks for the first side (say, 10 cm).
- Set your compasses to 8 cm. Put the point on one of the marks. Draw an arc.
- Set your compasses to 6 cm. Put the point on the other mark. Draw another arc that crosses the first one.
- The arcs cross where the third corner goes. Join the corners with straight lines to finish the triangle.

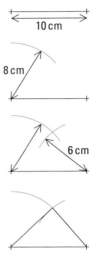

If you have been accurate, there should be a right angle at the top.

2 Draw the following triangles.

Some of them may be impossible!

- **(a)** 10 cm, 3 cm, 9 cm
- **(b)** 6 cm, 8 cm, 8 cm
- **(c)** 7 cm, 7 cm, 7 cm
- **(d)** 10 cm, 5 cm, 4 cm
- **(e)** 3 cm, 3 cm, 12 cm

3 A parallelogram can be made by joining two triangles together. See if you can draw this one.

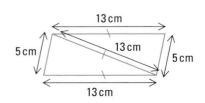

4 Draw a rhombus using this method.

❷ Measuring and Estimating Mass

Suppose you have a balance and the following weights: 2×1 g, 5 g, 2×10 g, 50 g, 2×100 g, 500 g.

Calculate how you could balance objects weighing 1 g, 2 g, 3 g, etc. until you find a pattern. Write down the pattern.

Example	3 g object
Answer	You could do it by putting the two 1 g weights with the sweet and the 5 g weight on the other pan.

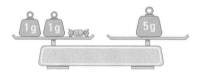

What extra weights would you need to balance heavier things?

❸ Calculations

A4 graph paper

1 A hardware shop sells cable by the metre. The prices are shown in the table.

Cable	Phone	Mains	Speaker
Price per metre	45p	70p	£1.25

Draw a graph of length and price. Use A4 graph paper with the long side vertical.

→ Horizontal axis: *Label*: 'Length (m)'. *Scale*: 2 cm = 1 m. *Range*: 0→8 m.

↑ Vertical axis: *Label*: 'Price (£)'. *Scale*: 2 cm = £1. *Range*: 0→£10.

Your graph should have three straight lines.

2 The shop also sells cable by weight.

Cable	Phone	Mains	Speaker
Price per kg	£18	£7	£25

Draw a graph of weight and price. Use A4 graph paper with the long side vertical.

→ Horizontal axis: *Label:* 'Weight (g)'. *Scale:* 2 cm = 100 g. *Range:* 0→800 g.

↑ Vertical axis: *Label:* 'Price (£)'. *Scale:* 1 cm = £1. *Range:* 0→£20.

Your graph should have three straight lines.

3 Using your graphs, or by calculating, work out what one metre of each type of cable weighs.

Chapter 18 *Time*

❶ Time Calculations

1 Copy and complete this table. Write your working underneath. Assume you will live to be 80.

	1 hour	1 day	1 week	1 month	1 year	life so far	whole life
Seconds in ...							
Minutes in ...							
Hours in ...							
Days in ...							
Weeks in ...							
Months in ...							
Years in ...							

2 Why is the **life so far** column difficult to fill in?

❷ Timetables

Use the information below to copy and complete this bus timetable.

Central Station to Brigham Centre									
Central Station									
Shopping Centre									
Warren Grove									
Brigham Marina									
Brigham Centre									
Brigham Centre to Central Station									
Brigham Centre									
Brigham Marina									
Warren Grove									
Shopping Centre									
Central Station									

The bus route **Central Station to Brigham** runs as follows on Mondays to Fridays.

The first bus leaves Central Station at 7.30am. Five minutes later, it arrives at the Shopping Centre. Eight minutes after that, it arrives at Warren Grove. Ten minutes later, it arrives at Brigham Marina. Six minutes after that it arrives at the centre of Brigham.

The journey back to Central Station takes the same time.

The second bus leaves Central Station at 7.50am. After that, there is a bus every half hour until 6pm. Then there is one more bus, leaving at 6.30pm, but this does not stop at Warren Grove.

Brush Up Your Number 11

● Calculation Shortcuts

Find a shortcut for each question. Show your working.

1 26 + 999	**2** 372 + 999	**3** 5200 − 999
4 8524 − 999	**5** 17 × 999	**6** 56 × 999
7 12 × 500	**8** 63 × 500	**9** 28 + 19
10 57 − 19	**11** 45 + 39	**12** 76 − 29
13 65 + 98	**14** 145 − 97	**15** 358 − 96
16 320 + 990	**17** 2300 − 990	**18** 2500 + 990
19 8 × 90	**20** 25 × 90	**21** 68 × 90
22 24 × 25	**23** 84 × 25	**24** 200 ÷ 25
25 700 ÷ 25	**26** 1000 ÷ 25	**27** 2100 ÷ 25

Chapter 19 *Perimeter and Area*

❶ Perimeters

L-shapes are made from two rectangles joined together, like this.

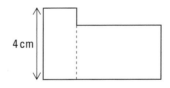

1 How many different L-shapes can you sketch that have a perimeter of 24 cm? Here is an example.

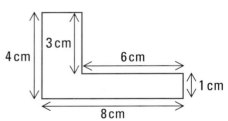

2 What is the perimeter of this L-shape? It can be done! Describe how you found the answer.

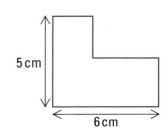

❷ Calculating Areas of Rectangles

Jenny is making a rectangular pen for Daisy, her cow. She is using the cow shed wall as one side of the pen. She has 26 m of wire netting to make a fence round the other three sides of the pen.

Investigate the different rectangles she can make. One is shown here.

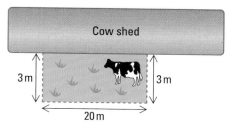

Which one gives Daisy the biggest area to graze in?

❸ Calculating Areas of Parallelograms and Triangles

A4 squared paper

On squared paper, draw one of your initials.

You can use rectangles, parallelograms and triangles.

R might look like this.

Divide the letter into separate shapes.

Work out the area it covers.

Try it with your other initials.

Try a whole word.

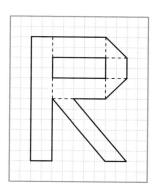

Chapter 20 *Volume and Capacity*

❶ Volumes of Cuboids

This table shows the dimensions of two cuboids that each have a volume of $60\,cm^3$.

Length (cm)	Width (cm)	Height (cm)	Volume (cm^3)
10	3	2	$10 \times 3 \times 2 = 60$
10	6	1	$10 \times 6 \times 1 = 60$

Copy the table and add the dimensions of other cuboids that also have a volume of $60\,cm^3$. Add as many as you can. Just use whole numbers.

❷ Capacity

Cubic units of volume match the capacity units.

> **Key Fact**
> $1\,cm^3 = 1\,ml$
> $1000\,cm^3 = 1l$
> $1000\,l = 1\,m^3$, because $1\,000\,000\,cm^3 = 1\,m^3$.

Lots of containers are shaped like cuboids: cartons, tanks, etc.
You can work out how much liquid they can hold. First work out the volume in cubic units. Then change to capacity units.

Example	A juice carton is 6 cm long, 4 cm wide and 8 cm high. How much juice does it hold?
Working	Volume of a cuboid = length × width × height $= 6 \times 4 \times 8$ $= 24 \times 8$ $= 192\,cm^3$ $1\,cm^3 = 1\,ml$, so $192\,cm^3 = 192\,ml$.
Answer	$192\,ml$

Work out the capacity of each container, in millilitres.

1

15 cm
10 cm
3 cm

2

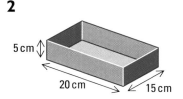

5 cm
20 cm
15 cm

3

18 cm
7 cm
7 cm

4

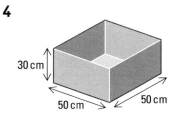

30 cm
50 cm
50 cm

5

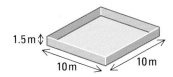

1.5 m
10 m
10 m

6

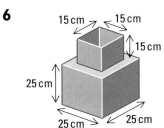

15 cm
15 cm
15 cm
25 cm
25 cm
25 cm

Brush Up Your Number 12

● Money

Copy and complete this table.

Item	Cost	Cost of 12	Cost of 24
Scissors	£3.50	£42	£84
Screwdriver	£2.25		
Hammer		£39	
Chisel			£63.60
Pliers		£52.20	
Saw	£6.36		
Knife		£29.88	
Plane			£479.76

Chapter 21 *Averages*

❶ Mode and Median

I (a) Jai writes a list of numbers.

50	80	70	50	40	50	30	70	20	20

Find the mode of Jai's numbers.

(b) Madeleine adds I to each of Jai's numbers.

51	81	71	51	41	51	31	71	21	21

Find the mode of Madeleine's numbers.
What has happened to the mode?

(c) Prakash takes 3 away from each of Jai's numbers

47	77	67	47	37	47	27	67	17	17

Find the mode of Prakash's numbers.
What has happened to the mode?

(d) Trudi adds 10 to each of Jai's numbers. What is the mode of Trudi's numbers?

(e) Trudi didn't have to count the frequencies to find the mode of her numbers. Describe the rule you think she used.

2 Repeat question I, finding the median each time.

3 Anthony **doubles** each of Jai's numbers. What happens to the mode and median?

4 Sasha **halves** each of Jai's numbers. What happens to the mode and median?

5 Think up some other rules you could use on the numbers. Test them out.

❷ Mean and Range

1 (a) Jai writes a list of numbers.

50	80	70	50	40	50	30	70	20	20

Find the mean of Jai's numbers.

(b) Madeleine adds 1 to each of Jai's numbers.

51	81	71	51	41	51	31	71	21	21

Find the mean of Madeleine's numbers.
What has happened to the mean?

(c) Prakash takes 3 away from each of Jai's numbers.

47	77	67	47	37	47	27	67	17	17

Find the mean of Prakash's numbers.
What has happened to the mean?

(d) Trudi adds 10 to each of Jai's numbers. What is the mean of Trudi's numbers?

(e) Trudi didn't have to add and divide to find the mean of her numbers. Describe the rule you think she used.

2 Repeat question 1, finding the **range** each time.

3 Anthony **doubles** each of Jai's numbers. What happens to the mean and range?

4 Sasha **halves** each of Jai's numbers. What happens to the mean and range?

5 Think up some other rules you could use on the numbers. Test them out.

③ Comparing Sets of Data

Squared paper or graph paper

This section shows you how to draw a mean/range diagram to compare sets of data.

Here is the comparison table for the shot putters from **Learn About It** on page 295.

	Mean (m)	Best (m)	Worst (m)	Range (m)
A. Putter	14.5	18	11	7
B. Chucker	16	22	9	13

1 You need a scale on which all of these numbers will fit. It needs to go from 7 to 22, at least.

Draw this scale and label it as shown.

2 Above the scale, draw a line going from Putter's worst to best distances. This illustrates the **range**. Place a dot on this line to show the mean. Label this line 'Putter'.

3 Now draw another line representing Chucker. Use a different colour for each line.

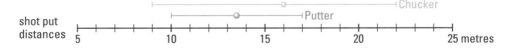

4 Work through the other questions from **Practice**, making mean/range diagrams. You will have to think carefully about the scales you use.

Brush Up Your Number 13

● Fraction Calculations

Remember that, to multiply fractions, you multiply the numerators and the denominators.

So $\frac{2}{3} \times \frac{4}{5} = \frac{8}{15}$.

You may need to cancel your answer.

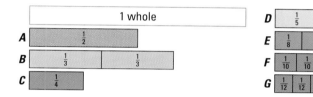

Copy and complete this multiplication square.

Use the fractions from **Practice** C on page 303.

Write your working underneath. The first one has been done for you.

×	A	B	C	D	E	F	G
A	$\frac{1}{4}$						
B							
C							
D							
E							
F							
G							

Chapter 22 *Chance*

---

① Theoretical Probability

A4 graph paper, long side horizontal

You can show any probability you work out on a scale.

Look at this spinner.

$\frac{3}{10}$ of the spinner is blue.

$\frac{7}{10}$ of the spinner is green.

$P(\text{blue}) = \frac{3}{10}$ or 0.3

$P(\text{green}) = \frac{7}{10}$ or 0.7

These can be put onto the scale.

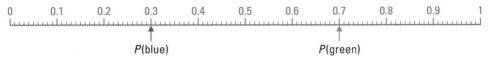

Draw probability scales for the spinners in **Try It Out** B on page 306.

Use graph paper. The lines should be 20 cm long.

➋ Predicting Results

This diagram shows another one of Zorah's charity games. It's a dartboard.

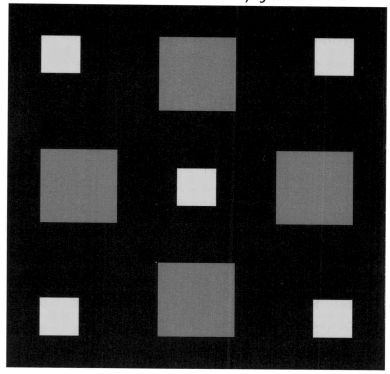

The probability of hitting a square on the dartboard depends on its area.

Here are the parts of the dartboard, and what you win.

1 Work out the area of each colour (you will have to measure the sides first).

2 Work out the probability of hitting each colour.

Area	Outcome
Red	Win 20p
Yellow	Win 50p
Black	Lose

3 It costs 10p for one throw. Work out what profit Zorah makes on 100 throws.

4 If you have time, design your own dartboard. Work through the steps above to see if will 'work'.

❸ Experimental Probability

Improbable protractor

Drawing pin, pointer, card, compasses, protractor

You can use probability to estimate an angle!

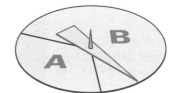

1 Make a spinner with 2 sectors. Label them A and B. You can choose the angles, but **don't** measure them!

Copy and complete this table, calculating the probabilities.

Outcome	Tally	Frequency	Probability
A			$P(A) =$
B			$P(B) =$
	Total	100	1

2 When you have worked out the probabilities, multiply them by 360°. This gives an estimate of the angles. Copy this table and complete the second column.

Angle	Estimated	Measured
A	$\times\ 360° =$	
B	$\times\ 360° =$	

3 Now measure the angles with a protractor and complete the table. How good were the estimates?